SEP 2 4 2015

T **D R Toi**
223 Southlake Pl
Newport News, VA 23602-8323

DIVINE NUTRITION

The Madonna Frequency &

The Food of Gods

Divine Nutrition
The Madonna Frequency

THE FOOD OF GODS

Produced by Jasmuheen &
The Self Empowerment Academy

http://www.jasmuheen.com/

First Edition – April 2003
E-Book produced – April 2003
Second Edition – August 2003
Third Edition – January 2005
Fourth Edition – September 2014

ISBN: 978-1-84799-847-7

INSTIGATING, RECORDING & SUMMARIZING
HUMANITY'S CO-CREATION OF PARADISE

*Please respect the work of the author
& help S.E.A. promote planetary peace ...*

for more copies go to:
http://www.jasmuheen.com/books-mp3s/
for more copies as a hardcover book go to:
http://www.lulu.com/spotlight/jasmuheen

INTRODUCTION

As I began to collate the data for this book I realized that everyone is hungry for something and that it is our lack of fulfilling nutrition that has created much of the disease and disharmony on our planet today. I also realized that lack of education sustains this state of disharmony and disease as many people are simply unaware of how to tap into a source of nourishment that will create the physical, emotional, mental and spiritual health and happiness that we all desire.

While much has been written and researched on balanced physical nourishment and how to create physical health, very little has been written about nutritional sources that can satiate all of our hungers on both a cellular, and also on a soul level. Nor have many simple pragmatic tools been shared that will bring deep fulfillment to our door.

While I have written two other books in the Divine Nutrition Series, in this book I would like to present a very simple, easy to understand method of satisfying all our hungers while also introducing a basic system that – if an individual is prepared to get themselves tuned to the right channel – can also free people from the need to take nourishment from physical food if this is their desire. However, the formulas, lifestyles and meditations in this book can be utilized by all – the only difference is that for those wishing to still partake in the delight of physical food, we recommend a vegetarian diet for health, sensitivity and resource sustainability reasons.

The Food of Gods book and its research and recommendations apply to anyone who is hungry for love, or health and happiness, and/or peace and prosperity. I call this hunger being at 'Level 1' in the Divine Nutrition Program. 'Level 2' is where we satisfy this hunger and gain health and happiness and peace and prosperity. Level 2 is gaining and applying the tools to get the nourishment we need to attract these things into our field. Then we have 'Level 3' of the Divine Nutrition Program, which is where we refine ourselves even further and learn how to be free from the need to take physical food and how to exist more freely on the Violet Light spectrum of the Theta – Delta wave. Both are discussed in this book and tools are provided to successfully achieve both paradigms.

As many who have followed my story are aware, after a life time of training, in 1993 I began my experiential research – and subsequent recording and reporting on – my journey into the field of "The Food of Gods". Although I had been accessing this field consciously for over 22 years in order to receive an endless stream of love and healing guidance, the field's gift of pranic nutrition had yet to be explored. We cover this journey and how it relates to us personally and globally in the first two books of this series – *Pranic Nourishment – Nutrition for the New Millennium* (also known as *Living on Light*) and *Ambassadors of Light – World Health & World Hunger Project*.

In this third book we bring the Divine Nutrition reality into perspective with Dimensional Biofield Science and of course we talk further on my favorite topic – which is the God within us all, that force that is all powerful, all loving, all knowing and everywhere, that force that drives our breath and guides us and gives life to all the fields, nourishing and sustaining all that is born, a force that also expresses Itself as Divine Mother love or what I call the Madonna Frequency field. To this force I give my allegiance, my love and my time, for to know It is to love It and to be one with It allows all our questions to disappear and our inner being to feel truly nurtured and fulfilled.

On this level, "The Food of Gods" journey is entirely experiential, and is one which leads us deep within the Dimensional Biofield, into what the Yogis call 'the ultimate reality' a place beyond the realm of our logical mind. A biofield is the auric field of radiation that surrounds all systems of life, and the field that occurs when two of more systems are magnetized together.

My personal assignment with this research field was:

a) To live it and prove to myself that my physical body could exist healthily purely on prana or Divine Nutrition alone, and be free from doubt so that I could stand tall amid the controversy and skepticism (that I was unaware was destined to come), and then

b) to gather and share all the research I could find to support this journey and make it easier for others to understand, and finally,

c) to find a solution to world health and world hunger problems, and lastly

d) to continue to bridge the metaphysical fields with the mainstream field of science and medicine by sharing any new research and now

e) to deliver a way that is safe, practical and easy for the interested masses to gain another level of freedom – freedom for the need to use so much of our world's resources, freedom from disease and freedom of choice, freedom from starvation and finally freedom from our emotional, mental and spiritual states of anorexia.

Points (a), (b), and (c) were covered in the first two books of the series, and points (d) and (e) will be addressed here. Nonetheless, this is not a field that one person is to conquer alone as bridging the worlds is part of a global game of evolution. It is not necessary to have read the other two books to understand what we share in this one.

Each of us has a role to play and each of us carries a piece of a massive program for change, which in itself forms a natural path of our evolution. In time all that we have discovered will be accepted as every day fact and this will come into being from individual exploration coupled with normal standard research by those open to these fields.

All I can ask is that all is done with respect and with the good of all in mind. If we all act with honor and integrity looking for 'win, win, win' solutions as discussed in our 'Biofields & Bliss' Series, our world can progress into a state of true civility and hunger, poverty, war and violence will become a thing of our past.

So while *The Food of Gods* provides information that we have received intuitively from being in the Theta – Delta field (some of which can hence only be substantiated by someone who can access these channels and who has the desire to experience this particular gift) we will also introduce enough basic Dimensional Biofield Science data to hopefully bridge the realms.

How long it will take to prove what we suggest is really up to the world of science, however proof is in the living and as more and more of us turn to the channel of Divine Love for our nourishment, the quicker our inner and outer worlds will be in peace.

Psychologists and metaphysicians have provided copious literature on how to satisfy some of our human hungers and the reasons for them, yet our focus here must remain on providing tools and data on the purest source of nourishment we have, which is Divine Nutrition and the Food of Gods. When presented in its entirety this still remains a novel – and still mainly experiential – field of research.

In order to move deeper into this discussion we need to make certain assumptions of our readers and these are:

a) That you believe in a force that is all knowing, all powerful, all loving and everywhere including within each of us, for without this belief much of what we propose may seem too far-fetched; although the Dimensional Biofield Science aspects may at least provide some food for your future thinking.

b) That you are open to know more of this force and yet are able to trust your inner instinct and use discernment for we are exploring realms where only your intuition will be able to confirm what is true.

As this is my 18th book covering metaphysical topics, much of the basic esoteric teachings have been covered in the book *In Resonance* and we have explained the science of it all in the *Biofields & Bliss* Series which includes our Planetary Peace Program. As we are not interested in convincing the reader of anything in this book, it is easier if you have done some type of metaphysical reading, although we keep our presentations of the following research relatively simple.

We also recommend the 'try it and see' approach as all meditations and programming codes that we recommend are safe and can only bring benefits to your life if applied.

As we wanted to present a practical book to convert a human bio-system to the Divine Nutrition channel, some of our previous research from the first two books in this series and from the Biofields & Bliss series, have been repeated here. For those who have read all of our previous research manuals we ask you to forgive this necessary repetition.

In the writing of this book I was initially torn between wanting to present a simple recipe of level 2 nourishment that will guarantee health and happiness for all and at the same time take the Divine Nutrition controversy – with its gift of level 3 pranic nourishment – a little further into the realm of science. Ever since my journey began with this I have intuitively hungered to bridge the worlds of science and metaphysics and I hope that my hunger to do this allows me to fulfill both objectives. However the problem that we still have is that modern day science is still too uninformed to make the necessary assessments within the metaphysical fields. Firstly a scientist has to expand their own consciousness to obtain what they need to know and the quantum field needs further exploration and respect before the metaphysical field can be understood, and secondly the fields are not stable, they are static and always changing and even the witnessing of an event will change it.

Dimensional Biofield Science is the science of understanding life in all the dimensions – the 1st, 2nd, 3rd, 4th, 5th, 6th, 7th and onward. The human life wave as a God in form exists in all dimensions simultaneously although many still see themselves as a 3rd dimensional model only. For those who are hungry to know and to be more – this book is for you.

Namaste – Jasmuheen

DEDICATION AND ACKNOWLEDGMENT

To Konrad Halbig and his wife Karen I will be eternally grateful for their decision to publish the first book in this series, and then to later stand tall amid the controversy that the release of this information would bring.

I also give my thanks to the German people whose hearts were touched by my early research enough to walk the path with me and who then proved by their own experience that what I had come to know was also true for them. To the millions who have walked before me and beside me exploring all these fields, I also give thanks, for you have made the journey easier for us all.

To my publishers in Germany, Italy, Croatia, France, Spain, Brazil, Belgium, Sweden, Greece, Hungary, Romania, Poland, Russia, and Japan, I also give my thanks for your courage to bring such a controversial subject to the public and thus anchor this data deeper within the global field. Evolution has a way of being supported, regardless of our capacity to deal with things that may challenge what we know.

I would also like to thank those who allowed me to gather and share the research of the Qigong and Pranic Healing networks, to also thank Dr Deepak Chopra for his patient attempts to bridge the world of modern and ancient medicines, and Dr Sudhir Shah (thank you for your willingness to share your research on Solar Feeding) and Dr Karl Graninger for the twenty years he dedicated of his life to study inedia. The studies of these people and all the others credited in my book *Ambassadors of Light*, has also made my journey easier and for all of their work I remain eternally grateful. Also thanks to Dr Masaru Emoto and his research in *Messages from the Water* which added another layer of credibility to our work and to the Master Mantak Chia for his openness and willingness to share his research and life's work with me and for being such a delightful presence in this world.

I give thanks also to those who know that what really brings nourishment to us all, is not the chemical reaction of food substances in our system, but the internal Presence of an intelligence that is so wise and loving that to merge with It allows us to satiate all our hungers. May we all continue to acknowledge and be nourished by this Source.

I also wish to give thanks to my family for supporting me all these years as I pushed my physical body and bio-system through extreme cycles in a bid to discover and expand my own limits, and for dealing so graciously with all the controversy that my often very public research has delivered to our door. I love you all dearly.

Lastly to all my organizers who – regardless of the controversy – have continued to bring me to their countries year after year so that I could continue to share of our research, again I love you all. And to those whose prayers have kept this (and me) alive, we just wouldn't have come so far without you! Thank you for feeding me on the inner planes with your love and support.

2014 Update

As I began to prepare this book for publication into the Chinese language, I realized that so much has unfolded over the last 11 years since I wrote all that this book contains.

These days I prefer to use the term Essence rather than DOW - or the Divine One Within - for the divine force is everywhere, within us and around us as the very Baseline frequency of all creation.

These days we also talk about being nourished from the outside in or from the inside out or a bit of both which is great for both our health and planetary resources. Imagine if we could safely reduce our current food consumption in the West by up to 50% and the impact this would have on our planet? All of this and much more we have now added at the end of this book along with testing methods to ascertain your prana percentage which will allow those called to this to have a safe conversion.

These days there are around 50,000 people in our world who now have this freedom of choice as to whether they wish to receive their physical body nourishment from physical food, or direct from prana or by utilizing a little bit of each just for the game of pleasure.

These days we have new methodologies coming through a variety of different people in many different countries as having this freedom of choice is so beneficial to us and also to our environment so it is a field of research and possibility that will continue to be explored.

As at 2014, cancer, diabetes, obesity and so many other dis-eases are on the rise especially within the Western world and yet a simple change in lifestyle can alter all of this and also end all suffering in our world. The greatest changes I have witnessed over these past 21 years since I began to be nourished in this way, has come from the lifestyle that we recommend to achieve this increase in the pranic flow so that it is flowing strongly enough through us to nourish us. As people apply this 8 point Luscious Lifestyles Program they get healthier, happier and more harmonious and this is a joy to witness.

But what is prana? Called the microfood of life, according to http://www.wordiq.com/dictionary.html, "prana is the vital air, or breath, of the human body, as visualized in Hinduism. It is also interpreted as the vital, life-sustaining force of both the individual body and the universe. Its first expounding came in the Upanishads, where it is part of the worldly, physical realm, sustaining the body and reliant on the mind. Prana suffuses all living form but is not itself the soul."

And according to the Qigong Masters from China, the first recorded case of someone being nourished purely by chi was recorded some 6,000 years ago. From there, cases we discovered in India and now it has finally come more into the West. So we hope you enjoy all that we offer here regarding some of our own experiential research into this topic!

THE FOOD OF GODS

Contents

DIVINE NUTRITION PROGRAM – Level 3 Nourishment:

Tools & Techniques

Chapter 1

Everyone is hungry for something …

Everyone is hungry for something whether it's definable or not, however most human hungers are easy to recognize. Many people are hungry for love while others hunger for wealth. Our hunger for health and happiness also dominates our time. Right now some people hunger for retribution, while others cry out with a hunger for harmony and peace, or for justice and truth and kindness to prevail and to not send their loved ones to war.

Some people hunger for sensual satisfaction while others seek the spiritual, ready to eat enlightenment like others consume their daily food, for they are driven by a hunger that is harder to explain. Hunger expresses itself in so many ways depending on its depth and the desires that drive it. Whatever the problem in life, scratch the surface of the issue, and you will find that someone is hungry for something.

Hunger for power sees the conquest of others while hunger for knowledge sees our growth. Hunger for wealth sees the exploitation of others, while hunger for altruism sees wealth's redistribution. Hunger for communication sees our union with others, while hunger for true food sees us often in lack. Hunger for wisdom sees us reach deep within ourselves as life then tests us to apply it. Hunger for truth leads us to discover that the Holy Grail is within containing its elixir called Spirit.

Hunger for Spirit reveals to us the Divine One Within who reveals Itself to be a master computer controller of a very complex bio-mechanism that pulses with fields that hold life – a 6.3 trillion cell mechanism that vibrates at a set speed that in turn determines the various realities we experience throughout the term of our life.

Satisfying these vast hungers has consumed the thoughts and time of leaders and sages and the curious alike, though few rarely make the time or have the desire to look at this game in greater depth. Often many are just too consumed with satisfying the hunger for survival to really find enough nourishment to begin to thrive. Those that do are either pre-programmed to do so, or stumble upon understanding the game of true nourishment through some big change in life.

The common finding among those who seek perfect nourishment is that as soon as one hunger is satiated, another is usually revealed, adding layer upon layer to the complex jigsaw of life. Keeping all our hungers properly fed becomes a time consuming passion and an art.

Feeding all our hungers takes time, attention, will-power, desire, focus, dreaming and scheming, money, energy, co-operation and union with others, communication and programming and to do so well we need a fair degree of basic skill.

Feeding our hunger successfully so we are free from feeling hungry on any level, requires holistic education for to satisfy ourselves we need to understand who we really are. To ignore any aspect of how our being, as a 6.3 trillion cell mechanism functions, is like living life in the dark and denying our sense of sight. If we have never experienced sight we do not know what we are missing, but if we have then we have a greater adjustment to make. The fact is our DOW – our Divine self – wants us to know It for It is the force behind the mechanism that breathes us and keeps us alive.

Although our DOW exists as an underlying creative frequency throughout all our cells and atoms, often Its presence has become a much weaker beat as in Dimensional Biofield Science, what we focus on will always grow. Because we have ignored the boss of our system for so long and instead focused on feeding our hungers via more material methods, Its energy field has been tuned to a more 'basic maintenance' mode.

The DOW in basic maintenance mode breathes us and listens to our thoughts and generally lets us play and experiment and suffer as we learn and grow. Until we begin to ask questions like "Who am I? Why am I here? Is there a higher purpose to this existence? Can we all live in peace on Earth?" Or "How can we all get along?" Or something similar, our DOW remains relatively dormant and is unable to release Its full potential until It is invited.

Thankfully each human bio-system has been equipped with its own perfect and limitless supplier of true nourishment for our DOW has the power to satiate all our hungers. When we work consciously with DOW power and the river of Grace It naturally commands, our lives become a streamlined flow of ease and joy where nothing feels like a problem and everything operates in perfect harmony and balance within the whole.

While we can satisfy our hunger for love or health or wealth, until we satisfy our natural hunger to know our DOW we will never feel fulfilled. Every being has been programmed to know its DOW for our DOW is our bio-systems intelligent creator, a force that some call God and it is not until we remember It and merge consciously with It that we can be fulfilled. The Sages call this way of being nourished as accessing the true food of the Gods.

Identifying our Hungers:

Basically our hungers can be grouped into four categories:
Physical Hunger;
Emotional Hunger;
Mental Hunger and
Spiritual Hunger.
And then we have our community and global hungers as well.

The fact is that unless all these hungers are satisfied we will always feel restless as each human being has been encoded on a cellular level with both the knowledge and the tools to satisfy all hungers. In other words we come equipped and are self sustaining. Releasing this knowledge and these skills happens via our life's journey and via specific actions and desires.

Physical Hunger is an obvious one and it presents itself as a feeling of emptiness in our stomach that remains there until we give it food. The type of food we choose either allows the body to remain healthy and regenerate itself or go into overdrive and try to deal with the toxicity that comes from choosing food or liquid substances that the body finds unnatural. While a copious amount of research has been done into correct physical nutrition, what we wish to move into in this book is utilizing another source of nourishment that the body can access in order to keep healthy and be disease free. The good news is that accessing this type of nourishment also satisfies our emotional, mental and spiritual hungers for this is the nature of DOW power and the Divine One Within holds the key to a limitless source of nourishment.

The reasons for our hungers are as varied as we are, some of it goes back to being unfulfilled in our previous experiences, some to just never getting enough – like a person who felt unloved as a child and who may feel emotionally insecure and becomes hungry for love and approval. Or mothers of children who choose to remain out of the work force when their children are young may feel hungry for mental stimulation while others feel hungry for a creative outlet. Teenagers are often hungry to be let loose in the world to experience all that life has to offer them while people who are in their sunset years may feel hungry for their youth again.

Similarly on a more metaphysical level, some souls hunger for an experience of life in a denser Beta field world while others hunger to leave it.

There are a myriad of types of hungers and reasons for our hungers and in order to understand some of these it is helpful to look first at some of the reasons why we block our ability to be nourished, next it is helpful to explore the natural cycles of human awareness which allow us to either be open or closed to the type of information held in the 'Divine Nutrition Series' and also the different sources of nourishment that we have available to us which I classify as either conventional or non-conventional.

Before we proceed with the Divine Nutrition Program, let's look a little deeper at the classification of the 3 nourishment levels that we can access. While I dislike categorization as they can further separate our species, for the purpose of this book it will be easier to make the below referencing.

LEVEL 1 in the Divine Nutrition Program (DNP):
A level 1 bio-system is a hungry one. It dies at an average age of seventy and experiences a slow system break down over time. It is susceptible to physical, emotional, mental and spiritual dis-ease and its health and happiness and peace and prosperity levels fluctuate. Level 1's rarely leave the Beta frequency field.

LEVEL 2 in the DNP:
A level 2 bio-system is a system that is being nourished enough on all levels so that the individual experiences sustainable and fulfilling levels of health and happiness and peace and prosperity. Level 2's tend to keep their brain wave patterns in the Alpha – Theta field.

LEVEL 3 in the DNP:

A level 3 bio-system is an individual who is free from the need of many of Earth's resources, who can – if they wish to – sustain themselves without the need of physical food and whose system remains healthy and disease free. Some 'level 3's' are also free from the death and aging process. A level 3 bio-system is also using many of their 'paranormal' powers and tends to sustain their brain wave patterns in the Theta – Delta field.

Chapter 2

Divine Nutrition Gifts, Brain Wave Patterns & Our Paranormal Powers

In order to understand 'The Food of Gods' with its gift of Divine Nutrition, we need to examine our brain wave pattern range as after a decade of experiential research I have found that there are literally two secrets to the successful access of this realm. The first is our personal frequency which is determined by our lifestyle and the second – which also influences our personal frequency – is the field of our brain wave patterns. The rate, or cycles per second that our brain wave patterns operate in, and also their amplitude, can determine how well we are being nourished in life and, if tuned in a certain manner, can also reveal another source of nourishment as yet relatively unexplored by the western world.

During a visit to India in 2002 and a meeting with Dr Sudhir Shah and his research team, I was given what I feel to be an important link in understanding the Divine Nutrition journey. I had already been guided to write this book with the focus on future research that I felt still needed to be done in the 'Divine nourishment field', when Dr Shah's personal research into brain wave patterns triggered me into a new level of understanding. In order to accept the food of Gods as a source of pure nutrition, we need to understand more of how the body and our brain works and we will address the area of Brain Wave pattern research in more detail later.

Brain Wave patterns and the Divine Nutrition Program:

Briefly, there are four main brain wave patterns which are:
- ❖ the Beta brain wave pattern at 14 to 30 cycles per second – level 1;
- ❖ the Alpha brain wave pattern at 8 to 13 cycles per second – level 2 & 3;
- ❖ the Theta brain wave pattern at 4 to 7 cycles per second – level 2 & 3 – and lastly,
- ❖ The Delta brain wave pattern at .5 to 3 cycles per second – level 3.

Although research on the differing type of brain wave patterns that occur between yogis and someone untrained in working with consciously altering their brain wave patterns, is now being done; what has not yet been explored is:-

What can happen within a human system when the slower in frequency, but higher in amplitude, brain wave patterns are sustained for long periods of time; in other words what happens to a person's life when they choose to anchor themselves in the Theta brain wave field? And …

How is this anchoring done?

All of this will be discussed in later chapters but now let's address the gifts that life in the Theta field can provide us with.

Paranormal Powers:

Research has found that when the Theta – Delta frequency pattern is held, the following attributes are evident in a person's life. These attributes are sometimes classified as paranormal powers that can be seen as:-

- ❖ Pre-cognition – the ability to sense what is about to occur;
- ❖ Telepathy – the ability to pick up unspoken mental-plane communications;
- ❖ Bi-location – the ability to be in two places at once, or to send a holographic projection of oneself somewhere else;
- ❖ Clairsentience and empathy – the ability to sense or feel what others are feeling;
- ❖ Clairvoyance – the ability to see between the worlds with our third eye;
- ❖ The ability to heal through touch or over distances plus much more.

The Theta – Delta pattern is the home of our latent paranormal abilities and when accessed allows our inner resources of Divine Nutrition to flow. In the metaphysical world, which power/s a person has often depends on the role they have agreed to play in the cycles of human evolution.

When the Theta and the Delta brain wave patterns are sustained not only does the veil go down between the conscious and subconscious mind allowing reprogramming of the whole bio-system in a more effective way, but we also begin to tap into other realms of reality, where issues like the following become more real for us:

- ❖ Divine radiance – where we can increase or decrease our auric emanations so that our presence nourishes others in a healthy way.
- ❖ Divine intentions – where we understand the power of our intentions and will in co-creation and use them with wisdom for the good of all and are hence supported by powerful and nourishing universal forces.
- ❖ Divine guidance – access to an inner plane system of reliable help.
- ❖ Divine prosperity – access to all the abundance we need to be fulfilled on all levels.
- ❖ Divine transmissions – the ability to enjoy two way communications with beings who are permanently anchored in the Theta – Delta field and to do so via empathic or telepathic means.
- ❖ Divine co-creation – the ability to, and action of, creating in a way that stimulates and releases the highest potentialities into manifestation.
- ❖ Divine Grace is an inexplicable energy that is incredible to experience, Grace is the oil that smoothes the way in life.
- ❖ Divine communication – communion with the God within and the inner plane Holy Ones

❖ Divine manifestation – the ability to recognize the will of the Creator and to manifest according to the Divine Plan's current agenda which is our conscious co-creation of paradise on Earth.
❖ Divine bliss – true emotional, mental and spiritual nourishment.
❖ Divine nutrition as in pranic feeding and the freedom it brings and
❖ Divine revelation – the zone of true knowing beyond limited perceptions and realities.

The above are some of the benefits that come from accessing the Divine Nutrition channel and we will elaborate on these later.

I call these gifts that we receive when we are in tune with the Madonna Frequency. The Madonna Frequency is the frequency of Divine Love and Divine compassion. The Madonna Frequency is the deliverer of the true food of the Gods, because (although this is totally unscientific in explanation) the metaphysical fact is that what allows us to be nourished – and maintain pure health without the need of taking physical food or vitamin supplements if this be our life choice – is an energy which can only be described as pure Divine Love and I believe that this energy of Divine Love is triggered automatically when a person maintains the Theta – Delta brain wave patterns.

I once met a man who said to me: "Why do you speak so much of the Divine? It's always 'Divine this' and 'Divine that'. And you say that we are Divine beings and maybe that is true for you but I certainly am not Divine."

I could have responded and quoted John 14.2 and said as Jesus did: "I shall go to the house of my Father to prepare for you an abode. The house of my Father has many abodes. On that day you shall know that I am with the Father, the Father in me and I in you. You are God". But that only impresses those of the Christian faith. What about the Buddhist who believes in a Supreme Intelligence rather than a God as we know it and what has this to do with the science of measuring brain wave patterns and Divine Nutrition?

When the abode is well prepared or tuned, then Divine Nutrition flows and is physically released within us especially when we consciously tune our brain wave patterns into the Theta – Delta fields. And Divinity?

Divinity is a state, an experience, a feeling of awe and recognition and wonder and appreciation when we find our self in the Presence of something that truly is sublime. Does it exist? Can we all experience this? This depends on our desire and also our capacity to perceive it yet most amazingly, if we believe in the Divine and ask It to reveal Itself to us, It does particularly when we meet It half way by consciously tuning ourselves into the Theta field where It expresses Itself more freely.

I like the game of logic, I like the game of trust and faith, I like the quantum game that says we can alter events just by the viewing of them and I like the fact that we can test the idea that we are Gods in form and that what we focus on comes into being if we all believe in it enough and do what is required to retune the fields. I like the idea that this means that if we unify and focus collectively then we can co-create anything on this Earth. I also like the experience of the vastness of creation, the knowing that God is everywhere and that this includes within us and as such all is naturally Divine. The role of the modern day metaphysician is now only to absorb the proper nourishment to support us as we act as if we are Divine. I also like the fact that with proper nourishment, enjoying our 'para'normal powers will become a common aspect of all our lives.

It's interesting to look at the idea of 'normal' or what is considered acceptable to the status quo. In our modern day world it is normal to suffer dis-ease and bio-system breakdown and decay. It is normal to die at around age 70 and to experience emotional highs and lows. Violence is tolerated as an everyday fact as is the suffering of our children. Personally I would like to think that as we learn how to stop blocking our inner nourishment flow, that these things become abnormal rather than every day. All it takes is education to inspire us to understand and make more supportive choices which are easier to make when we understand the natural cycles of human awareness.

Chapter 3

Cycles of Human Hungers and Awareness

Like many metaphysicians in this world, I was born with an inbuilt hunger to be in the Theta field of life even though many in my personal field were oblivious to such drives. However in the metaphysical world there are reasons and also natural cycles to our hungers that are outlined in diagram 1 at the end of this chapter. These can also be seen as stages in our lives and when these are understood our drives are easier to explain and handle.

Stage 1: Operating in the Beta Field and always being hungry on some level.
LEVEL 1 in the Divine Nutrition Program (DNP):

This is the state of the mass of human consciousness. It is the 'I need to survive here' stage of 'looking out for number one'. In the Western world where we have more choices, our pre-occupations here are 'where will I work', 'where will I live', 'who will I marry', 'should I have children', 'how many' etc. Then we may enter into the stage of the doing of this which is followed by the looking after our self and our family as well as we can. Here we may be struggling to survive – as per the 3 billion or more people in our world who often exist on less than $1 USD per day – or we may be surviving quite nicely thank you yet something within us somehow still feels a little empty.

In this first stage our brain wave patterns are resonating at the Beta frequency of 14 – 30 cycles per second and our focus is generally consumed by a 'me, me and mine' mentality. When we are in this frequency field the idea of Divine Nutrition and living by Its Light usually seems ridiculous, unfeasible or something that belongs to some future dream world that is maybe populated by yogis and enlightened beings. Essentially it is unimaginable as a choice for us and just not part of our personal reality.

Stage 2: Discovering the Alpha Field and sometimes feeling hungry.
LEVEL 1 & 2 in the Divine Nutrition Program (DNP):

Once our hunger for survival has been met, and even sometimes while we are still striving to survive, a human being may begin to seek to thrive rather than just survive. This next stage often occurs due to lack of emotional, mental and/or spiritual nourishment or sometimes due to a near death type experience. Here we may ask questions like "Who am I?", "Why am I here?", or "Surely there is more to life than just paying the bills and raising a family?"

These types of questions are prompted by that part of us that is limitless, all knowing and who is here as a Divine being who is having a human experience and who wishes us to wake-up and become more aware. When we think like this we stimulate our brain wave patterns into the Alpha zone of a more reflective, meditative consciousness which often opens the door for higher knowing to flow through.

In this stage we also move into the 'me and them' awareness of yogic duality where we realize we are not the centre of the universe and that others exist and have needs as well and that we can co-exist with these others either in harmony or disharmony. In this field of awareness our choices become apparent and we may start to glimpse the fact that we are not victims but are the master of our own destiny. In Stage 2 our brain wave patterns are firmly anchored in the Alpha zone of 8 to 13 cycles per second although we may dip into the Beta zone when we allow our selves to be stressed from time to time. This stress becomes greater when we are pulled back into the Beta field. In this stage we know by experience, that when we meditate, and take time out and make different choices that the 'feel good' Alpha vibes return.

In this stage we are usually aware of the benefits of a healthy, fresh food, and maybe even a meat free diet; of the benefits of treating the body as a temple and exercising it and also the benefits of yoga and regular meditation, and time spent in solitude and contemplation; and perhaps we are even aware of the nourishment we receive when we are kind and compassionate to others and to ourselves.

In this stage we are beginning to understand that life mirrors our own consciousness and that we can control the journey of our awareness as personal growth issues become important. Here honesty and self assessment and questions like "Am I really happy?" and "If not, why not?" and "What can I do to change this?" may consume us. As mentioned, entering the Alpha field can even be triggered by a 'mid-life crisis'. In this stage we have usually had some sort of feeling or experience of being guided by a higher power in our life, or we have been involved in 'co-incidences' and synchronicities that we cannot explain.

Stage 3: Discovering the Theta Field and rarely being hungry.
LEVEL 2 & 3 in the Divine Nutrition Program (DNP):
The more time we spend with our brain wave patterns anchored in the Alpha zone, aware that we can co-exist compassionately and be in harmony with others, the more at peace and fulfilled we become – particularly if we have learnt to listen to and trust our inner voice or 6th sense of intuition, which is the guidance of our authentic self – our DOW.

In this stage we have moved into the field of unified consciousness where we may even feel 'at one' with everything as if we are just one small cell in the body of some Divine organism that seems to pulsate with a compassionate, intelligent and loving awareness. In this stage we have realized that how we spend our time, and what we pay attention to, will directly influence the type of experiences that we attract in life. By this stage we have become aware of the power of our thoughts to create reality and hence we now choose thoughts that create the type of life where we feel as if we are thriving and in tune with a greater game. In stage 3 we have trained ourselves to see the God in all life and to recognize the perfection of creation and the natural cycles of all life, as we feel the tantra of life and duality and feelings of separation disappear and we realize that our DOW is eternal and that death is just an illusion.

In this stage our brain wave patterns are firmly anchored in the Theta zone of 4 to 7 cycles per second. In this field Divine Revelations and Holy Visions are more common as are visitations with Holy Beings that reside on the Inner realms and who are accessible when our 6th sense of intuition and our 7th sense of knowing are activated and tuned to their channels. We tune to them via the power of programming, and the conscious direction of our will and intention, and our success at connecting with them is determined by the purity of our heart levels which then magnetize the pure of heart to us. The more we spend time in this field, the more we wish to 'give something back', to serve and be of use to others and to have our presence contribute positively in this world.

It is in the Theta field where the Shaman as a master of ecstasy, or the yogi as a student of the Divine, comes into his or her true power. Simultaneously as we begin to witness the vastness of creation we realize that the more we think we know, the more we see just how little we know.

Stage 4: BEing in the Delta Field and never being hungry.
LEVEL 3 in the Divine Nutrition Program (DNP):

In this stage all our questions disappear as our inner being has been flooded with such powerful nutrition that we hunger no more. Our physical body has been flooded by so much light, love, joy and Divine ecstasy that every cell is vibrating at the frequency of a true God in form; in this stage our emotional body has been flooded with such an unconditionally loving Presence that we find ourselves experiencing a deep knowingness and awe of the beauty, perfection and immensity of creation. Our mental being may or may not retain conscious awareness in this field as this depends on how deep we dive into the Delta zone, however bathing in this field changes us permanently and on such deep levels that we can not explain our experience there and often lose our words when we try.

In this stage we often oscillate between the Theta and Delta fields as it is difficult to retain the desire to function in, or partake of, the physical world when we are immersed in the Delta zone – in fact our awareness of the physical world usually disappears when we bathe in this frequency field. This is the realm of the 'All That Is' and of perfection consciousness, for it is the home of the Gods where pure nourishment and creative possibilities flow endlessly.

The Food of Gods is a timeless mystery that is delivered throughout our system when our brain wave patterns are resonating from deep within the Delta Field. As already mentioned, it is a quality form of nourishment that feeds our human soul and also our cells. In spiritual terms this energy from the Delta Field, in its purest essence, is love. In Dimensional Biofield terms it is simply a brain wave pattern that can unlock inner doors that when opened, and programmed, have the ability to flood our atoms with a supreme type of nourishment that we call Divine Nutrition.

Known as Manna and Prana and Chi and the Universal Life Force, on an alchemical level this Delta field essence also expresses itself via a wave of Grace, where magic and co-incidence rule via a synchronistic and harmonious flow. Able to be aligned with and experienced, the wave of Grace of the Delta Field adds a level to life that provides us with the purest nourishment we need.

Stage 5: Freedom
LEVEL 3 in the Divine Nutrition Program (DNP):
I would like to add another stage here which is the stage of true freedom. When we have explored and experienced the benefits of stages 1 to 4, one of three things occurs:

1. First we have learnt to be free from the things that block the Divine Nutrition flow.
2. Next, if we haven't completed our work here, we are intuitively guided to anchor ourselves firmly in the Theta field and to be a radiant example of impeccable mastery in a way that nurtures the world and from this centre of focus we learn again how to compassionately serve. The 'I' disappears and is replaced by the 'we'.
3. Lastly, if we have completed the work we agreed to do on this plane, when we find ourselves anchored in the Theta – Delta wave, we may be given the opportunity to leave. I used to joke that when this time came that God would send a cosmic limousine to collect us and until that happened we needed to relax and have some fun and get on with fulfilling the things we had come to do. What instead occurs is that we become so filled with the love and light, that is the true food of the Gods, so that we are overwhelmed by, and merge into, a band of pure magnetic love that seduces us from our body. In other words we ascend and are given the opportunity to ascend into a realm of pure light and leave our physical form.

Cycles of Human Awareness:

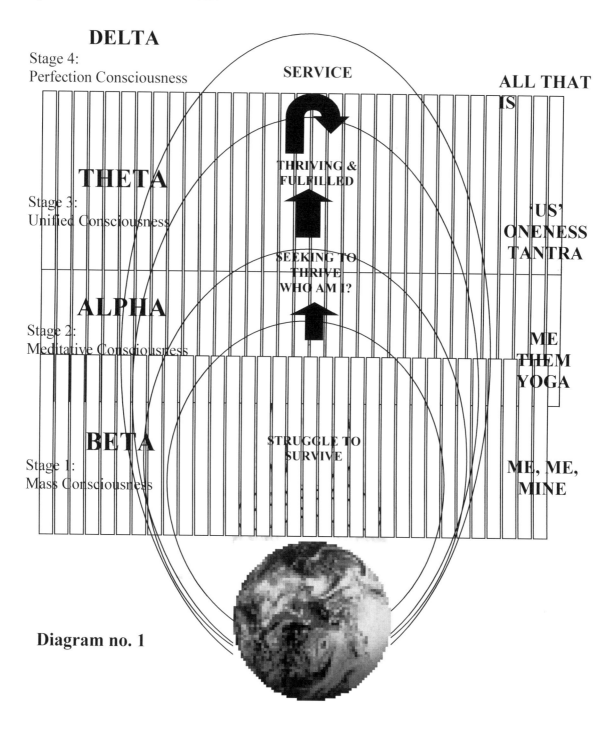

DELTA

Stage 4:
Perfection Consciousness

SERVICE

ALL THAT IS

THRIVING & FULFILLED

THETA

Stage 3:
Unified Consciousness

'US' ONENESS TANTRA

SEEKING TO THRIVE
WHO AM I?

ALPHA

Stage 2:
Meditative Consciousness

ME THEM YOGA

BETA

Stage 1:
Mass Consciousness

STRUGGLE TO SURVIVE

ME, ME, MINE

Diagram no. 1

Chapter 4

Blocking our Nourishment
The Atrophy of Life

In his book *Self Matters* current daytime TV guru and Oprah Winfrey supporter, Dr Phil McGraw, shares that only people who choose to listen to their authentic self (their DOW) end up fulfilled; as their 'fictional self' – the aspect of our self that is molded by our culture and conditioning, does not have the capacity to give us what we require. He states that because our fictional self is usually too caught up with fulfilling everyone's expectations of us, we often end up completely out of touch with our true nature. I believe that the continual ignoring of this authentic self leads us into a state of emotional, mental and spiritual anorexia and the atrophy of health and happiness levels in our life. The ignoring of our authentic self is the no 1 cause of all dis-ease on Earth today and our lack of holistic awareness, and/or disbelief in Its power, blocks Its ability to keep us properly nourished.

There are many factors in life that we encounter and allow to block our access to the Divine Nutrition Channel. Apart from feeding the physical body toxic substances that are chemically at odds with what it needs, there are also the 'fear and judgment' blocks that are part of the toxic feeling and toxic thinking game. Fear of death, fear of change, fear of being different, or the judgment of self and others – all of these impede the nourishing flow of our authentic self's unconditional love.

Lack of nourishment means we are always dancing with our death as this lack feeds the atrophy of life and with the lack of nourishment of human contact and love; our Divine Self cannot operate at Its maximum potential. Unaware of Its true power and role in our life, we choose to block our inner voice, and the food It offers, by forgetting It is there or by treating our Divine (authentic) Self as if It were an external God that only talks to the priests and the Holy instead of as a part of who we are. We ignore It by our material world focus, we seek Its answers when in need and then relegate It like an unappreciated friend into the deeper valleys of our mind where only a bath in the Theta – Delta waves can release It from the prison of our ignorant actions. We choose lifestyles that perpetuate death and disease as if our life was never a precious gift from an imaginative and loving Source that endlessly breathes life.

The atrophy of our bodies, minds and inner joy being, happens through both our negligence and the fact that certain experiences have been pre-selected – or at least the learning of their outcomes. In other words even our ignorance can be a source of food for ignorance often allows us to make choices from which great suffering and then learning can come.

The cycle of life – and us upon it; the cycle of Earth as a planet kept alive by the food of the sun; the cycles of a sun fed by a Central Sun; the cycles of the inner and outer galaxies; and the cycles of universes held and unfolding within universes – all are just cycles in time. A Divine heart beats, a Divine breath creates sounds and words and magical rhythms of life and so it all goes on with people seeking answers to superficial and superluminal questions while others seek nourishment for their cells and their souls. While some block the call of true nourishment, others blossom and open to it and the game goes on – again just cycles in time. All unfolds perfectly with no right or wrong – just another rhythm of life, and each rhythm adjusts itself to mirror the consciousness of our mind. How we as individuals choose to be nourished is quite irrelevant in the greater scheme of it all – as is our suffering and learning, or lack of it, and our pain – and yet it is not irrelevant to us as we are here now, alive and able to dive through the depths of it all.

It is easy to criticize ourselves and others and ask why we block our nourishment from the one Source that nurtures us all, is it ignorance or arrogance or simply amnesia of this Source? Is it just lack of holistic education? And who's to say that all the death and disease that we perpetuate aren't a perfect part in a natural cycle of our learning called life? Perhaps our senses have become so dulled by the Beta field that we've become insensitive to Its true call. Yet as more of us remember our Source, the clearer our choices become – we can breathe in Its power and blossom or we can ignore It and experience the 'normal' cycle where we see our lives atrophy and die.

The Dance of the Dying

I began a new year – 2003 – with my mind filled with such questions for death was at my door. So many loved ones moving on slowly or moved on – a dying pet, a dying father, a dying marriage, a dying life. Although it all sounded difficult there was so much to be thankful for, for I was witnessing a feast of change, of human emotion and control, and assessment and recognition, and questioning and just dealing with it all. At least I had a ton of tools to work with, tools that I could utilize to tune myself through it all with minimal negative side affects – tools that I would like to share in this book.

Things like too much melancholy is never good for the soul and fear in particular, of change or of the unknown – puts our energy fields into a classic Beta cycle of static that is almost like a burning at the stake, those times of crucifixion by fire that our fanaticism created in the time of less enlightened past, a darker cycle in time. And yet death can bring rebirth when we truly let go and agree to change and to move on. Marriages, like lives, can be reborn by giving them the nourishment that they need – yet only when two people listen to their authentic self, can our relationships truly blossom. The first step to feeding our selves properly is to recognize when we are not being fed and then having the courage to change things so that we are and to not block a needed transition – for the death of something is always followed by rebirth.

The bonding that can occur in the time of a dying is a joy to experience and witness. It's a time to be real and honest and to assess and re-choose and value and do hand in hand – up to a point – for the true dance of both dying and rebirth is always done alone.

Fear of loss and fear of death can inhibit the way we love which can inhibit the way we are fed. A few years ago my youngest daughter declared as we lovingly buried our first pet rat to whom she had become extraordinarily close:

"That's it! I am never going to have another pet – all they do is die – and I can't stand the pain of it all." Yet I knew that her pain would atrophy her heart and prevent her from experiencing the nutrition that unconditional love can fill it with so that same afternoon I brought two new baby rats home for us to love.

My pet rat Mondi has been the most loyal and loving friend. From the moment we met eyes we became quite entranced with each other. "Hi!" her eyes and whiskers said. "God, it's great to meet you!" At least that was the feeling she induced within me as my inner child giggled in excited anticipation. I just knew we'd be great friends, and we were.

There are times in life that ask us to act with a certain dignity and Grace. The dance of dying is one of them. Seeing Mondi waddle around at the grand old age of ninety plus, with her brown fur tinged with grey, and eyes that tell me she is tired, touching my caring soul. Then when I channel my love to her small form I feel her body strengthen and feed and it's an amazing sight to behold – almost 'vampire-ish' yet in a very gentle way. One blast of love seems to give her a new lease of years – at least in rat terms. And how can we deny our loved ones real food? As she nestles into my hand I cup her back gently in both hands so that my fingers can stroke her on her brow and I am reminded of how precious it all is – this bonding between animal and man. Its gift is the sheer joy of connection and getting to play in the field of another intelligent life, for rats are incredibly intelligent. The rat was the first creature to answer the call of the Buddha.

Adopting a rat as a friend is a very wise idea for anyone interested in the interplay with another intelligent species, or for someone who wishes to experience a little more of the unconditional love food of life. For a start they are great examples of work and play, and seeking and finding, and responding, and having fun, for they are always ready for a game. Mondi loves it when I hold her upside down, lying on her back, legs in the air, while I tickle and stroke her. I'm sure her little belly just quivers at my touch as she soaks up lots of the nourishing chi energy that flows from my fingers. Our hands can be as holy and healing as we wish, and there are times to recognize this and use them as such for even our hands can channel the true food of the Gods.

Nestled against my heart chakra I'd open it further and begin to flood her fields with my love as if a big lighthouse beam is on. Mondi always sits there and drinks it up, as I talk soothingly to her, interested in her day and telling her of the new home at the beach where I have begun my solitude time of life for my dying marriage and hungry self are being re-born by a silent sojourn by the sea.

Unplugged from technology, my time out time is bliss and my heart has begun to release Its joy again. I know Mondi also needs some beach air and more time with me as she figures out her needs. Is death a negotiable process? Perhaps it is. Yet watching somebody go through the dance of the dying, and knowing there is nothing you can do but give them love and support in whatever way they need, is a very interesting experience. Developing the sensitivity to feed others what they need can develop in us the ability to nourish our selves as well.

* * *

As I lean on my dying father's bed we look lovingly into each other's eyes and recognize the reflection of our own souls. It's been nice between us, precious somehow, particularly since my mother died as we've had so much more time to enjoy together, to bond as fathers and daughters can do. My mother's presence always filled his eyes with light and after she died a part of him went with her, leaving him as someone incomplete. Meeting his new wife gave him a few more happy years to his life yet he dearly wished to move on and so he bargained with his God, asking and praying and now his time had come.

"I'm calm," he'd said, "And so is she." He continued while looking lovingly at his wife as she shuffled out into the corridor of the ward.

"The hospital is nice." We all agreed, well prepared for this next game unsure of the roll of the dice.

"The doctor wants to talk to you all tomorrow, I can't tell you anymore, but I know and I'm calm," he sighed as if he was glad there was set time – time to prepare. "No pain, the doctor told me and no dementia."

"Yes, I agree – this way will be much better. Your system will just become weak." We nodded in silent agreement having guessed the outcome of his tests. Later I asked, "Do you have no will to fight this? I'm sure it can shrink and disappear." I said pointing to the tennis ball sized tumor that now blocked his stomach entrance and intruded into his esophagus.

"No, I'm happy and calm," was his reply.

"A new adventure …" we both said at once, and giggled like a couple of kids.

"Are you nervous?" I asked.

"No, I'll see them all … your mother, and Paul and Nina."

"And your mum and sister too."

"Yes," He grinned.

"Scared?" I asked and then said, "It's really just letting go."

"Only of the fire," he responded. And I realized he didn't mean the brimstone type as hell just wasn't part of his agenda.

"OK, I promise."

"What?" he asked.

"To check there are no eyelids fluttering before we send you into the crematorium fire." We laughed again and said in unison: "Deal."

I saw the nurse from the corner of my eyes. Perhaps she thought it all a little strange, yet we'd been preparing for this time for years.

How does a tired and hungry soul leave the human form? In the civilized dying game a Lama will meditate and leave at will. For others we simply break the body down over time, as everything breaks down over time unless it is properly nourished with food that can keep it alive and whole. Sometimes the allotted time and learning games synchronize like a book to be closed when it's been read and its message has been imparted with the turning of each page.

I'd been thinking of the stages of life, our personal cycles in time, and how sometimes the load can weigh us down. Or when a chapter has been digested and we are suddenly open to a new life, a way of being nourished and feel complete in the 'I am pleased with who I am and what I have created' line that we eventually must look at in life.

"How long does he have?" I asked the doctor as he later tells us all the options.

"Three maybe four months, depending on what he decides – we need to keep him nourished and curb the losing of weight. Otherwise he will just waste away and suffer other complications."

Later as I kiss and hug my father helping him to sit up and enjoy his cooled down cappuccino, he looks at me and smiles.

"Next month, I'd like to go next month. Yes I think it will be next month."

"I wonder if we can order it? Or if there is a calendar that says, 'oh yes, there's Arnie he's due out any day. When did he clock in? Aha! And when is he due to clock out? Uhuh! Thirty days? Forty days?' Sounds civilized, like retrenchment papers being served." My father chuckled quietly to himself and closed his eyes to rest.

And so I watch and wait, and Dad watches and waits, and each day he gets a little weaker. Sometimes he's full of fun with the familiar twinkle in his eye, and other times he grumbles his way, shuffling through it on tired old legs that say they've seen better days. I look at the once tall proud man of Viking stock who used to carry me into bed each night after I had fallen asleep listening to the classics on our old gramophone. A gentle giant he'd tuck me in and kiss me sweetly on my head as if I was some strange precious creature, a boy-girl who'd come unexpectedly from his loins, as after my older sister came they swore they'd have no more.

As I watch I see a caring man who'd once spent months transforming a rusty old second hand bike, delivering it looking bright and shiny and new, for my seventh birthday. I remember how he'd sing so much, in his brilliant tenor voice, that the walls in his workshop reverberated with his song, often when he was miles away, as if concrete had ears for opera or maybe the bricks just absorbed the passion of his sound.

I've spent a lot of time reminiscing as I sit on the balcony of my new beach apartment and write. 'The Food of Gods' is my focus and I look at what true nourishment is.

If food that is prepared with love tastes better, and is more nurturing for us, what about just love?

Surely pure unconditional love is the most nourishing food of all?

And what of the difference in the lives of someone who is nourished by food and good loving, compared to someone who has good food but no love?

What about food for the heart?

What about food for the mind?

And lastly, what about food for our souls?

Cells and souls, is there perfect nourishment for them both?

These are the questions that flow through my mind as the gentle sea breeze caresses my face and I sigh again thankful that I have time to think and be and no longer do.

* * *

The desire to nourish ourselves begins long before our birth. It carries over as an imprinting from another time as molecules re-gather to create a new form. The Ancient Wisdom says that half of all the atoms in each new life are re-gathered from our previous form, like old clothes cast aside then collected to dress us once more.

Regardless of such beliefs, from the moment we exit the womb, we are driven by our desire to be fed – to feed on the love of our mother, to feed on the milk of her body, to feed on her touch, to feed on the sound of her voice and to feed on her smell. Then slowly, all our senses come alive to absorb the food of the world and often it takes decades to discover what truly feeds us, and what drains us, and makes us emotionally cold and also old.

There are so many conflicting signals in the world and so the first real food comes from discernment and listening to that inner 'I know'. When we listen we are fed, when we ignore it we starve and for most of us who are born in this Beta world, we begin to die the moment we are born.

Still, there is something so blessed about witnessing the process of a new life coming into the world, and more than one mother has found herself staring in awe and wonderment at her new born child, as the feeling of such love fills her heart and her soul, feeding that need to breed that Mother Nature gifted.

There's also something so blessed about watching the process of death. Completions and endings make way for new beginnings and experiences that will feed the soul, for the true food of the soul is the living of life and the sharing and caring that it brings.

Food for the mind comes as answers to questions no matter how great or small. Food for the heart comes in waves of love that flood through us deeply enough to release the true gifts of our soul – for the soul is programmed to reveal itself within waves of love, as like will always recognize like, and our hearts and souls are both are programmed only to be fed by love.

If death is like holidays and life is like school time, then death is also food, for it feeds us a time of rest, to step back – independent of form – and assess the game of life and plan the next round. True food nurtures us giving us both chemicals and insights that provide us with the strength to grow. With the food that comes from the Gods, there is no separation for it nourishes all aspects of our being, and as such we also need to recognize all the Sources that true food can come from, particularly as we expand our viewpoints to look at what is truly nourishing.

The expansion of our thinking, moving from limited thinking to lateral thinking and limitless thinking, obviously feeds our mind for the mind of humanity has huge capabilities, and how well we are nourished on the mental plane depends on what levels we are operating. Many people are driven by unconscious desires and needs, never really knowing who they are or stopping to question what their motivation is for many of the actions that they do. Many are driven by subconscious realities that bring hungers seeking to be fed.

Rarely do we do absorb enough of the food of Gods to dwell in the level of the super-mind, except when we are being selfless, and have tuned ourselves to the channel of kindness and compassion; for the higher emotional spectrums that we have built within us of mercy, compassion, kindness, altruism, unconditional love etc. walk hand in hand with the higher aspects of our thinking on the mental plane. These are the thoughts that say to us, why we are here? Can we live in harmony? Can we co-exist in peace? Can we all get along? And when we sincerely want to know, the intelligent universe that surrounds us gives us the food we need to actualize it all and grow. These are the thoughts that also awaken and feed our DOW.

Mind Mastery versus Boxing & Limitations

In my mid teens I met an Indian Guru who I saw regularly over the next decade as I was hungry for not just what he had to say but also for the energy that radiated from him, an invisible force field that seemed to touch and feed my soul. Yet I realized over time that he always had the same thing to say, it was just delivered via different parables and analogies of life. The nourishment of the Food of Gods is like that, it just comes in different packages and forms depending on our needs; and true wisdom, like the repetitive message of the guru, is always very simple and once we know, we know.

When I was two I was hungry for physical food that was free of the vibration of fear for the meat served at our table had been slaughtered without with blessing or awareness that I was used to from when I had lived before. Unable to express the reasons for this intuitive rejection I just did what children do and struggled to be heard, as of course my mother thought my health depended on the eating of meat, and that without meat I would wither from malnourishment and die. Our lack of awareness of alternative sources of protein simply sustained our conflict and her insistence on an action that ignored my 'authentic self', resulted in a slow death on another level as spiritually I began to starve. Spiritual starvation always happens when we ignore the guidance of our DOW.

As I grew family life nourished me creatively and intellectually and my affectionate mother was always there with the food of tactility and love yet I was always hungry for more. It took decades to discover what this hunger was for as a teenager it seemed I had it all – a loving family, a healthy body, good grades at school, popularity and friends, a quick mind and sound reasoning skills, independence and even lots of love. It took awhile to isolate and discover where this hunger was coming from, and then to work through the maya of the religious minefield to fulfill what I found was a hunger in my soul. It was as if my soul had a voice that kept crying out to me in the silence and saying "There is more! There is more! And I want you to have it, I need it, you need it!"

Having finally discovered how to feed all aspects of myself via the nourishment sources we discuss in Chapter 6, I have come to witness the tendency that many have to suicide.

For example: To allow our minds to bath continually in negativity, and judgment, and the boxing of others and the disappointment that happens if they don't fulfill our expectations, is mental suicide as is the choice we make to always see the half empty glass rather than see it as being half full.

To choose to feel stressed out when events in life feel overwhelming, when meditation and its gift of Alpha – Theta pool bathing allows us to feel more detached and act rather than react, can be seen as emotional suicide, as can continually choosing to interpret events in life in a way that promotes anger, hatred or fear. To choose to feed the body physical foods that research shares can create cancer and decrease our lifespan can also be seen as a form of suicide.

Of course the above can be seen as a judgment and we all have the free will to choose how we wish to think, feel or act when we have been educated to the alternatives, for education is the key. This means education in the fact that we are more than just our minds and bodies and emotions and education into the fact that all our bodies need proper nourishment and education regarding how to do provide this in a way that is honoring of all. Once this education has been given, with its practical tools, then there really is no excuse any more for – as Gods in form – it is up to us to choose and create the life we desire to have on this physical plane and in doing this both our personal and our global needs have to be assessed. *(There are more practical tools for this in the Biofields & Bliss series.)*

For forty years I hungered for enlightenment and to have the experiences that the Holy Ones have shared. The sort of experiences that I have personally had during my life in the pursuit of this, are certainly not rare and many have been driven by such hungers that they themselves may not have understood. While I have succeeded in satisfying all of my hungers, a consequence of this is that I have also been boxed by others who have judged me too different to the norm. This feeling of judgment, when we are not yet in our own power, can be absorbed into our own energy field as toxicity, making us feel isolated or 'less than', or unacceptable, which in turn blocks our personal Divine Nutrition flow, for self acceptance and self love are required for this nourishment to work freely. Hence we will address how to dissipate these projected energies from our fields in a later chapter.

Absorption versus Radiation

The blocking of this nutritional flow can occur also due to overwhelming the bio-system with the absorption of outer plane frequencies that drain us rather than nurture us. As we sensitize our self enough to be constantly tuned to the Divine Nutrition channel, we need to address the issue of how we move in, and interact with, the world. As systems of energy we are constantly radiating and absorbing frequencies from the inner and outer realms and when learning to live effectively in the various energy fields and dimensions, many questions arise.

For example, if all life radiates energy:

❖ Do we have to absorb the random and often limiting imprints from the Beta field or even the Alpha field? No.

❖ Is it possible for a human being, knowing the benefits of the Theta and Delta fields, to exist purely in these frequencies while the majority of the world maintains the pulse of the Beta field? Yes.

❖ Also is it possible to exist in any field and not be overwhelmed by it? Yes.

❖ Can we absorb what we want from all worlds on a frequency level in a positive way? Yes.

❖ Is it easier to radiate a constant stream of energy into the world, and have it transmute everything it touches, rather than us absorbing energy randomly that we then have to transmute? Yes.

How do we do all of this? By applying the tools in this book as the great news is that due to the mechanics of Dimensional Biofield Science we have control and choice over what we wish to absorb or radiate in a field. Is there proof in this? Yes most definitely for as we apply this science our life changes for the better which is a tangible personal experience that can easily move us beyond all doubt.

Also as more of us tune to the Divine Channels for our nourishment, the global field also becomes better nourished and this is a change that can be measured via the Schumann resonance. This now proves that the old Beta field of mass consciousness, and hence the Earth's frequency itself, has changed and is now running at an Alpha resonance of about 7.4 cycles per second. This means two things, firstly that the Earth's frequency is now providing a nurturing base for humanity to bath in and catch up to and match individually; and secondly that all the Earth healing work that our grid engineers, geomancers and light workers have been doing for the last few decades is bringing positive results for those with eyes to see.

This change has also been helped by a number of other factors. For example: The Maharishi's organization has been supporting Dimensional Biofield technicians to hold open the inner doors, via meditation and lifestyle, to the Alpha – Theta – Delta field. This has resulted in the flooding of the Beta field with purer Alpha and Theta Delta frequencies – according to the capacity that each Dimensional Biofield technician has for field imprinting. Every Field Technician's abilities to consciously alter the fields will differ according to their keynote, which is affected by their day-to-day lifestyle. However, we need to understand that the predominant field of the people on Earth is still the Beta – Alpha mix, and that maintaining a pool of Theta – Delta for us to exist in and actually thrive on, can happen if we use certain simplistic but powerful devices that are guaranteed to work.

The first field control tool that we have is our attitude, where we change our mind set by asking: do we wish to absorb or do we wish to radiate? As every living thing radiates energy, when we absorb these energies indiscriminately from the world our inner field key-note changes – sometimes in a way that nurtures us and sometimes in a way that drains us – and it is up to us to choose how we wish to be affected and what we wish to absorb.

If we absorb enough mental, emotional or physical pollution, we get stressed out, ill or run down and generally become unhappy. Even if we absorb selectively, by living a specific and often restrictive lifestyle, we can still end up with a field imbalance, an inner field that is imprinted too densely by the Beta field in a way that no longer suits us. Sometimes when we are well tuned to the Alpha field we can still be hungry as our capacity has expanded and so we begin to naturally thirst for more of the frequencies – and associated realities – of the Theta field.

Our capacity for these frequencies is always changing and expanding once we move out of our self imposed boxes and limitations – physically, emotionally and mentally and spiritually. For example, a person who exercises every day has far greater capacity physically than a person who exercises once a year. A person who meditates every day has far greater sensitivity to and capacity to magnetize the Alpha – Theta – Delta waves than someone who constantly engages in Beta field activities and is never in stillness. This is why a Beta field person, who has never meditated and never experienced the love waves of their own Divine Being pulse through them, has great difficultly in comprehending the game of Divine Nourishment and living on Its light.

The Beta field is the field of poverty, violence, social injustice, emotional highs and emotional lows, and is generally a field of man-made, self-inflicted chaos. A Beta field person can increase their capacity to see, hear, feel and be nourished by the gifts of the other zones through a simple change in lifestyle that includes meditation, mind mastery and maybe even yoga.

The Alpha field reveals the Zen of life, allowing us down time, to chill out and re-set the direction of our own life, to assess the imbalances and re-address them hopefully for the good of all. Time in the Alpha zone improves our health and happiness levels and is step one in the direct and conscious feeding our soul.

The Theta field brings co-incidences that no longer seem to be random and time spent here attracts events filled with symbolism and deep, meaningful possibilities for it is a field of infinitely creative potential, a field of Grace, true nourishment and love. This is the field through which all Holiness and true messengers come. This is the zone from which all the Holy books were born.

And the Delta fields bring it all, for from its field springs paradise and the 'garden of Eden' of the Bible's God. The Delta zone is also the home of the Elohim and the Archangels and pure lore.

The opening of the inner doors and the heart and crown chakra plug in meditations, allows for our inner fields to be tuned constantly to the Delta and Theta fields on an energetic level, thus providing a very strong foundation for the elements to gather around us and respond. (These meditations are provided in Chapter's 6 & 7)

Once the inner doors are open and the system is plugged in, a new and potent radiation begins to rule the game, and the mindset needs to be one of 'walking through life imagining ourselves as transmission stations radiating Divine Love, Divine Wisdom and Divine Power – through every cell and pore and atom of our body – into the external fields'.

As all is interconnected in the fabric of the fields of life via an energy matrix finer than a gossamer web and as we know that what we focus on we feed, then our mindset and attitude are crucial in accessing the field of Divine Nutrition and sustaining Its healthy flow.

I would like to add that one of the main keys to access the Theta – Delta field is our purity of heart. This means that our emotional field needs to pulse with the signals of sincerity, humility, surrender and compassion – things that cannot be taught except in the class called 'life' and via our interaction with living beings. Unfortunately this interaction can also close our heart and fill it with emotions that block the Divine Nutrition flow which is based on the universal Law of Resonance. (see diagram at the end of this chapter)

The matter of Theta – Delta feeding requires specific fine-tuning to be successful and depends on what an individual desires to achieve and is destined to achieve. As we have shared, it also depends on:

- ❖ How open our fields are, and
- ❖ What part of us needs to be fed, as Divine Nourishment can come to us on many levels?

Due to the fact that we still exist in a predominantly patriarchal world, in my opinion balanced nutrition for our physical, emotional, mental and spiritual aspects can only come from the Madonna Frequency Field and until we are all nourished on all these levels, war, violence and chaos will remain part of our day to day world.

Yet regardless of how our world is operating at this moment we can control our own fields. We can walk through life absorbing everything that comes our way until we are a mixed match type vegetable soup of energies or we can cleanse our fields and plug our selves in to the Divine Nutrition Channel and radiate the nourishing frequencies of Divine Love and Wisdom into this world. To absorb or radiate is simply a matter of choice that comes from the utilization of the type of tools we offer in this book.

Later we will look at specific Bio-Shield Devices that we can use to shield our selves from frequencies that we feel are no longer nurturing. We will also move on to look at how to 'Weave a Field' which means how to create specific types of energy fields for true nurturing and how to also re-weave an existing field so that when we exist in it, we are more receptive to the benefits of being in the Theta – Delta wave.

Diagram 2:

Blocking our Nourishment due to our field signals. Whatever we store, we radiate out into the surrounding fields which then (as energy expands and contracts), attracts like frequencies and comes back to its source of origin – us.

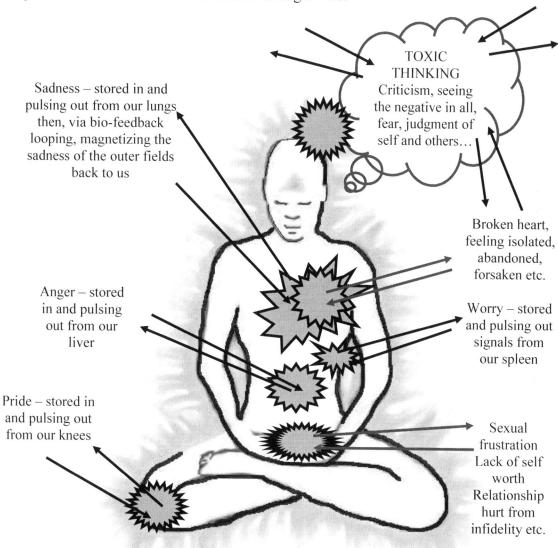

TOXIC THINKING
Criticism, seeing the negative in all, fear, judgment of self and others…

Sadness – stored in and pulsing out from our lungs then, via bio-feedback looping, magnetizing the sadness of the outer fields back to us

Broken heart, feeling isolated, abandoned, forsaken etc.

Anger – stored in and pulsing out from our liver

Worry – stored and pulsing out signals from our spleen

Pride – stored in and pulsing out from our knees

Sexual frustration Lack of self worth Relationship hurt from infidelity etc.

The more our cells and organs are filled with unresolved toxic emotions and the longer we have an unchecked constant stream of toxic thinking, the more we block our ability to attract, hold and radiate the nourishment levels that we need to achieve and maintain emotional, mental and spiritual health. Choosing positive thinking patterns and flooding our bio-system with Violet Light will retune our cells to attract a more nourishing field.
More on this in Chapter 6.

Chapter 5

The Nourishment of Prana –
Feeding like the Gods

Everything new that comes into being always has a history and sometimes something that seems new is often found to be ancient – this is the way with the path of Divine Nutrition and its gift of physical, emotional, mental and spiritual body nutrition. The say when new information comes first it is ridiculed, then opposed then finally accepted and so it has been with our journey to offer this way of being to the world yet we continue to do so, safe in the knowledge that what we share has the potential to bring humanity into a state of true freedom. Freedom from the need to eat, to drink, to sleep, to age or be dis-eased or even die, is the second level of the Divine Nutrition Program yet the full potential of the benefits of Theta – Delta field living is yet to be fully explored. I am sure there are a myriad of other gifts that will come to us, particularly when we get a mass field tuning.

I look back over the last decade, at all the people I have met who have challenged me or inspired me to do more research, to go deeper within myself and to understand more about Divine Nutrition and prana power, and to them I give my heartfelt thanks.

Everything of course is so much easier in retrospect, and the 'if onlys' can forever haunt us in our dreams. "If only I had known then what I know now, if only I had done this or that, if only I had been more prepared."

I used to say that if I had known what was destined for me in the field of 'The Food of Gods', first I would have become a doctor, and then I would have become a priest. Both would have been so advantageous in dealing with our skeptical world, except that sometimes the naivety of pure faith is one of the requirements to access Level 3 of the field of Divine Nutrition. Perhaps too much intellectual knowledge may bind the door of our heart.

It has always been demanded of the pioneers of our world that we have courage and trust and faith – for defying the odds, expanding boundaries and challenging the status quo while we maintain personal balance and integrity is an interesting task and one for either the brave hearted or just naïve.

When I first became public with my experiential research in the 'Level 3' field of Divine Nutrition, people said that my naivety protected me and in retrospect I think it's true, for faith allows many to surf the waves of life unaware of the resistance that lies beneath the tides of change.

In retrospect my journey was clear from the beginning, it was to bring the focus back to the power of the Divine, for 'The Food of Gods' offers so much more than our freedom from the need to take nourishment from physical food. The fact that the Divine Nutrition Channel can provide love and healing and guidance has unfortunately been overlooked in the public response to the phenomena of pranic feeding. This book is my attempt to bring it all back into perspective and to also provide a safe, step by step program for all who desire it, to plug into the Divine Nutrition channel.

Is there a simpler way? Probably.

Do we know it all? Not by a long shot but this is what we have understood to date.

Do we recommend more experiential and scientific and medical research? Definitely!

Are the pioneers of new ways of being perfect? No. Most of us are just individuals who are learning as we go, who are open to explore the mysteries of life and who are strong willed and pure hearted enough to walk a path less trodden.

People often say how advantageous it would be to have all the facts and steps of a plan, with logic and motivation, goals and outcomes, all laid bare, before they proceed to fulfill a given task. Unfortunately in the realm of service, for initiates exploring the field of the Gods, this is rarely how it's done. The journey of trust and faith walk hand in hand in every spiritual warrior's life and the entry key to the higher realms, and the kingdom of the Gods, is an energetic mix of sincerity, humility and surrender. These are virtues that only the doing and living of life can deliver to our door. The desire to experience more and the discipline to tune ourselves to the Divine Nutrition Channel are also keys that we need but the benefits are worth it.

Some say there is no such thing as destiny, that life is what we make of it, and that it is always our choice to take advantage of what comes our way, whether it is for personal or global gain. Yet in the world of Gods anything that is dreamed can become real and avenues to do so have been long laid down over time. Certain pathways have been trodden yet rarely completely explored, for the fields of creative possibility are indeed endless. As such each pathway acts as a field of magnetic attraction that pulses out invitations to those with the desire to explore, for the law of resonance will always allow like minds to be attracted and like fields to merge and play.

A person who acts with integrity will always be free of regret, especially when they act with a purity of heart and a desire to deliver something that is beneficial for all. Yet this will not shield the pure of heart from the anger, ignorance or confusion of those who will be challenged by a newer or purer view. So it is, and so it has always been, and so perhaps it will remain. And so it is that the information contained in the 'Divine Nutrition: Living on Light Series' has, and will, challenge many industries from the medical and pharmaceutical to even the holistic health industry – as when we really tap into this field of nourishment all dis-ease and disharmony disappears. As the reality of Divine Nutrition and ways to easily access it become more widely accepted, then many in the medical and nutritional fields will eventually face unemployment for the individual and global demand for their services will lessen over time. This is just a natural path of our evolution and proof of the innate intelligence that we possess that allows us to learn and grow.

One of the joys of life is that we do all learn and that we can refine things and we can make them better. The fact that there have been problems for some people, due to lack of preparation and other reasons, when they have attempted the initiation I discussed in Book 1, has led me to search for a simpler, less challenging program for people to undergo to ensure their success in accessing the Divine Nutrition field.

Before we move on to look at the different forms of nourishment that we have available to us, I would like to clarify the difference between the living on light and 'Divine Nutrition: Food of Gods' reality.

- ❖ This can best be summed up by the following points:
- ❖ The most important difference with our focus on Divine Nutrition is that It has the ability to feed us *on all levels* and that
- ❖ We can still benefit from increasing Its flow through our bio-system *even if we continue to choose to enjoy eating*. Allowing this Divinely Nutritional stream to be increased in our system means that we can be fed emotionally, mentally and spiritually and as such the techniques and guidelines shared in this book, will benefit us all by freeing us from our current personal and global emotional, mental and spiritual states of anorexia. As already mentioned, I have come to call this Level 1 of the Divine Nutrition Program.
- ❖ Providing the tools and research to do this is my real focus in the world and just part of my life's work for I know that when we learn to nourish our selves enough – and from free and purer sources – then our planet will blossom into a state of paradise for all. Committing my life just to the issue of 'to eat or not to eat' is too limiting an agenda for me particularly since I have seen what really can be achieved when we access the food of Gods Divine Nutrition channel.
- ❖ Once we have increased the intensity of this flow and directed it in a manner that will give us a pure and never-ending source of emotional, mental and spiritual nutrition, *we can then choose to accept one of the additional gifts of this flow, which is It's ability to physically nourish our cells* which is Level 3 of the Divine Nutrition Program and a choice that few are drawn to make. To me this ability is a very small gift of the food of the Gods and I feel that our focus needs to be on all of the gifts. However, while this may be an acceptable option for the bulk of humanity in our future, at the moment we are still in the pioneering stages of this in the Western world and much more research needs to be done. All pioneering work requires, 'guinea pigs' or test subjects, of which perhaps you – the reader – may be one. How do you find out if you are? Keep reading and in Chapter 11 we will provide a technique for you to find out.
- ❖ Prana, of chi, or the Universal Life Force as in Reiki, all have as their underlying vibration, or base frequency, pure love and light and when these flood our bio-system, they stimulate the release of the same things within us. These are the frequencies that can sustain and nourish physically, emotionally, mentally and spiritually.

In order to understand how we can be nourished on all levels of our being we need to look at both the conventional and non-conventional Sources of nourishment that we all can access. These Sources can feed anyone interested in either Level 2 or Level 3 of this program however for Level 3 success we need to apply the additional recommendations in Chapter 11.

Chapter 6

Nourishment Sources & Types
Conventional & Non-conventional

There are a number of sources from which a human bio-system can be nourished to create physical, emotional, mental and spiritual health and happiness some of which are conventional and others are more non-conventional. A conventional source of nourishment is a source that is understood readily by the status quo and accepted as being 'normal' due to our educational history and community habits. A non-conventional source of nourishment is usually something known and utilized by metaphysical students and those of the Ancient Mystery Schools and these will be our main focus here. I call the below Level 1 & 2 Sources.

Some obvious Level 1 & Level 2 sources of nourishment are:

- ❖ of 1a. Conventional ***Physical Food***, a diet which research has proven needs to provide the perfect blend of vitamins and minerals to keep the physical system healthy.
- ❖ 1b. Its non-conventional counterpart is ***pranic nourishment*** which is the ability to be nourished from an inner source of Divine Love and Light. To do this successfully we need to utilize many of the tools we will soon discuss.
- ❖ 2a. ***The Food of Love***: This food nourishes our emotional body and often comes from contact with a one-on-one loving and tactile relationship – usually with a 'mate' or lover. Research has proven that babies who are fed and also cuddled a lot gain weight quicker than babies who are fed the same food but cuddled and held less.
- ❖ 2b. A more non-conventional source of the food of Love is ***unconditional love***. I call it non-conventional as the ability to love unconditionally in one-on-one human relationships is rare yet unconditional love provides the most nourishing food of all. Most people find it easier to love their pets or friends unconditionally than their family or life-partner. Lack of unconditional love means that our unfulfilled expectations and judgments can create dis-ease and block the Divine Nutrition flow.
- ❖ 3a. ***The Food of Family***: The conventional source here is our ***blood-line family*** and people's lack of true family nourishment has kept therapists in business for years. In metaphysics, due to our karmic connections with our blood-line

family, the food we receive from our interaction with them is usually via learning experiences that allow us to grow emotionally, mentally and spiritually. For example: Being ignored as a child may push someone into the world of entertainment, where they in turn may then nourish millions with their on-stage presence, and at the same time their 'inner child' is fed via the mass adulation of audience acceptance, which can balance out their childhood lack.

❖ 3b. The non-conventional Food of the Family is the food that comes when we work with the reality a *global family*. This means relating to everyone we meet as if they are as potentially nourishing and important to us as a blood-line relative can be. This is part of the 'love thy neighbor' game that Jesus spoke of that is required today in the unification of humanity. Everyone knows the nourishment factor of an extended family of friends and treating all people and even animals as if they are loved and cherished brothers and sisters can provide us all with an incredible source of food. This however takes mind mastery as to do this we need to choose to celebrate our differences rather than judge each other with the familiar cries of "If you acted and thought like I do, I would understand you and maybe accept you and be more loving towards you."

❖ 4a. *The Food of Success*: The conventional sources of nourishment through success are the wealth and status gained that feeds the emotional and mental aspects of our bio-system and success in the western world of business in particular focuses on these things. In the corporate game of the past decades for many there has been the 'every man for himself' attitude, the 'take but not give back' game, and 'don't look too closely at the impact of actions on the whole' game. Hence we have the current backlash with terrorism due to global starvation of the compassion energy and how the 'affluent big-brother success' game has been operating.

❖ 4b. The non-conventional food of success comes from operating in a more *balanced* way and knowing that true success is managing to co-create health, happiness, peace as well as prosperity and, most importantly, doing it in a way that nurtures all.

❖ 5a. *The Food of Sex:* Practicing conventional methods of sexual exchange creates pleasure and can birth life but does not nourish the bio-system anywhere near as well as it could if we apply the more non-conventional …

❖ 5b. *The Food of Sacred Sex:* We will discuss the food that comes from adding the love and spirit energies to the sex energy soon and provide a mediation tool to do this successfully.

I have often said that the 4 greatest western Gods are the God of Money, the God of Fame, the God of Power and the God of Sex. These four Gods are worshiped daily and religiously by millions who seek to have their stomachs full of security, peace, love and happiness. The problem is that these Gods cannot deliver the nourishment we need and so we – as individuals and as a planet – have developed emotional, mental and spiritual anorexia.

Non-conventional Level 2 & 3 Sources of Nourishment

Our physical body consciousness desires us to be fit and healthy and strong for the bio-system was actually built and programmed for self regeneration, health and longevity. Our pituitary and pineal glands, as the master glands in our body, operated on the original program of only producing life sustaining hormones to support this yet, like all cells of the body, they constantly listen to what we are thinking and obey us as masters of the bio-system. Consequently over time these glands began to produce the death hormone to mirror our modern day beliefs that we have to die. We discussed this in greater detail in the first book in this series and physical immortality – while a by-product of nourishing life – is not our focus now, for what I wish to provide in this book is simply a way of being nourished that can benefit us all personally and globally.

The greatest source of physical, emotional, mental and spiritual nourishment comes via our day to day lifestyle. Creating physical health, fitness and strength depends on a number of factors and much research has already been done in this field, for example we know that drinking pure water, eating fresh healthy – preferably vegetarian – food, exercising regularly and engaging in meditation to deal with mental and emotional stress, are all extremely good for us. We also know as metaphysicians that time spent in silence in nature and that exercising self mastery and mind control via re and de-programming our bio-system, is also beneficial in the creation of mental and emotional health, as is the use of devotional music or chanting and mantras. Add daily service and prayer and we have a basic health and happiness lifestyle recipe. *(All these things have been discussed in detail in* the Four Body Fitness: Biofields & Bliss *book as the 8 point lifestyle plan we call the Luscious Lifestyles Program or L.L.P.)*

Even when we have attained a degree of satisfaction for our physical hunger by adopting eating and exercise and relaxation habits that keep the body healthy and happy, we still need to address our emotional, mental and spiritual hungers which the above lifestyle also will attend to.

So let's address briefly then more deeply other non-conventional sources of nourishment and how to consciously tune ourselves into the Theta – Delta field as there are many sources of nourishment and many simple tools for us to use to gain the benefits of feeding from this zone.

Some examples that we will elaborate on shortly are:

* ❖ *Breathing* – using the love breath meditation and the Ancient Vedic Holy Breath tool. Both these techniques increase the amount of chi and prana in the body and expand our cells capacity to attract and radiate chi from the Theta – Delta field.
* ❖ The *Inner Smile* Taoist Master practice: this technique prepares our organs and bio-system to get and stay connected to the Theta – Delta field by tuning them to the frequency of unconditional love.
* ❖ The *Body Love* Tool – this is a way of again expanding our atoms and cells to accept and receive more Divine Nutrition.

❖ *Lifestyle Love* Tool: A Perfect Diet Program for physical, emotional, mental and spiritual nourishment. This includes the use of water, diet and exercise to create a bio-system that again is capable of being well tuned and accepting and coping with energy of the Theta – Delta Field without burning out the electro-circuitry of the bio-system. This lifestyle can also be applied as a cleanse and detoxification program as we apply 'The 3 > 2; 2> 1' and 'The meat > vegetarian > vegan > fruit > Divine Nutrition Prana Power' preparation system.

❖ Nourishment via accessing *solar energy* and wind and Earth and plant prana

❖ Healing Sounds, Mantras and *Programming Code* Tools: For the emotional and mental tuning to the Theta – Delta Field and accessing appropriate nourishment for these aspects of our self. This includes the Taoist 6 Healing Sounds plus the use of specific mantras and the "Perfect Health, Balance, Weight, Image" programming code.

❖ The Nourishment of the *Microcosmic Orbit* Tool.

❖ The DOW POWER Tool of the *Violet Light* & the *Divine Amrita* & *Pituitary & Pineal Gland Activation*.

❖ Nourishment and Our *Purity of Heart*.

❖ The Nourishment of *Ecstasy* Tool and Elemental Equilibrium.

❖ Nourishment from the Food of the Goddess.

The above are just a few non-conventional sources that we will now focus on as tools of nourishment that can contribute to fulfilling all our hungers. Below we will look at each in more detail and provide what you may require to hook into and experience being nourished by each source. Where the techniques need greater clarification and more detailed outlines for more perfect practice, we have referred you to their original source for you to access more detailed explanatory data and techniques.

In Chapter 11 we will begin to look at the specifics of life for people wishing to be free from the need to take nourishment from food also. However the below non-conventional Sources of Nourishment are available for all who wish to enjoy the health, happiness, peace and prosperity that comes to us automatically when we are truly nourished in life.

Non-conventional Nourishment Sources & Tools
To be used for Level 2 & Level 3 Nutrition

BREATHING

1. Breathing – *using the love breath meditation and the Ancient Vedic Holy Breath tool. Both these techniques increase the amount of nourishing chi and prana in the body and expand our cells capacity to attract and radiate nutrition from the Theta – Delta field.*

Our breath is one of the most powerful tools we have for the feeding and fine tuning of our bio-system. Free, and at our constant control, we can utilize various breath techniques to achieve many things from calming and de-stressing the bio-system to leaving the body to travel through the inner planes via bi-location techniques and 'astral travel', to fine-tuning our energy fields to be in the Presence of the Holy Ones and more. While there are many techniques of breath work, for the Divine Nutrition program, I recommend the below two.

Divine Nutrition Program – Technique no. 1:

This technique is designed to tune us to the Divine Love channel from which the Food of Gods flows. I call it the **Love Breath meditation**. See Diagram no 4. and apply the steps below. Do for at least 5-10 minutes each morning and evening or until you really feel as if all you are is love and all you do comes from this love. Do the below meditation every morning and as much as you remember to do it and see how you feel after a month or so …

❖ Step 1 – imagine yourself connected on the inner planes with a beam of pure love that flows from the heart of the Divine Mother into your heart chakra.

❖ Step 2 – Inhale of this love deeply and chant as you reclaim "I am love" keep chanting this mantra over and over with sincerity.

❖ Step 3 – Exhale this love slowly out into your body and chant "I love" over and over with sincerity as you imagine this love filling every cell and then flowing out from your auric field in your outer world.

❖ Also with this tell your body over and over until it tingles "I love you, I love you, I love you, I love you" as per technique no. 3.

Together this exercise opens your cells and atoms up to receiving pure Divine Mother Love as it strengthens your Divine heart and your ability to attract, hold and radiate love in this world. It also changes your brain wave patterns from Beta-Alpha to the Theta – Delta zone.

This is also a great technique to use if ever you feel uncomfortable around someone or judgmental towards them and if you wish to feel more compassionate. It is also a good technique to remind us of who, and what, we really are when our masks and personas are stripped bare.

This is definitely a 'try it and experience the difference' tool which takes some focus and discipline. As we have shared in other manuals, a basic breathing technique like this one which uses the "I am love, I love" mantra, is also a wonderful way to train what the Indian yogis call our 'monkey' mind to remain still and focused. Many people are unable to focus their mind on just their breath for more than a minute or two without finding themselves thinking of work, or shopping, or other things, yet mind mastery is absolutely necessary to find and access the food of Gods channel. Untrained in the art of stillness, the Western mind in particular requires this type of training as a pre-requisite for attaining inner and outer peace.

Divine Nutrition Program – Technique no. 2:

The Ancient Vedic Holy Breath. Over 5000 years old this technique achieves a number of things. Firstly what actually breathes us is our DOW – the Divine One Within us who is here to have a human experience and who utilizes our physical, emotional and mental bodies to do so. Without Its energy we could not and would not exist and when we match Its breathing rhythm we begin to glimpse Its power. Using this tool is also like saying to your DOW "Are you there? I really want to feel you."

- ❖ Take a few moments and sit in stillness then:
- ❖ Breathe through your nose with deep, fine and connected breaths, no pausing as you inhale then exhale so that you are literally circular breathing.
- ❖ Once you have an even rhythm, move your awareness to the energy behind your breath and just watch and feel your breathing rhythm.
- ❖ Remember you are focusing now on the inner force that breathes you and you will know when you have found Its rhythm as you will begin to feel Its waves of love pulsating through you.
- ❖ After awhile you will no longer be focused on deep, fine connected breathing and instead will feel as if you are being breathed.

With training you can find the bliss of your DOW's love beat within maybe four or five breaths. Imagine being able to switch yourself into the bliss zone this quickly.

For those already trained in the art of meditation, I recommend that you do both of the above techniques sitting in the middle of some chaotic scene like peak hour traffic. Again this is focus training as it's easy to be a yogi and meditate in the stillness of nature however many live in busy cities where experiencing a constant state of inner peace can at times be a challenge. Maintaining mastery in all situations in life is also basic training for the modern day yogi*.

* While in India the female yogi is known as a yogini, throughout this text I choose not to discriminate as to me a yogi is neither male nor female.

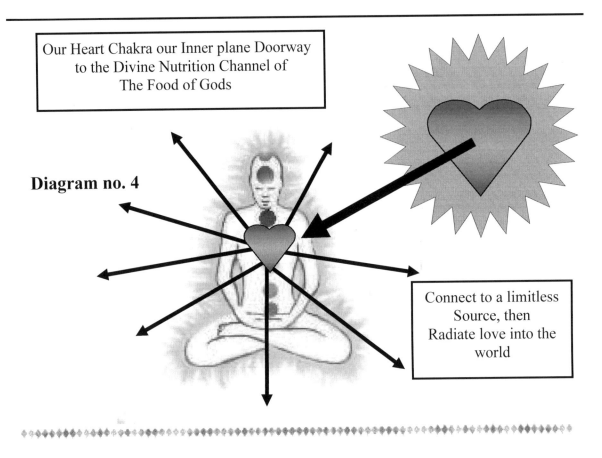

Our Heart Chakra our Inner plane Doorway
to the Divine Nutrition Channel of
The Food of Gods

Diagram no. 4

Connect to a limitless
Source, then
Radiate love into the
world

SMILING

2. The Inner Smile *Taoist Master practice: this technique prepares our organs and bio-system to get, and stay connected, to the Theta – Delta field by tuning each organ to the nourishing frequency of unconditional love. It also opens the inner doors to an experience of a more conscious and positive mind-body communication.*

Divine Nutrition Program – Technique no. 3:
- ❖ Sit quietly and imagine that you are in your body, as if your mind has taken you inside somehow and you see your lungs before you.
- ❖ Imagine beaming a great big smile at your lungs and at the same time
- ❖ think how thankful you are for the job that your lungs have been doing for you your whole life – filtering the air you breath, extracting the chi or pranic particles from the atmosphere around you.
- ❖ Say over and over to your lungs as you smile at them, "I love you, I love you, I love you" and/or "thank you, thank you, thank you".
- ❖ Do this with your brain, then your heart, then your kidneys, your liver and your sexual organs until you have smiled at every organ in your body.
- ❖ Do this daily and soon your organs will begin to feel appreciated and loved and will co-operate quickly with your new programming codes.

BODY LOVE

3. *The* **Body Love Tool** *– this is a way of again expanding our atoms and cells ability to accept and receive more Divine Nutrition in its purest form which is love.*

Divine Nutrition Program – Technique no. 4:

Every morning and evening take 5 minutes to tell your body that you love it by sincerely chanting over and over "Body I love you, body I love you, body I love you." When said sincerely, from a point of really appreciating every part of your body – from your head to your toes – after a while your body will tingle in response as if to say "Do you? Do you really?" and your response of course will be "Yes I do!"

Although this is a simple tool, it is one of the most powerful we have for gaining the physical bio-systems co-operation for the co-creation of health and happiness. In metaphysics love is the foundation for all change and expansion.

LIFESTYLE

4. *The* **Love Lifestyle Tool***: A Perfect Diet Program for physical, emotional, mental and spiritual nourishment. This includes the use of water, diet and exercise to create a bio-system that again is capable of being well tuned, and accepting, and coping, with energy of the Theta – Delta Field. This energy needs to be downloaded safely without burning out the electro-circuitry of the bio-system. Diet refinement is also to be applied as a cleanse and detoxification program while applying 'The 3 > 2; 2> 1 system, then the meat > vegetarian > vegan > fruit > Divine Nutrition Prana Power and programming code system.'*

Divine Nutrition Program – Technique no. 5: *The Love Lifestyle Tool: A Perfect Diet Program for physical, emotional mental and spiritual nourishment:*

One of the first steps for successful Theta – Delta field feeding and accessing this pure food of the Gods is the adoption of the Luscious Lifestyles Program of Recipe 2000➔ – as we mentioned earlier. Briefly, the L.L.P. entails a daily lifestyle of the following points:
1) Meditation
2) Prayer
3) Mind Mastery
4) Vegetarian Diet
5) Exercise

6) Service
7) Spending time in Nature
8) The use of devotional songs and mantras

While all of the above was discussed in great detail in the *Four Body Fitness: Biofields and Bliss – Book 1*, I would like to add the following:

The **meditations** given throughout this book will actually suffice to effectively tune our emotional, mental and spiritual fields, and open the correct channels, for Theta – Delta field feeding. Meditation allows us the stillness to experience DOW power.

Pray. Not only does prayer heal, but this daily communication with the cosmic computer called God keeps the pranic flow strong within us for this is the universal law of resonance where like attracts like. Focus on Divinity allows all that is Divine to be fed by our attention.

Mind Mastery and **programming** is the most complex part of this lifestyle. In Dimensional Biofield Science, light rays act as computer hardware that is then operated and directed by specific software programs that are comprised of thought, will and intention. A basic fact in Dimensional Biofield Science is that all thoughts, words and actions – that are beneficial for all – will be supported by the purest and most powerful fields. See below for the Perfect Health, Balance, Weight and Image Program, required for successful Divine Nutrition Feeding. The control of our thoughts and the direction of our perceptions of the world, are crucial to this success.

A **vegetarian diet** tunes us to the fields of kindness and compassion which are a natural part of the Theta – Delta field. A vegetarian diet also improves health and decreases our draining of the world's resources, as it takes 20 times the resources to put animal products on the table compared to vegetables and grains. Until we have mastered our bio-system, it is also much better for our health as has already been proven. To continue to support the unnecessary slaughter of life can create a block to accessing the purest frequencies of the Food of Gods as it dilutes the energy flow from this channel.

Exercise keeps our physical fields strong, and hence allows us to attract, hold and radiate more of the Theta – Delta field frequencies – hence we become a clearer and stronger transmitter of these frequencies and more able to imprint quite powerfully in the world.

Service also keeps us tuned to the kindness and compassion channel and attracts more love and support to our personal field.

Spending **silent time in nature** is one of the most amazing foods for the soul, as it really allows us to gain peace, quiet, solitude and feed off the pranic particles that are generated by nature and the trees, sunshine and the Earth. This is part of Surya yoga.

The use of **sacred music chants and devotional song** also keeps us tuned to the Theta – Delta fields as both de-stress our physical, emotional and mental bodies, and allow us to feel and recognize the Divine in its purest form. We discuss the influence of healing sounds in more detail later.

This 8 point lifestyle plan – the Luscious Lifestyles Program or L.L.P. – promotes fitness on all levels and keeps our personal field tuned to the Divine Love, Divine Wisdom channel and in time, anchors our brainwave patterns in the Theta – Delta field. This in turn affects our personal keynote and frequency and attracts more Grace into our life allowing us to make a more joyous and easy transition into personal and global paradise, which is the true gift of being nourished by the food of Gods. This lifestyle plan is a key requirement for both Level 2 and Level 3 nourishment.

Creating a fit bio-system is a necessary step to accessing the Divine Nutrition channel and we can begin with creating physical fitness through diet and exercise and drinking water which we all know are good for us. So much has been written about physical cleansing and detoxification and both are required to prepare the body to receive the pranic flow and we look at this in greater detail in Chapter 11.

Additional Tools for HEALTH & LONGEVITY

To begin this preparation now, I personally also recommend the following which can be applied immediately:

Divine Nutrition Program – Minimization Technique no. 6:
The 3 > 2; 2 > 1 system:

This means that if you currently eat 3 meals a day cut back to 2, or if you currently eat 2 meals a day then cut back to 1. The reason for this is that research has proven that if we halve our calorie intake we can increase our lifespan by 30%. Also it means that we immediately reduce our consumption of the world's resources by 30% just by having 2 meals each day instead of 3.
Our body will also feel better as it will have less digestion time and IF we choose a healthy diet we will begin to detox slowly and also lose weight if required – unless of course we do the programming for perfect weight as in point 8 of this chapter.

Concurrently with this I recommend:
Divine Nutrition Program – Conversion Technique no. 7:
The 'meat > vegetarian > vegan > fruit > Divine Nutrition Prana Power' system.

This means immediately stopping your consumption of red meat (as per the reasons discussed above and in greater detail in the *Ambassadors of Light* book the Divine Nutrition Series) then when you are comfortable with this – in maybe 3 to 6 months – stop your consumption of all other animal or marine flesh.
Next after you have adjusted to the 'no meat or chicken or fish' diet – in other words if it has a face don't eat it, then cease your consumption of all other animal derived products such as cheese, eggs, butter, honey etc. and become a vegan. For level 2 nourishment you may settle here but for those open to level 3 nourishment….
Next when you are comfortable with this go to raw foods only, and then only fruit and then finally light liquids such as water and herbal tea and prana only. This conversion

process can take up to 5 years depending on where you are right now with your dietary habits.

The slower you take it, the easier will be the emotional adjustment and the general detoxification of your system. However dietary preparation is not enough to plug into the Divine Nutrition channel. All that we recommend in this book needs to be applied particularly the step by step plug in program with its meditations, energy grid work and programming codes in Chapter 11.

The adoption of a vegetarian diet is usually a natural choice of someone tuned to the kindness and compassion frequency, particularly when they have been well educated as to alternative choices and have made the conscious decision to no longer support the slaughter of life.

Please note that even those interested only in Level 2 nutrition so that they can experience the health and happiness, peace and prosperity agendas, experimenting with raw food and even a fruit only diet can be wonderfully beneficial for your bio-system as the cleaner and lighter the physical form, the better you will feel on all levels. If however you are going to live on only fruit for periods of time, then you need to plug into the Violet Light spectrum to receive all the nutrients you need. (See techniques 12, 13 & 14). Also there are many alchemical rewards for those who learn to master their baser natures.

◆✦◆◆◆◆◆◆◆ ✦◆◆◆ ✦◆✦ ◆◆◆◆ ✦✦✦ ✦◆◆◆◆◆◆◆◆◆◆◆◆◆◆◆◆◆◆◆◆✦◆◆◆◆✦◆◆◆◆◆◆ ✦✦ ✦✦◆◆◆ ✦◆◆ ✦◆◆◆◆ ◆◆◆◆◆◆◆◆◆◆ ✦

SUN FOOD

5. *Nourishment via the access of* **Solar Energy** *and wind, Earth and plant prana.*

This is probably the most well researched area that we have to offer information on, as Dr Sudhir and his team in India have now spent a number of years looking at Solar Energy Nutrition and how it operates in the body; and the Master Choa Kok Sui has been researching Earth and plant prana in his path of studying pranic energy for healing. Both of their research was discussed in the *Ambassadors of Light* book as is the research of many other doctors who have been studying the pranic field.

I recently asked Dr Sudhir Shah what led him into studying the field of solar nourishment and he answered: "Nature. I had an opportunity to monitor prolonged fasting as per Jain religious method of Shri HRM (Hira Ratan Manek) for 411 days; on scientific basis. That led me to postulate alternative ways to sustain a body when a person is not on routine food-calories. There was only one explanation i.e. cosmic energy utilization."

In his first hypothesis on the subject he wrote: "Out of all cosmic sources, the SUN is the most powerful and readily available source and has been used for energy, by sages and Rishis since ancient time, including lord Mahavir, Tibetan lamas and other Rishes. Again, how the SUN energy is received:- The Brain and the mind are the most powerful recipients in human body and the retina and the pineal gland (the third eye or the seat of soul as per Rene Descartes) are equipped with photoreceptor cells and may be considered photosensitive organs. As plant kingdom thrives on chlorophyll and photosynthesis, directly dependant on the Sun, similarly some photosynthesis must be taking place when we hypothesize the Sun's energy.

"Through complex ways and distinct pathways this energy must enter the body. There is a pathway from the retinas, to the hypothalamus, called the retinohypothalamic tract. This tract brings information about the dark and light cycles to the suprachiasmatic nucleus (SCN) of the hypothalamus. From the SCN, impulses along the nerve travel via the pineal nerve (Sympathetic nerves system) to the pineal gland. These impulses inhibit the production of Melatonin. When these impulses stop (at night or in dark, when the light no longer stimulates the hypothalamus) pineal inhibition ceases, and Melatonin is released. The pineal gland (or the third eye) is therefore a photosensitive organ and an important timekeeper for the human body. The unexplored process of energy synthesis and transformation from the sun energy perhaps partly occurs here.

"We should also examine this aspect carefully, as this leaves scope for an important discussion – whether each and every individual can use sun energy and if so, can they do this efficiently? Only time can answer this. But it is possible that each individual has a different genetic code and also each body has different physical capabilities. Hence, one may be able to receive this Solar energy more readily, can transform and store it in a better way and also can utilize more efficiently and even recycle it – while another person may not be able to do it to the same extent. Hence, experiments must be taken up, if it is possible on a randomized base upon volunteers with a control population. However, leaving this component aside for the time being, it is possible that many people can do this experiment very successfully under supervision. Prior to this a body checkup and particularly a retinal-ophthalmic checkup is mandatory and under strict medical guidance, a graded time bound experiment upon volunteers may be taken up."

Dr Shah sums up his research into solar nutrition as follows: "If this theory can be generalized, then it can change the destiny of mankind. First of all, the food crisis will be solved. Through activation of this supreme energy in body and the transforming of it in the electrical, chemical and the magnetic forms, a person can not only become free of diseases but can gain positive health with a vibrant aura. His luster can impress even enemies enough so that their enmity may dissolve. With the improvement of mental and intellectual capacities one may be able to use brain-power up to 90 to 100 %, as against to 3 – 10% as we normally do. There will be reign of peace and prosperity. As there is no food, the bad thoughts and ill feelings will be stopped, so eternal peace is bound to follow.

"This will also question the routine common calorie mathematics. By this, there is a challenge to the routine calorie based science. Its limitations are highlighted, at the same time the complex issues of obesity and malnutrition can be readily explained through the concept of solar energy. It is possible that obese people, though not eating excess food, still receive energy from cosmic sources thus explaining their obesity. The concept of cosmic energy can be used for the total upliftment of mankind at the physical, mental, intellectual, supramental and Spiritual levels. Extensive scientific research work therefore should be immediately taken up by appropriate authorities, including bio-scientists and medical personnel, who can then answer all these issues."

Dr Shah's full report can be downloaded free from: http://www.jasmuheen.com/wp-content/uploads/2011/06/LIGHTAMBASSADRYRESEARCHBOOKLET.pdf
Dr Shah's shares more in the research section of this book.

Divine Nutrition Program – Technique no. 8:
Accessing solar energy & nature prana for feeding:
On a practical level we recommend that in order to access solar or plant and Earth nourishment you do the following:

- ❖ Spend a few minutes every dawn and dusk time looking directly into the sun. Your body will absorb the sun's nutrition via the pores of your skin and through your eyes. It will then take this nourishing light directly into your brain and circulate it via your pineal and pituitary glands and through the hypothalamus.
- ❖ Next do this while lying in the ocean – this is highly recommended by the Indian yogis as the combination of solar feeding while immersing the body in the ocean's ionic particles is very nourishing. Doing Surya yoga* on the beach is also very nourishing.
- ❖ Walk regularly along the ocean shore to absorb wind prana or in high mountains and breathe deeply of the fresh sea or mountain air.
- ❖ Hug trees particularly big strong healthy ones. Connect with the tree via your heart chakra and send it love and light and ask for a mutual energy flow connection and support so that the tree can experience your experience in the world and you can feed off its strength and pranic force field. Trees and all plant life are living fields of intelligence that just happen to exist within the confines of a different molecular structure than the human bio-system. They operate via a group consciousness and are not as individualized as we are and they love receiving our carbon dioxide as much as we benefit from breathing in the oxygen they generate.
- ❖ To access Earth prana, walk barefoot daily on the Earth and consciously absorb the pranic energy through the souls of your feet. Then give some back by imagining that with every step you take on this Earth, pure Divine Mother love is flowing from her heart to yours and into your body and down your legs and out through the souls of your feet and back into the Earth, to be utilized as the Mother Earth requires and desires. This sets up a nice biofeedback looping arrangement of give and take. Absorb prana and give back love and gratitude for you may wish to thank the elements of the Earth for lending you their molecules and atoms for the original creation, and continual sustenance, of your body.

* More on Surya Yoga in Chapter 9.

SOUNDS

**6. a) The Taoist Healing Sounds *for emotional tuning and organ cleansing, b)*
Programming Codes *including the Perfect Health – Balance – Weight – Image Code –
why and how to apply it.***

Divine Nutrition Program – Technique no. 9:
a) The Taoist Healing Sounds:

Taoism, along with Confucianism, is one of the two major religious traditions that have shaped Chinese life for more than 2,000 years. Broadly, a Taoist's attitude towards life can be seen in the accepting and yielding joyful and carefree sides of the Chinese character. This attitude offsets and complements the moral and duty conscious purposeful character ascribed to Confucianism. Taoism is characterized by a positive attitude towards the occult and the metaphysical, whereas the pragmatic Confucian tradition considers these of only marginal importance, even though their reality is not denied.

The founder of Taoism, Lao-tzu, historically remains an obscure figure. The principal source of information about his life is a biography written in about 100 BC. He was said to be a court official advising in matters such as astrology and divination, and was in charge of the sacred books. The name Lao-tzu seems to represent a certain type of sage rather than an individual name, and the relevant books of instruction seem to have a number of authors.

The 6 Healing Sounds of the Tao have been developed to release the denser frequency emotions that we often store in our organs. The nourishing frequency of the food of Gods is held in every cell and every atom, however if our cells are filled with toxicity from the 'swallowing and storing' of unresolved emotions, or from chemical toxicity from poor dietary choices, or from too much negative and judgmental thinking, then the subtle frequency of the Divine Nutrition channel can be literally swamped and overwhelmed by these more dense and coarser energies. Successful nourishment depends on clean cells and organs. As like attracts like via the Universal Law of Resonance, the purer the frequency of each cell, the purer the energy field that each cell can attract hold and radiate.

The Taoist masters have discovered that each healthy organ is associated with a particular color, sound and frequency and that the organs are weakened by physical, emotional and mental toxicity. They have also discovered that there are six cosmic healing sounds that help to restore, balance and cleanse the vital organs and circulate the body's chi by redistributing any heat build up that gets caught in the cooling sacs – fasciae – that surround each organ.

The Tao masters share that by using particular sounds, visualization, light and intention, we can alter the vibrational mix of each organ For example the sound "Sssssss", said with the tongue behind the teeth, works on the lungs which, as many are aware, store our sadness and grief. The sound "Choooooooo" works on releasing the emotion of fear from the kidneys and its associated organ, the bladder. The sound "Shhhhhhh" works on releasing anger from the liver and its associated organ the gall bladder.

Rather than go into great detail here, we recommend that you read and apply the precise teachings of the Taoist 6 Healing sounds as per the booklet *Cosmic Sounds – Sounds that Heal* by Mantak Chia. This section is just a brief introduction on the ability of sound to cleanse, rebalance and nourish our organs.

WORD POWER

b) Programming Codes:

As we discussed in the book *In Resonance* specific sounds, sacred songs and mantras have long been used to nourish the bio-system with certain frequencies. We know that the sound "Aum" feeds the crown chakra energy centre by tuning it to the Divine Wisdom channel. We also know that the sound "Ahhh" nourishes the heart chakra by tuning it to the Divine Love channel particularly when used intermittently with the Love Breath meditation and its "I am love, I love" mantra. Programming codes are in essence specific mantras or sentences that are used to reprogram the way the body consciousness sees itself and how it functions.

One of the dynamics of Dimensional Biofield Science is the power of words – Shabda Yoga – and in order to successfully access the Food of Gods we need to understand the importance of imprinting the various energy fields with specific telepathic programs. It is assumed in metaphysical circles that the DOW is a being of supreme intelligence, love, wisdom, great integrity, compassion and all the other virtues we would assign to one made in the image of the God of Gods and that our DOW is one whom we can trust implicitly.

The codes that we offer in this book have developed over a substantial period of time and are very particular programs that involve having an understanding of cellular memory, of past, of present and even future life times – such as our genetic imprinting and covert and overt social influences, plus influences of the media, education and our general conditioning. Depending on our family and cultural influences, and our day to day life experiences, some bio-systems run in a circle of very limited options, concepts and realities, a loop that is constantly being reinforced by the lowest common denominator of the most dominant status quo field. In other words we are only as good as the worst among us as we all influence each others as cells in a quantum field called the body of God.

Hence, the need to take an honest look at life, reprogram our limiting beliefs and adopt a change of attitude to support our new beliefs, are all crucial in reprogramming the mental aspect of our bio–system. To access the Divine Nutrition channel we need to open the inner plane doors that support this type of feeding and also ensure that we are well connected enough to this channel to have it deliver enough creative power to sustain us, in perfect health and happiness on all levels, as this is what being truly nourished is all about. The Divine Nutrition channel of the Food of Gods is a channel that is incorruptible with a limitless supply of power, exactly like a pure 'cosmic computer type God'.

Many people in the west – due to lack of awareness of their mind/body connection, limiting repetitive self talk patterns, self judgments, judgments of others, negative thinking etc. – have created confusion in the cells of their body, whose natural programming codes were originally imprinted to operate without limit. We have been running with so many limiting beliefs for so long, which we have rarely challenged, so that our physical, emotional and mental bio-system has reprogrammed itself into the game of atrophy and decay. As such, one of the most powerful sources of emotional and mental nourishment that we have today is the thinking pattern that we choose.

However the true power of reprogramming our bio-system and the success of any code must begin with a belief that as we are a God in physical form, only then will our bio-system listen and obey when we instruct it to do something. Below is the main essential code for stabilizing our weight, our health and the Divine Nutrition flow and we recommend its daily use as our circumstances in, and influences by, the world tend to change each day.

Divine Nutrition Program – Technique no. 10:
The Perfect "Health, Balance, Weight and Image" Program:
While this also has been touched on in my other books, it is repeated here as it is an essential program for maintaining the Divine Nutrition flow. This programming code is used to stabilize our weight when we are no longer taking physical food, it is also used to keep our bodies in harmony on all levels and whether we eat food or not and it is used to eliminate any disruption from past life cellular memory. It is also used to free us from the limitations of perception that we absorb from the world re the changing and superficial fashion of image.

The command itself is to be used daily and involves sincerely chanting over and over: "Perfect Health, Perfect Balance, Perfect Weight and Perfect Image NOW." Repeat as you connect each finger in turn with the thumb in a repetitive mudra.

There are 2 things to be aware of for this code to work.

❖ Firstly we stress again that the above program *must* be said as if you are a God in form, the Master of the bio-system whose job it is to obey you.

❖ Secondly the intention behind the words must be accepted and understood. This is as follows:

PERFECT HEALTH: The intention behind this is like saying to your bio-system and your DOW, that your DOW has your permission to bring you into a state of perfect physical health, perfect emotional health, perfect mental health and perfect spiritual health. It is also said with the intention that you as owner of the bio-system will live the lifestyle required to support perfect health (as in the Luscious Lifestyles Program of technique 4 in this chapter). It is true that people have attained instant and spontaneous healing when their sincerity and humility levels peak at a set frequency so both are important here.

PERFECT BALANCE: This is giving permission to your DOW to bring you into perfect balance on all levels of your being through all lives, with joy and ease and Grace and to keep you in balance with our fields. Remember our DOW is an all powerful, all knowing master computer controller of our system if we allow it to be. This is a powerful program for those who a) trust in DOW Power and b) understand multi-Dimensional realities and c) have spent time processing limiting or negative cellular memory.

PERFECT WEIGHT: This means I surrender my weight to my Divine Self and ask it to make me the perfect weight that I need to be. Strangely enough when said with sincerity and conviction of this, people have actually put weight on without taking any food.

PERFECT IMAGE: This means that I surrender my image to my Divine Self and give it permission to "radiate through me Its perfect image into the world" rather than me being influenced by the status quo and its idea of beauty. We add this code as we know that true beauty comes with DOW radiance.

The Perfect Health, Perfect Balance, Perfect Weight and Perfect Image programming code is used daily and said while connecting each finger to the thumb so that the program works with the hand mudra and is absorbed directly into the energy field of the body. For those familiar with the Chi machine, this program is most effective when done when the chi rush comes at the end of the oscillation cycle. More on this is covered in the section on Bio-Shield devices.

There are of course, other specific programming codes that are crucial to successful Theta – Delta wave nurturing but as these relate not just to improving our health but also specifically to the area of pranic nourishment, where individuals can be free from the need to take physical food, we will address these in chapter 11.

＊✦＊✦✦✦✦✦✦✦✦＊✦✦✦✦＊✦✦＊✦✦✦✦✦＊✦✦✦✦✦✦＊✦✦✦✦✦✦✦✦✦✦＊✦✦✦✦✦✦✦✦✦✦✦✦＊✦✦✦✦✦✦✦✦✦✦✦✦✦✦✦＊✦✦✦✦✦✦✦✦✦＊✦✦✦＊✦✦✦✦＊✦✦✦＊✦✦＊✦✦✦✦＊✦✦✦✦✦✦✦✦＊✦

SACRED SEX

7. The Nourishment of the Microcosmic Orbit

Receiving nourishment via our dietary choices has long been an accepted choice and as mentioned, well researched. Humanity's love of food has well been documented as has the physical outcomes of the ingestion of certain food choices. Billions of dollars each year are spent dealing with the treatment of diseases that are now manifesting from poor dietary choices which, when combined with lack of exercise and modern day stresses, are proving lethal.

Similarly research has now moved on to look at the factors of emotional and mental stress regarding a person's health and even longevity and personally, I have spent the last 30 years of my life looking at the factors that contribute to an individual's health and happiness levels. The best formula I can provide, after 33 years of Level 2 experiential research, is the Luscious Lifestyles Program as it is the only recipe that caters for our physical, emotional, mental and spiritual health and happiness desires.

Food and sex have long been a source of both need and amusement for many. Humanity's ability to both pro-create, and also enjoy sexual sharing without the desire for the creation of life but just for pleasure's sake, is another well researched field. Again billions of dollars are spent entertaining these human desires – from top class restaurants to fast food outlets, to the relatively new sacred sex classes to the various soft and hard-core pornography outlets. Humanity's needs in these areas seem endless and due to lack of proper nourishment, these needs are creatively self fuelling.

What has not been looked at in depth in the western world is the nutrition that can come from the utilization and redirection of our sexual, emotional and spiritual energy streams. Yes, according to some research and ancient teachings, sexual activity can be a form of Divine Nutrition when utilized in a certain way.

We have discovered that accessing Divine Nutrition is a process of an Inner Alchemical flow, whose force is triggered and released via our lifestyle – a part of which is meditation and using programming codes. The ability to draw Divine Nutrition from the inner realms through our atoms and into the cells is simply a process that utilizes energy differently to what we've been taught in the western world. Another example of utilizing energy to feed and strengthen the body is the Taoist Healing Love practice as taught by Mantak Chia.

I had the pleasure of spending time with Mantak in November 2002 when our group met there to discuss and launch the Madonna Frequency Planetary Peace Program and during our time together I had the opportunity to talk to him extensively about the Taoist practices and the flow of Divine Nutrition.

I call those who no longer take their nourishment via physical food the Light eaters and one of the problems many have experienced over the years is their inability to remain grounded, as the energies we are accessing to nourish our bodies are so refined that we not only feel as though we are existing in two worlds, but we often feel as though the material world is too foreign to spend time in. Hence many Level 3 light eaters prefer a life of silence and solitude. However as many of us have specific work that requires us to be very involved with this world, how to be more grounded is something that needs addressing. As such I thoroughly recommend the practice of qigong and the Taoist practices so that we can maintain our focus in the world and not feel too alienated. Exercises like the 'Iron Shirt' and many others are a wonderful way to ground us in an energizing manner.

Another common problem has been our absorption of energies that are not too our liking when our sensitivity levels become too high. We have discussed this in detail in the 'Absorption versus Radiation' section of the 'Blocking our Nourishment' chapter. We can also combat this by utilizing the various Biofield devices as discussed in chapter 11.

However as there are comparatively far fewer Light eaters in the world today than there are sexually active people, I have decided to include the below information in this chapter as the Microcosmic Orbit practice is a very powerful source of nourishment for us all whether we are choosing to eat food or not. Also when we allow ourselves to be nourished only by prana – as in Level 3 of the Divine Nutrition program – our sexual energies change.

Like many of the Taoist Masters, much of Mantak's research focuses on the use of Chi or prana to nourish the body from both an internal and external energy source. By increasing and then circulating the chi in specific ways throughout our system we can access the Divine Nutrition channels while remaining grounded and active in our modern day world.

The Taoist training methods conserve and transform chi or energy and use it to create a sacred and Holy temple within the body that then acts as a storehouse for chi for individuals to draw upon and consequently always maintain peak health. By integrating the energy flow through the brain, through the sexual organs and all the organs via a specific circuit or energy flow, all our organs can be nourished and maintain optimum longevity and also performance.

In his book *Healing Love – Cultivating Sexual Energy* Mantak writes:
"Taoists say that orgasmic energy is the best distillation of the body's essences, drawn from all the organs, glands and cells by the amazing electrochemistry of the arousal process. The body thinks it is going to create new life, a child, so it releases its premium energies to start new life."

According to Mantak even the simple practice of smiling to all the organs – and the technique I use of telling the body daily "I love you, I love you, I love you" over and over with sincerity – also improves health and vitality and nourishment flow. (See techniques 2 & 3 in this chapter.) Obviously this needs to be accompanied with a lifestyle that proves to the body that you love it and are prepared to treat it with honor and respect.

Mantak shares that the sexual energy in particular tends to compound or amplify our base emotions so the more we choose to feel love and think positively the more this enhances our energy generally. Because of this, the Taoist teachings also promote mastery of the mind, and also our emotions, and recommend the 6 Healing sounds to cleanse the organs so that the chi they store and carry can be used more beneficially for the body.

Nourishing the bio-system through utilizing the energies of the procreation centers, of the spiritual centers and of the heart centre means that we can promote, deliver and sustain perfect health on all levels or achieve a younger appearance despite our age.

As many metaphysicians are aware, the three most powerful energies that our body generates are:

1. The Procreative energy for the establishment of new life, an energy that is generated and increased through our sexual arousal and union.
2. The Spiritual energy that is generated when our sixth and seventh senses – and their corresponding pituitary and pineal glands – have been activated and our crown and brow charkas are open, tuned and strong.

And thirdly we have

3. Our Love energy as generated through our heart charka (see Purity of Heart – point 9 of this chapter)

When these energies combine and circulate through the body, via metaphysical techniques including the Taoist energy tools that Mantak teaches, they can be directed to nourish our cells, organs and even the bone marrow of our body.

Apart from basic breathing tools, the Microcosmic Orbit as covered in Mantak's book *Sexual Reflexology – the Tao of Love and Sex* is a wonderful way to blend and transform these powerful energies into a more nourishing substance for the body rather than waste this energy buildup as per traditional western sexual practices. For those interested in these practices we recommend you read the above book. The microcosmic orbit is a simple way to circulate these energies and refresh, nourish and activate the brain, the nervous and hormonal system and the organs, particularly when we are tired. As Mantak says "The sexual energy is instant energy (food) for the brain."

He also writes: "If both partners have opened their microcosmic orbit, the natural polarity between man and woman is greatly amplified and the energy flow much more powerful, because these master channels feed all the vital organs and their associated meridians.

"This balancing and nourishing exchange is the heart of the Healing Love practice and part of what eventually leads the dedicated student beyond sexual pleasure to longevity and immortality."

While I recommend Mantak's book on this matter, below is a very simple meditation that will allow us to circulate these energies and nourish ourselves with their power. First we do it on our own and then with our partner if desired.

Divine Nutrition Program – Technique no. 11:
Microcosmic Orbit Meditation:

Diagram 5

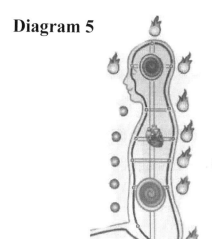

Sit comfortably upright, back straight in silent meditation.

❖ Do the love breath chanting "I am love" on the inhale and "I love" on the exhale as your draw a never ending source of love into your heart and then send this love down into your sexual organs.

❖ Do the inner smile technique. Smile to your heart, to your breasts, to your sexual organs, to your brow chakra, to your crown chakra.

❖ Place your tongue on the roof of your mouth; slide it gently backwards as you do when you are seeking to taste the Divine Amrita (as per the meditation in that section – technique no.13).

❖ Begin to contract and release the same muscles that you use to stop and start the flow of urination.

❖ Imagine as you contract that you are drawing the energy from your ovaries down into your perineum or up from your testes.

❖ Visualize a color to this energy you are drawing.

❖ Keep contracting and releasing these muscles and feel the energy of procreation building up.

❖ Next as you keep contracting your perineum, imagine sending this energy up to the base of your spine.

❖ Keep contracting and releasing and building up more energy and keep sending it to the base of the spine where you imagine it being held and mixed with the kundalini energies.

- ❖ Then imagine shooting this energy up as you contract – from the perineum to the base then straight up the spine though the ascension chakra, which is ponytail height at the back of the head.
- ❖ Do the same again but this time imagine it shooting up your back, through the ascension chakra and into the crown chakra.
- ❖ Imagine a new color to this energy and keep your tongue on the roof of your mouth as you keep contracting and releasing and sending more energy up your spine, into the crown and then imagine it flowing through the brow chakra.
- ❖ Then imagine this energy flowing from the brow chakra and into your heart chakra, finally mixing the sexual, spiritual and love energies together. You can follow this energy flow with your mind and direct it with the chant "sex, spirit, love; sex, spirit, love". The idea is that if we take the sexual energies and add the spiritual and love energies then we come into perfect balance on an inner energy level.
- ❖ Finally as you keep contracting and releasing those muscles and sending more energy up the spine, through the spiritual centers and in to the heart, you imagine this energy now flowing from the heart in a perfect orbit back to the perineum and then back up the spine again.
- ❖ Keep repeating until you feel the energy flowing quite naturally in a circular orbit – known as the microcosmic orbit. As the flow accelerates imagine a color to this energy and trust that the color that comes to you is perfect for you now.
- ❖ Eventually you may feel as if the energy flow is happening naturally without your need to contract or release your muscles anymore.
- ❖ Once you have mastered this on your own you can add this practice to your sexual sharing when either seated on your partners lap or they are on yours, or when lying down together. The only change with a partner is that once the flow has begun, we can then send this energy into their heart chakra – from ours – and imagine it flowing down their body, up their spine etc; or we can send it in through our brow chakra to their brow chakra – always keeping the figure 8 symbol of infinity shape through the bodies as the energy crosses over.
- ❖ I recommend that the solo practice of the microcosmic orbit be done for 5 minutes daily as a morning 'inner breakfast' routine.

The blending of the energies like this with the symbol of infinity pattern helps bring us into a more harmonious sharing state and opens our telepathic connection especially when we send the energy through the brow centre. It also allows us to be more sensitive and in tune with each other as well as opens the doors for both heart and brain orgasms.

(For the exact practice of this please read Mantak Chia's books on the Microcosmic Orbit and Sexual Healing.)

The Tibetan Lamas have long utilized the microcosmic orbit to not just redirect their unused sexual energy when they are being celibate, but also to have it feed their bone structure including their bone marrow, their organs, their meridians, blood lines and their complete physical bio-system, as the blending of these three powerful energies through the body releases a very powerful force of nourishment from a storehouse of energy that we naturally have within us.

Interestingly enough, when the human bio-system enters into the vibration of compassion and unconditional love, and then combines this with sexual arousal energy, a new chemistry is created in the body that has a resonance of 8 herz. This is the frequency bordering on the Alpha – Theta state which resonates at 4 cycles per second to 7 cycles per second. In this new chemical state every cell of the body is nourished with Divine Love and feels completely fulfilled as happens automatically when we are tuned to the Theta field.

The practice of sacred sexuality among metaphysicians is becoming a more common way to nourish ourselves but what is less commonly understood in the journey of Divine Nutrition, is the role that the Violet Light and the Pituitary Gland and the Pineal Gland play.

DOW POWER

8. The DOW POWER Tool of the Violet Light & the Divine Amrita & our Pineal & Pituitary Gland activation: Techniques no. 12, 13 & 14.

DOW Power is activated naturally via the above 8 point lifestyle in technique 5, and the programming codes in technique 10 which keeps our bio-system tuned and open to the Divine Nutrition Channel. As our DOW is the original 'boss' of the bio-system, acknowledging Its Presence, tuning to Its frequency field, working consciously with It, loving and being loved by It and merging and surrendering to It, is one of the smartest things we can do if we are interested in experiencing lasting health and happiness and discovering inner peace and prosperity.

DOW Power is the main source of Level 2 and Level 3 nutrition that each of us can connect to and be sustained by physically, emotionally, mentally and spiritually – for as we keep reiterating, the Divine One Within us is literally, God. If we had no DOW Power driving our mechanism we would not be alive but DOW Power can do much more than just breathe us. In order to be successfully nourished by DOW Power with its ever open access to the Divine Nutrition channel, we need to adopt certain attitudes, do specific meditations – as per the ones in this manual – and also utilize regular prayer practices so that our lines of communion with the Divine Nutrition channels stay open and our prayers need to be sincere and from the heart.

Attitude is also one of the most important areas of consideration for obtaining the nourishment we need. Research has proven that people who think positive live longer and also that those who eat less live longer.

In a recent interview with Dr Shah that I did for my free online magazine, The ELRAANIS Voice, he writes: "Attitude decides the progress of a person, a religious commune, an institute, a house or a family etc. The importance of attitude can't be overemphasized. A quote from Charles Swindoll should suffice.

"The longer I live, the more I realize the importance of attitude on life. Attitude to me is more important than facts. It is more important than past, than education, successes, than what other people think or say or do. It is more important than appearance, giftedness, or skill. It will make or break a company....a church....a home. The remarkable thing is we have a choice everyday regarding the attitude we will embrace for that day. We cannot change our past. We cannot change the fact that people will act in a certain way. We cannot change the inevitable. The only thing we can do is to play on the string we have, and that is our attitude...... I am convinced that life is 10% what happens to me and 90% how I react to it. And so it is with you..... we are in charge of our attitudes."

Although we will hear more from Dr Shah later and also discuss the benefits of accessing the Food of Gods, Divine Nutrition channel; providing the perfect nourishment for humanity to create health and happiness and peace and prosperity for all, will result in a paradise planet as we discuss in the following excerpt from the *Biofields & Bliss book 2 – Co-creating Paradise*:

"According to metaphysics, there is only One Force that has the capability of creating PARADISE on Earth. There is only One Force that can unite us in a way that reveals our higher nature and common bond. There is only One Force that is incorruptible.

"There is only One Force that drives our breath that fills our atoms and that gifts us with seven senses to experience the beauty of having form. This One Force is the Master Computer Controller of every 6.3 trillion cell mechanism – every individual human being. This One Force is all-powerful, all knowing, all loving, all capable, all being – within and without. I call it our DOW – the Divine One Within. It is also our DOE – the Divine One Everywhere.

"All our DOW wants is for us to KNOW It. To know, to dare, to do and to be silent, allowing the Radiance, which It is, to talk for us revealing It's magical Grace ... This means 6 billion people co-existing in harmony, guided by the one force that exists in all and is common to all for the DOW is beyond mind, ego, cultural and genetic influences."

Our DOW & The Violet Light:

How our DOW physically, emotionally and mentally expresses Itself is through waves of love and light. The love is what we feel when we sit and meditate and seek the experience of Oneness with our DOW in silence, nourishes our physical and emotional bodies. The light is what we see when we focus on our third eye and activate our pituitary and pineal glands plus the hypothalamus – which acts as an inner television screen, which in turn allows us to see this Violet Light of our DOW. And it is this Light which nourishes our mental body as it carries with it Light Codes and Light packets of information from the Source of Supreme Intelligence that many call God.

Diagram 6: The Ancient Wisdom's Three Fold Flame of Violet Light is said to exist in our heart chakra. Traditional diagram above left.

The Tao, the Violet Light & the North Star:

In the teachings of the ancient Tao, it is said that the Violet Light spectrum comes to our physical Earth through the fixed point of the North Star and that when we connect with this star we are free from the pull of the natural life/death cycles of the Earth. The Taoist talk about the Source of Supreme nourishment as Wu Chi, a centre of universal energy from which both heaven and Earth are born.

The Taoist masters say that there are 3 gateways in the body to receive Wu Chi nourishment and these are the Upper Tan Tien which is our brow chakra, the middle Tan Tien which is our heart chakra and the lower Tan Tien which is our sacral chakra and that when tuned, these three energy centers connect the heaven and Earth within us. The Tao heart has seven layers, seven electromagnetic fields and seven states of compassion.

In his booklet on *Darkness Technology* at http://www.universal-tao.com/dark_room/index.html Mantak Chia writes on page 7: "The emanation of infrared light of the Big Dipper, combined with the violet rays of the North Star, has a positive, nurturing effect upon the bodies and minds of those who know how to access it. Taoists believe that the Violet Star, the Big Dipper and the other constellations form the 'Gates of Heaven'. All living things must pass through these gates to return to their source of origin, the Wu Chi, which is the state of Oneness with the Tao." According to Dimensional Biofield Science, the Tao or Oneness expresses Itself in a human bio-system as the conscious force that I call the DOW.

Mantak also writes on page 8: "The pineal, as Yang, is balanced by the Yin of the hypothalamus gland. The Taoists regard this as the main switch for the Universal Force.

When the spirit (DOW) awakens, it resides in the hypothalamus. When the pineal and hypothalamus are connected, they give out a powerful balanced force." The Taoists also talk of a spiritual cauldron or inner source of energy that when tapped into can heal and feed the body and sustain physical longevity or even create immortality if desired.

On page 11, Mantak also talks about how when activated "The pineal gland initiates a cascade of inhibitory reactions, permitting visions and dream-states to emerge in our conscious awareness. Eventually the brain synthesizes the 'spirit molecules' 5-methoxy-dimethyltryptamine (5-MeO-DMT) and dimethyltryptamine (DMT), facilitating the transcendental experiences of universal love and compassion."

Interestingly enough Mantak's research also shares that when activated the hypothalamus also regulates not just the blood pressure, body temperature, fluid and electrolyte balance, but also body weight via a process of dynamic equilibrium. Consequently, when the pineal gland is flooded with Violet Light and activated and connected with the hypothalamus, via light streams and programming codes, then the reality that we can consciously program "perfect weight" into the body appears quite natural.

Another interesting Taoist point is that the North Star controls some 500 billion stars of which Earth is one and that the universe has 6 trillion plus stars which equals and mirrors our body's 6 trillion plus cells. One of the most interesting points I have discovered with the Taoist teachings is that they say that only the Violet Light can be successfully programmed.

In Chapter 11 we will look at the Three-Fold Flame of Violet Light of Saint Germain and also the significance of the Maltese Cross.

VIOLET LIGHT

Feeding and flooding the Bio-system with Violet Light:

The flooding of our cells with the Violet Light of the Theta – Delta field is another tool of nourishment that produces some amazing results. As discussed earlier, clairvoyance, clairaudience, clairsentience, physical immortality, the ability to use 100% of our brain, enjoying a stress free healthy vehicle, the ability to be free from the need to age, or take water or food, or the need for sleep, and the ability to dematerialize, to bi-locate or to send a holographic projection; all of these states depend on us attaining and maintaining a deep Theta – Delta field connection, and keeping open certain inner doors.

As most metaphysicians are now aware, every cell has molecules that hold atoms which are 99.9% space. This space is a pocket of pure intelligence, a living organism filled with the consciousness of our DOW. By the use of the type of programs discussed and by using energy shifting tools, we can learn to open inner doors, or improve the download of data coming through doors that are already opened, or open fields to very particular frequencies where a bigger picture is continually unfolding. In other words using these metaphysical tools people can move into more positive realities that feed them in a healthier way.

When the DOW is invited to flood our system with Violet Light, it acts like a computer virus clean up program that can automatically heal and nourish us particularly when used with the programming code of Perfect Health, Perfect Balance etc.

Once these inner doors are open we can then flood the cells of our body with the pure Violet Light that streams constantly through our inner energy centers or chakras. This occurs more easily with the creation of our unified Chakra column. (See diagram 7 & 8 below) I call this system 'flooding'. Flooding can also operate via a system of bio-feed back looping once the original energy dynamics are established.

Divine Nutrition Program – Technique no. 12:
How to flood our bio-system system with the Violet Light and its Theta – Delta field frequencies:

I consider the following tool one of the most powerful and important in the Divine Nutrition Program as it is from this Source of Divine Love, Divine Wisdom and Divine Power that a human bio-system can gain perfect nourishment.

Firstly: Do the Chakra expansion exercise below and create one column or spinning tunnel of light with its inner plane connection. This is our Violet Light hook-in to the source of DOW power and it is best done after centering yourself with Techniques 1, 2 & 16 in Chapter 7.

Diagrams 7 & 8:

The creation of one spinning chakra column of radiating Violet Light.

Original drawing by Juan Li

- ❖ Step a: Imagine pure, Violet Light flowing in through your crown and flooding and expanding each chakra with its power,
- ❖ Step b: Imagine each energy centre growing and expanding with this nourishing light until each chakra touches the next one to form one spinning column of light.

❖ Step c: Imagine this spinning column radiating out millions of rays of Violet Light into your cells, then into your atoms.

❖ Step d: Then imagine that these Violet Light beams of energy are radiating through your atoms and opening the inner doors.

❖ Imagine that these rays expand to their maximum expansion* and then attract the Violet Light from the inner planes and then contract back.

❖ Step e: Imagine these Violet Light filled rays then flooding back further into the atoms, then into the cells, then into the organs, bloodlines, meridians and so on until all of your bio-system is flooded with this Violet Light.

❖ Step f: Imagine that this 'expansion, attraction and contraction' process occurs naturally and automatically just like breathing, keeping your cells tuned to the inner plane fields of Violet Light.

*Maximum expansion is determined by velocity and power and potency of the beam being transmitted.

The above meditation is required for both Level 2 and Level 3 nourishment.

Our daily focus upon the above spinning chakra system feeds it as a reality, making it stronger and when it is married with our breath, it begins to set up its own bio-feedback looping system which then automatically keeps our system tuned to the inner Theta – Delta channels. This occurs because it is the nature of these very frequencies – which comprise the Violet Light of transmutation – to magnetize the inner realm Violet Light back to themselves, for they are guided with a deep knowing that everything is part of one great whole.

The potency of this meditation and chakra column field again depends on our lifestyle and how well the steps recommended in this book have been applied. There are many ways to tune the physical system to the Theta – Delta field of the DOW where true nourishment is possible, and the benefits are indescribable. As more and more Theta – Delta wave energy is accessed the more we come to know just how little we know about the human bio-system as all known laws become just one layer of a much greater whole. Each level, each field has its own set of laws and dynamics, that are mathematical sub-sets of the field of the One from which all has been born – what some would call again the cosmic computer or God, or the original point of creation. As Deepak Chopra shares in his book *How to Know God* the physical field is a subset of the quantum field which is a subset of the virtual field.

In Dimensional Biofield Science millions of rays of light are constantly radiating through every cell and through our atoms into the inner universes and if energy expands and contracts and if like attracts like, then we can direct these energy lines of Violet Light to attract more of the Violet Light spectrum from within the inner realms.

Although the dynamics of the Theta – Delta field, and all other fields, are governed by universal law, all fields are open to re-tuning both into and out of the Theta – Delta field as all doors are constantly opening and closing to this zone. The 'how' is again simply due to our lifestyle and specific programming codes that act like a software program that we can use to run the physical bio-system hardware more effectively.

Biofeedback looping causes certain interactions with the field that changes the field resonance. A word that is similar to resonance is frequency, which in physics is where a number of waves pass a fixed point in unit time. It is also the number of cycles of vibrations undergone during one unit of time by a body in periodic motion. A body in periodic motion is said to have undergone one cycle or one vibration after passing through a series of events or positions and returning to its original state.

Our personal frequency is what determines how much or how little Divine Nutrition we can access and how long we can stay anchored in the Theta – Delta fields. Frequency can be adjusted so that the emotional and mental aspects of the bio-system literally find themselves existing within another realm, a realm of more refinement and subtlety that brings deeper levels of fulfillment than the general existence most people have in the Beta – Alpha field.

The purest light spectrum within the Delta Theta zone that we can access and utilize for the greater good is the Violet Light of the seventh ray of spiritual freedom. This is a particular band of energy, or photon energy, which has a particular frequency that is available through the inner plane network. It is a particular frequency or light spectrum that when downloaded and redirected throughout our physical, emotional, mental and spiritual bio-system creates powerful transmutation and change. However, this light spectrum only operates at its maximum potential when it is programmed with specific sounds and codes.

This explains why step 8 in the Luscious Lifestyle Program focuses on the importance of sacred sound, for sacred sounds have been utilized for thousands of millennia by the indigenous tribes and traditional religions since the world began. It has been done so in their knowledge of the power of sound in tuning the bio-system to the Theta and Delta fields, moving of course first from the Beta through to the Alpha.

An amazing example of the power of sacred sound on our bio-system was when my husband and I were once in Paris. We make a habit when we are on the road of meditating in churches and chapels, cathedrals or mosques or wherever we are drawn and I am usually guided to do some sort of Dimensional Biofield engineering that involves the fine-tuning of the different fields and so the outing becomes both purposeful and relaxing.

One of my favorite pastimes is sitting in forests, or parks and places of worship where the power of the Divine can be felt or seen or heard or sensed in some way. On this particular occasion we had found a church in the middle of Montmartre that had become a beacon of light that stood strong amid a street of tourism that offered clubs and sex shops. The Chapel was obviously used and felt most welcoming, for the energy when we sat within its walls was completely transforming. Feelings of a deep connection to a Divine Spirit that had been prayed for, and longed for, and invited in were evident within the walls of the tiny Church of St. Rita's, which was plain by comparison to the great cathedrals of St. Michel and Notre Dame, yet this simple church had a magic that the bigger ones with all their throngs of tourists somehow failed to possess.

After enjoying the Chapel and feeling it feed us with its Theta – Delta wave, we caught the Metro over to St. Michel – an amazing cathedral that was built for royal worship centuries ago. A place thronging with tourists because the stained glass walls are magnificent, the Church had such a strong Beta field which drowned out anything more refined. Suddenly, as we sat there watching it all, the PA system began to boom out Gregorian chants. Proud and strong and devoted and powerful, the monks sang in one voice with all their contraltos and vibratos, and everything they could muster, and suddenly the energy of the place lit up, the field became lighter and more alive as people began to sit. Everyone stopped talking and a sacred hush fell over the room. It truly was a miracle to behold, and suddenly we witnessed so powerfully just how sacred sound can quickly tune a buzzing Beta field into a calmer Alpha.

We talk throughout this book of the different waves and how much we are anchored in the Alpha, the Theta or the Delta field depends always entirely on our desire, our attitude and our lifestyle, and the things we have discussed so far. But there are certain field devices that can be applied with certain field actions that will bring about certain results. Again we need to take an honest look at our life to see what sort of programming codes we need to download or apply to get what sort of result so that we can then go deep into the science of field weaving of which the Violet Light is the preferred foundation.

The Violet Light has long been known in esoteric circles to be the most powerful transmuting tool, and it consists of three frequency bands. The first is a pink band of light that carries the energy of Divine Love; the next is the golden yellow band, which carries the imprinting of Divine Wisdom, and then a blue band that carries the imprinting of Divine Power. When Divine Love, Divine Wisdom and Divine Power blend together we all can come into a state of freedom where we can express our Divine Nature with honor.

Divine Love, Divine Wisdom and Divine Power are also the three frequencies of original creation, from which all life and intelligence has been born to move through the field of Akasha and support the creative processes that occur within the quantum field. As such the Violet Light band carries the energy of perfect transformation, perfect healing, perfect re-energizing, perfect alignment and perfect flow and so is nourishing on all levels.

AMRITA – THE NECTAR OF GODS

The DOW and Its nourishment via Amrita:

Apart from the pineal gland and the hypothalamus, the DOW can utilize another of our master glands to nourish us via a tool well known to the ancient yogis of India. When our pituitary gland is activated and flooded with Violet Light, it begins to increase its production of a sweet-tasting nectar – which is also known as the inner fountain of youth.

This liquid is known in the Ancient Vedic Scriptures as Amrita and is produced in very small quantities in a sleeping mind yet when the mind is awakened – the spirit mind that dwells in the hypothalamus – and when the master glands of the pineal and pituitary are activated to a higher potential, then the production of Amrita increases and is said to be powerful enough to feed and nourish the bio-system to a Level 3 status and free it from its need of physical food.

The technique to stimulate the pituitary gland and increase its natural production of Divine Amrita is a two part process and part 1 of the technique is well known among those who practice martial arts.

Divine Nutrition Program – Technique no. 13:

❖ Part I involves resting the tip of the tongue lightly on the roof of the mouth. Basically this connects the electromagnetic flow of energy through the body as in the Microcosmic Orbit tool.

❖ Part II requires us to then stimulate the pituitary gland by sliding the tongue backwards and eventually placing it far enough back to curl under the Uvula at the top of the throat, that little thing that hangs down like a U shape at the back of our mouth. To do this we need to stretch the muscles under the tongue so that it can reach back further however, the great thing with metaphysical tools is that the power comes with our intention not the technique.

❖ So if each day we slide our tongue back a little more with the intention that when the tongue is in this position we stimulate the pituitary gland to produce more Amrita, then it will do so.

You will know when you taste this nectar as it has an unforgettably sweet flavor. I recommend that you practice this technique daily as it activates the pituitary gland which in turn increases our access to the Divine Nutrition channel. Also when your tongue is in this position you are not only youthing your own body but you cannot talk which is a wonderful gift to the world. This is a great tool to use at work, in the car, in the shower, when shopping or anywhere you remember.

OUR GLANDS

Activation of our Pituitary & Pineal Glands·
Diagrams 9 & 10:

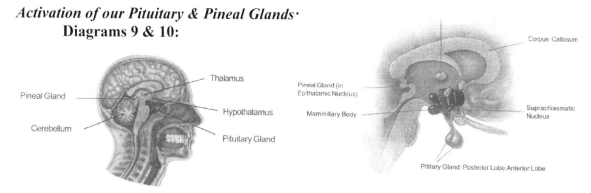

The above images are from Mantak Chia's 'Darkness Technology' Booklet.

Divine Nutrition Program – Technique no. 14:

The main tool we have for activating the Pituitary and Pineal glands is our lifestyle as per the Luscious Lifestyles Program. The vegetarian diet and service aspects of this program automatically increases our sensitivity to the Divine Nutrition channel and also attracts more of the love/wisdom/kindness and compassion frequency, which is the 8 herz vibration of the Alpha – Theta field. When these master glands are activated by also flooding them with Violet Light, our bio-system also attracts more of the higher elements of Akasa and Cosmic Fire which are the two elements connected to these glands and also the two elements that work with our crown and brow chakras. While the pituitary gland produces the Divine Amrita, the pineal gland produces a substance called pinoline which also tunes the brain to the Theta – Delta zone.

When activated and tuned to the Theta – Delta wave these glands act as Cosmic transmission stations allowing us to feed more successfully on the Violet Light radiation, that also streams not just through the North Star, but through our sun which acts as a giant radiating grid point that downloads the transmissions from the Central sun of the inner realms. Successful Level 3 nourishment is dependant on the activation of these glands.

Dr Shah writes of these glands: "While going through the details of recent scientific literature and also comparing it with ancient Indian spiritual texts, as well as western occult and new age, the following things are apparent.

"The activation of the pineal gland is the key step in our psychic, spiritual and energy transformation processes. Here in this gland, energy processing and re-distribution occurs. The pineal gland is the commander of all endocrine glands, therefore controlling the humeral system. It also regulates the circadian rhythm, sleep wake cycle and it also slows down the ageing process. It has psychic properties and is the seat of soul or mind – so called the third eye. It is the Agna (Ajna) chakra of the tantric system. Its activation can be done with prolonged yoga and meditation techniques or through the practice of solar energy. The latter does not use classic yoga steps. The pineal also inhibits growth and metastasis of some tumors. It has a stimulatory effect on the immune system. In birds and other animals, it has a magnetic material and is therefore the navigation center in birds.

"Scientists are looking at the magnetic, navigatory properties of the pineal gland in humans. So pineal activation and charging through solar energy is a vital step that is the doorway to the Cosmic energy highway. This may be Kundalini Shakti activation, in other words.

"Ever since mankind has started ignoring the psychically and Spiritually equipped pineal gland it has fallen on the merely physical-material plane and so endless pains have fallen on mankind. Mankind must now relearn to activate the pineal and the other psycho-spiritual bodies either through cosmic energy dynamics or through practice of Rajyoga or the Tantric ways or other such practices. Kundalini Shakti is said to be activated through these and happiness and bliss with peace are bound to follow. This light energy may be transformed into electrical, magnetic or chemical energies in body. Once processed, this energy must be transported and must be stored somewhere. Actually the ultimate form of all energy is light. Energy and light can be transformed into matter and back again to energy.

The hypothalamus is the commander of autonomic nervous system and pineal gland is in proximity to the autonomic nervous system, so it is logical that new energy transportation may either activate this system or it may use this system as a vehicle.

"The Parasympathetic nerves and its hormones and chemicals may be more useful than the sympathetic system. As the sympathetic system increases body needs (e.g. thinking, fighting stress, excitement etc.), the parasympathetic system is known to reduce the energy needs. It keeps the person serene and at mental peace and alters the metabolic requirements to a lower state and puts it to sleep. There may be other hormones or chemicals too and the role of the temporal lobe and limbic system also may be important. It may work as a regulator if not receptor and may be psychically involved in directing the energy in proper pathways. Deep into the limbic systems or in the parts of medulla oblongata, this energy may ultimately be stored and from time to time, may be recalled, charged or recycled. The medulla oblongata has all vital centers and therefore can be proposed as a store of vital energy.

"Thus there are energy receivers or receptors, processors, analyzers, transformers, storers etc. to explain the energy logistics (*of Divine Nutrition*). As this form of energy mathematics is different from what we conventionally are used to in the form of food and calorie mathematics; we will call this micro-food or mind utilization food (Manobhakshi Aahar Ttuûte ytnth). Here, we have talked about the Sun energy, but one may use any source from the cosmos, i.e. air, water, plants, Earth etc. This may be called Surya vigyan, but equally there is Chandra vigyan and Vanaspati vigyan as mentioned in our ancient texts."

Part of ancient yogi and Taoist master practice was to spend many hours and even years meditating in a dark cave for such actions were known to induce an amazing level of consciousness in the one meditating. Modern research has now revealed why as spending long periods of time in darkness allows for the accumulation and synthesis of psychedelic chemicals in the brain, such as pinoline, which affects the neurotransmitters of the brain and brings visions and dream states into our waking consciousness. As Mantak writes in his booklet on Darkness Technology:

"In the darkness environment chemical changes occur in the neuro-endocrine system as serotonin converts to melatonin which prepares the bio-system to receive the finer and subtler energies involved in higher consciousness experiences e.g. Divine communion, revelation and communication.

"Melatonin is produced in the pineal gland and affects the major organs systems, quieting the sympathetic nervous system and allowing for the daily rejuvenation of both the mind and the body. When excess melatonin is produced via prolonged periods in darkness, dream and sleep states then can bridge into waking consciousness and our higher truer nature begins to reveal itself and we feel reconnected to the Source of all nourishment and life."

As many esoteric cultures believe – the soul disengages itself from the body when it sleeps and merges into its higher purer form as a Divine spark which also occurs during prolonged darkness meditation time. This is called soul feeding time, for here the soul can drink deeply of the Theta – Delta frequency well, and receive the pure nourishment that it requires. Another benefit of the activation of the master glands in our body is that we can be feed, via our soul, in a more conscious manner during our waking time.

HEART

9. *Nourishment and Our* Purity of Heart.

If our desire is to be physically nourished by prana alone – Level 3 – then purity of hearty is one of the chief requirements for doing this successfully. A pure heart is something life provides us through living through our experiences here, and the choices that follow on from our perception of events. Our perception and how we choose to respond to people in life situations is a powerful tool to access the Divine Love channel if we wish to consciously magnetize more of this to our inner and outer fields.

In the metaphysical realms, the pureness of our heart determines what level of nourishment we can access to feed our spiritual, mental, emotional and physical bodies. What determines a pure heart and how we can attain this, and why it is important, are three important questions to answer in the Divine Nutrition game.

To try and determine a pure heart brings us into the realm of judgment which in itself is an energy that restricts our access to the Divine Love channel door as the Divine Love channel is actually a river of unconditional love that has no room for judgment. Remember that discernment and judgment are different energies – discernment is a necessary tool of freedom for any spiritual initiate whereas judgment, of self and others, can be a limitation. However, we can share action factors that help to purify the heart and attain both Level 2 and Level 3 nourishment.

Some of these are as follows:
- ❖ The desire and commitment to always fulfill the win-win-win game when relating to others and to deliver or set up outcomes that will be beneficial to all.
- ❖ The Love-Breath meditation which expands our capacity to attract, hold and radiate Divine Love.
- ❖ The commitment to, and action of, impeccability which means always doing the best we can in any given situation, and acting as if we truly are a master.
- ❖ Honesty with ourselves and with others in a loving and supportive manner.
- ❖ Sincere compassion towards and loving awareness of others – in other words genuine concern of the welfare of others
- ❖ Selfless service and the ability to give without seeking reward, and in an appropriate manner that nurtures another, without making them feel unnecessarily indebted to you – in other words to give freely of our time, care, love, money, etc in a positive empowering manner without self aggrandizement.

A pure heart is important as it unlocks the doors of the Theta – Delta fields and releases our highest potential, for true wisdom and Divine Power are only given to those who can value and use these gifts wisely. The true gifts of the higher mysteries and higher realms always come to the loving and the wise and the pure of heart.

A heart filled with hate or doubt or skepticism or judgment, or a heart that has been walled through hurt and is shielded to others, needs to be healed before it can access the higher kingdoms in all their glory. This means our psychic heart, which when walled or blocked eventually creates problems in the physical heart. Combined with toxic diet, toxic thinking and toxic feeling patterns, we have the high incidence of heart attack which is rising in our modern world. The number 1 killer of Western men and women these days are heart related problems.

ECSTASY

10. The Nourishment of Ecstasy Tool and Elemental Equilibrium:

We know that when the pituitary and the pineal glands are activated by the Violet Light and the Luscious Lifestyles Program, they keep the brain wave patterns anchored in the Theta – Delta fields. We also know that when the elements come into a certain state of equilibrium, we can free the body from the restrictions of age or the need for Earth's resources. Before we go on to discuss the nourishment that can be released through the body when we hit the maximum Delta field pattern of absolute bliss and ecstasy, I'd like to recap on the below.

The Elements & The Fields:

After a decade of research into Divine Nutrition I was revealed the reality of the Self –Sustaining Template. We touched on this device in my book BB1 and we will elaborate on this a little in the next section. However, upon closer investigation of how this Dimensional Biofield Device operates, I discovered the secret of Elemental Equilibrium.

How the elements come together as molecules around our light-body, and chakra system, is determined by our mental plane and emotional plane realities. When the elements of fire, Earth, water, air, akasa and cosmic fire are in perfect equilibrium; the bio-system moves into a different energy band and becomes self-sustaining, provided we have created the energy grids to support this and added the necessary programming codes for automatic activation when this equilibrium is reached.

This equilibrium is achieved and also maintained via our day-to-day lifestyle and mental and feeling states. When a being is sensitized enough to bridge all Kingdoms, then the Gods of the Elements can be called forth and instructed to rearrange themselves to support the perfect Elemental Equilibrium reality. This will then bring our bio-system into another level of freedom as the Food of Gods will nourish and water it in such a way that it is free also from the need to eat or age or sleep. This requires an extreme state of fine-tuning which is difficult to maintain due to our current global biofield mass frequency yet as more tune to the Divine Nutrition channel, the easier it will be to sustain these fields of reality.

In order to understand what the Food of Gods actually is and where it comes from, we need to understand the following which provides an elaboration on some of my earlier written material on the elements:

According to the metaphysics of the Ancient Wisdom, all the elements of this plane come from the Cosmic Monad. The physical universe is therefore an elaborated carrier of all the other six elements. The further the process of unfolding proceeds towards the material sphere, the weaker the influence of the higher elements progressively becomes as the influencing field of their Source of luminosity is reduced.

The following seven elements are to be understood as being interpenetrating and interwoven with each other. Each element emanates from the one before it and thus each successively contains growing complexity, containing not only its own characteristic individuality, but also the aspects of the preceding elements.

1) **Cosmic Monad**: The first and unmanifest Logos which breaks into the seven elements of: Earth, fire, water, air, akasa & cosmic fire. It is the Cosmic Monad from which the Food of Gods flows in its purest form. At this level of frequency and purity, it is too refined for our bodies to cope with, without burning out the electrical circuitry of our system, and hence must be stepped down through the inner plane grids for human utilization. (We spoke at length about the grids in BB2).

2) **Akasa**: The origin of the Cosmic Soul; the source of all intelligent order and laws in the universe; the second and quasi-manifest Logos.

3) **Cosmic Mind**: The source of all individualized intelligence; the third and creative Logos. With the activation of our hypothalamus, pituitary and pineal glands plus the flooding of the cerebral cortex and the cerebellum and all areas of our brain with Violet Light, and via specific programming into both the glands and the chakras – the brow, crown and ascension chakra at the back of our head – we can align our 'human mind' functions to directly link into the Cosmic Mind.

4) **Cosmic Karma**: The source of pure impersonal, universal compassion; the source of the impelling cosmic energies of the universe; the intelligently guided force of the hierarchical universe. The Luscious Lifestyle Program points of 'vegetarian diet' and 'service without thought of reward' help us to hook into this channel.

5) **Cosmic Vitality**: The source of cosmic vitality, permeating in all things. Again as the essence of the quantum field, this is the energy band from where the Food of Gods flows most easily.

6) **Astral Light**: The lowest functioning aspect of Akasa; the equivalent in the cosmic hierarchy of what the astral model body is to humans; the reservoir of all psychic, moral and physical emanations of the Earth. It is on this wave length that the Food of Gods can flow into our physical form via the Violet Light and through the higher aspects of our awakened mind.

7) **Physical Universe**: The body or garment of the six more ethereal elements preceding it.

These seven elements with their numberless sub-elements are aspects of the first element, the Cosmic Monad and are connected to the seven human senses, of which people who exist in the Beta field usually only use five. In order to access the channel of the Food of Gods, we need to activate our 6th and 7th senses and utilize the elements that work with them.

The relationship between the elements and our physical senses are as follows: Astral light : hearing ; 2. Air : touch ; 3. Fire : sight ; 4. Water : taste ; 5. Earth : smell ; 6. Akasa : Intuition ; 7. Sea of Fire : Knowing

For those open to the metaphysical aspects of this, in Dimensional Biofield Science, the quantum field is an aspect of Akasa, which is the second Element of the constitution of the universe. The first Element is termed a 'Principle' and is boundless, inconceivable and the root from which all the other six elements of the universe grow and each element evolves from the one preceding it. Akasa is semi-manifest, being the origin of the Cosmic Soul, the source of all intelligent order and laws in the universe. Akasa and Cosmic Fire are the elements of the Theta and Delta Field and all life, all intellect, all action, operates and exists, within the quantum field which is an aspect of Akasa.

Akasa is cosmic ideation, Spirit, the Alpha of Being. At the other end of the scale, the lowest aspect of Akasa, is astral light, cosmic substance, Matter, the Omega of Being. Akasa is the first born, 'the living fire', the Deity pervading all things. In dimension it is infinite, and is differentiated from space and time in that it is the material cause of sound. This is an aspect of Akasa called Aditi in Sanskrit, a higher principle than astral light. This is the melodious heaven of sound, the abode of the Chinese Deity Kwan-Yin, whose name means 'Divine voice'. This voice is a synonym of 'the word', speech as an expression of thought. Kwan-Yin is the magic potency of sound in nature, whose voice calls forth the elusive form of the universe out of Chaos. The Kwan Yin vibration is also an aspect of the Madonna Frequency.

The Food of Unconditional Love:

When the elements are in perfect equilibrium and programming codes have been set to match frequencies with certain pre-chosen channels, we can connect in to the Christed Grid of unconditional love that surrounds our planet, and is woven through our planet's heart, and we can feed off or draw nourishment from this grid. In essence the true food of Gods is unconditional love and the more we love ourselves unconditionally, and others unconditionally, the easier accessing this type of nutrition becomes.

For those who say "It's too hard to love others unconditionally" I recommend you open the door to this force by beginning with the loving of a pet. The creation of a close and loving bond with an animal such as a cat or dog or rat for example allows us just a glimpse of what unconditional love, is particularly when we take the time to appreciate the gifts that relating closely with these creatures can bring.

Albert Einstein once wrote: "A human being is a part of the whole, called by us 'Universe', a part limited in time and space. He experiences himself, his thoughts and feelings as something separated from the rest – a kind of optical delusion of his consciousness. This delusion is a kind of prison for us, restricting us to our personal desires and to affection for a few persons nearest to us. Our task must be to free ourselves from this prison by widening our circle of compassion to embrace all living creatures and the whole of nature in its beauty. Nobody is able to achieve this completely, but the striving for such achievement is in itself a part of the liberation and a foundation for inner security."

The Nourishment of Ecstasy:

When we attain a certain elemental equilibrium, through our lifestyle, programming codes, intentions, will and purity of heart, then we enter into the realm of the food that comes from the experience of ascension of enlightenment, where we become totally filled with light. This is an experience where the Food of the Gods is literally flooding through our bio-system and nourishing us on all levels simultaneously. In this space, so much love, so much light, so much joy and so much knowing flows through us filling every cell, every aspect of our being until all our questions disappear and all our desires disappear and all we feel is complete and truly full.

The yogis call this experience the 'ultimate reality' particularly when we go deeper into the Delta field and leave the mind behind. In this state we are the completeness of the now, no mind, no conscious awareness, just merged with the Oneness of the All That Is. Here we are bathed and cradled and cocooned and loved and retuned and nourished by the most Divine frequencies of Source, for we are literally in the Presence of the Divine Source of Creation. The only reason we know that we have been there is that:

    a) we feel so good when we return back to the Theta – Alpha field, and we have – at least temporarily – no more hunger and

    b) because of the lost time syndrome where perhaps we sat to meditate at 11am and when we return it is 1pm and intellectually we have no recall of where we have been but boy do we feel good.

Bathing in this bliss zone can last for seconds, minutes, hours or days and it touches each one who tunes into this state in a unique and profound manner. Over the last 30 years of my meditations surfing in the Theta – Delta zones, I have had numerous experiences of being filled with the light and love and joy and ecstasy of these realms. Sometimes I have retained full awareness and sometimes I have gone beyond my mental awareness zone. Each time is different yet each time is so nourishing that all I can feel is blessed. Due to our basic telepathic and empathetic natures, which are strengthened by such experiences, long term or proficient meditators can have an amazing range of experiences in these zones. Here the meeting of beings of great light is common as we learn how to match and hold frequency fields with those on the Buddhic wave, or the Christ wave, or the Madonna Frequency. All is possible in these realms for all doors are open and as we think things, they often manifest automatically before us, delivered by a universe that sees us as Gods in form.

There is one other element that determines how and when we have this experience and that is Grace. Frederick Buechner wrote something that touched me re Grace, he said:

"The Grace of God means something like: Here is your life. You might never have been, but you are because the party wouldn't have been complete without you. Here is the world. Beautiful and terrible things will happen. Don't be afraid. I am with you. Nothing can ever separate us. It's for you I created the universe. I love you. There's only one catch. Like any other gift, the gift of Grace can be yours only if you'll reach out and take it. Maybe being able to reach out and take it is a gift too."

I used to think that Grace was something intangible that swept through my life from time to time, leaving me in awe of Its power while bringing magic and joy and synchronicity to events that made it seem so obvious to me that some Higher Power had me at Its will and that somehow I'd just stumbled into Its stream of love and blessings. I have since learnt that while Grace can't be commanded and comes of Its own accord, we can definitely put ourselves in Its path by living an impeccable life with a pure heart and staying tuned to the Divine channels via our lifestyle.

Grace is an experiential medicine that frees us from our emotional, mental and spiritual anorexia. It is an addictive sustenance that feeds our spiritual body as It lets us know and witness that we are in perfect alignment with our Divine nature. The Catholic Encyclopedia says that "Grace (gratia, Charis), in general, is a supernatural gift of God to intellectual creatures (men, angels) for their eternal salvation, whether the latter be furthered and attained through salutary acts or a state of holiness." This state of Holiness comes to us naturally when we live the lifestyle required to keep us anchored in the Theta – Delta field.

To me Grace is a form of Divine Nutrition as It feeds my inner being when I see It in action. There is nothing I like more than to ride through life on a wave of Grace and once we have experienced this, no other way of Being compares. The true nourishment comes from knowing, seeing and feeling just how perfectly life can be lived when we are supported by this Divine flow.

✦✦✦

11. Other forms of Nourishment:

There are many other forms of nourishment available to us some that are well recognized and others less so. Laughter for example nourishes our heart, as does song. Healthy fresh fruits and vegetables, plus nuts and grains, can feed our cells the nutrients they need if we wish to be fed in this way. Exercise feeds the physical body with strength and flexibility, just as meditation feeds our spirit and emotional body and trains our mental body to focus in a nourishing way. Human contact such as kisses and hugs feeds our desire for touch just as watching a sunset at dusk on a beach may feed our hunger for silence or to be in the presence of natural beauty. These are of course, conventional forms of nourishment.

It is however, for the non-conventional forms of nourishment that humankind has become so hungry, for as our DOW awakens within us, Its dynamic Presence triggers the awakening of the DOW within all. Feeding ourselves via some of the non-conventional sources mentioned here speeds up Its awakening and with this are released our paranormal powers.

The above 10 points are just some of the tools used by metaphysicians the world over, throughout the ages, to provide forms of nourishment not readily understood or utilized by our modern day world. For those of us wishing to understand more of the science of the ancient wisdom and how Divine Nutrition is possible, we need to explore a little more of feeding via the Theta – Delta wave. Once we ourselves are well nourished then, through our personal energy transmissions, we can influence the nourishment of the world.

GODDESS FOOD

12. The Food of the Goddess

The Food of the Gods is pure love and wisdom and in its feminine aspect it becomes the Food of the Goddess. The food of the Goddess is cosmic glue, a field of pure unconditional love that allows life to exist in all realms, in all forms.

One of the more unconventional modern day sources of nourishment – and the one on which this book is based – is Divine Mother Love. Known also as the Madonna Frequency, Divine Mother Love has been projecting Itself through the fields of Earth through eons of time and long before we became a predominantly patriarchal society. I do not wish to get into a feminist type discussion except to say that tapping into the Goddess energy brings amazing levels of deep soul nourishment to our lives. I would also like to add that one of the major reasons for the high levels of global emotional, mental and spiritual anorexia today is due to the imbalance of the yin/yang – masculine/feminine energies in the Earth's fields. This imbalance has brought us violence, war, poverty, lack of compassion, greed and hunger on many levels.

One of the obvious ways to rebalance a field is to flood the field with the frequencies it is lacking and we can do this via the tools in this book. The Love Breath meditation in particular – technique 1 of this chapter – is a great aid in achieving this rebalance. Imagine 6 billion people freely breathing in and drawing Divine Mother love into their bio-system and releasing it into the Earth's fields as they breathe out?

One of the things that I am sometimes criticized for in my global work is being 'too political'. People tell me to stick with the spiritual however to me everything is spiritual – there is no separation and obedience to the Higher Laws of spirituality are the tools we have to successfully run all the systems of our world.

Throughout all esoteric circles mediums and those connected on the inner planes are receiving the same message. This is that we all need to radiate more love and more light into the world for only then will we come into balance. So a western world dominated by patriarchal systems and energy field radiations needs to now be flooded with matriarchal so that we can come back to the middle ground.

One way to do this is to recognize the gifts of the Goddess, understand the common historical connections and work with the relevant energy fields to bring our own lives into balance which will then reflect in the community and global fields. So let's look a little at this now and provide a brief overview of these energies.

When researching the history of the Goddess and the roles she has played throughout time in nurturing our world, we can identify a few common traits which you will recognize below as we share some of their legends and gifts.

First we have:
THE DIVINE MOTHER
- ❖ Creator and Sustainer of all Life
- ❖ The Source of Divine Nutrition
- ❖ Source of pure, unconditional Love
- ❖ The Source of mercy and compassion
- ❖ Goddess of One, mother of all gods and goddesses and humanity
- ❖ The Cosmic glue behind creation
- ❖ The Source of Grace and Joy

The Divine Mother radiates through:
THE HIGH PRIESTESS
- ❖ Directly representing the Goddess on Earth, the High Priestess ensures fertility and ongoing creation.
- ❖ The High Priestess is the great goddess herself and is seen universally as Kwan Yin (Asia), Isis (Egypt), Athena (Greece) and Rhiannon (Celts).
- ❖ All wise, all knowing she gives and takes life and reminds us of our innate inner wisdom and of the Divine spark within and asks us to radiantly manifest this into the world.
- ❖ The High Priestess embodies love, mercy and compassion.

Then we have:
THE TRIPLE GODDESS
- ❖ The original Trinity symbolizes the 3 faces of the Great Goddess.
- ❖ Stage 1: The VIRGIN as strong and self defined,
- ❖ Stage 2: the mother as the nurturing source of all nourishment and
- ❖ Stage 3: the crone representing death and transformation.
- ❖ The role of the Triple Goddess is to remind us of our sacredness regardless of our age for all stages are precious, and also to remind us that there is one multi-faceted Goddess, always present, always sacred.

Then we have some of the HINDU Goddesses who the Hindu's believe are all aspects of the One Divine Mother Goddess.

- ❖ DURGA – also called Devi in India where all goddesses are one as all are different aspects of the Divine feminine. Devi took the name of her enemy after she slew the evil demon Durga in battle while riding on a tiger.
- ❖ LAKSHMI – Goddess of abundance, the Shakti force of Vishnu.
- ❖ KALI – the triple goddess of creation, the animating force of Shiva, the destroyer. Kali's role is to face our fears.
- ❖ SHAKTI – the animating force of the universe, Shakti unites us with the Divine, cosmic, orgasmic energy of life.

Next we have some of the CELTIC Goddess:

- ❖ THE LADY OF THE LAKE – Celtic Goddess of consciousness and revelation, emotion, renewal and creativity, gives us the energy to rule our lives.
- ❖ MORGAN LE FAY – Represents a place of deep healing magic within us, ruler of Avalon, noted for her healing powers and prophetic vision, controller of destinies.
- ❖ ETAIN – Celtic moon goddess, wife of Midir king of the underground, symbol of fertility. Teaches us to be shining wherever we are.
- ❖ ARIANRHOD – Welsh triple moon goddess, keeper of the heavens and cycles and changes of time. Nurtures us thru dark night of soul changes.

And some of the EGYPTIAN Goddesses:

- ❖ ISHTAR – Babylonian Creator Goddess, the Source of all life. Queen of heaven, giver of Light, represents being active and strong.
- ❖ ISIS – Moon Goddess, mother and giver of all life. Goddess of agriculture, medicine and wisdom, Isis represents total femininity.
- ❖ HATHOR – The mother of all Gods and Goddesses – goddess of love, mirth, beauty and sensual pleasure. Sustainer, destroyer, creator.
- ❖ BAST – Earth mother Goddess of abundance and of relaxed play. Protector of women in childbirth, mother of Light and independence.

Some of the ROMAN Goddesses:

- ❖ Fortuna – Goddess of Abundance and Destiny.
- ❖ Flora – Goddess of Nature and pleasure, teaches us to honor inner and outer growth and the beauty of spring and flowers.
- ❖ Venus – Goddess of Grace and physical and spiritual Love, Venus guides us through both our calm and stormy emotions.
- ❖ Minerva – Goddess of knowledge, dawn, war and wisdom. Patron of the arts, crafts, guilds and medicine. Works with the nature symbols of wisdom, the owl and the serpent.

And some of the NORTH AMERICAN INDIAN Goddesses:

- ❖ Changing Woman – Brings abundance and teaches harmonious living and of love, hospitality and generosity. She also brings the wisdom of nature and teaches the honoring of our cycles – a shape-shifter.

- ❖ Eagle Woman – allows us to soar beyond stereotypes and break limiting bonds yet still be wise and nurture. Represents spirit, valor, spiritual sight.
- ❖ Spider Woman – creates by thinking, dreaming and naming – reminds us that good comes from everywhere, brought the Cherokee sun and fire.
- ❖ White Shell Woman – Turquoise woman – protects us from our enemies, created the Navajo, teaches us how to see life's joy and beauty in all things.

And of course, some of the GREEK Goddesses:
- ❖ APHRODITE – represents freshness, renewal and hope and the feminine being in all her glory – her realm is relationship and feeling and mature love. The Goddess of both spiritual and passionate love.
- ❖ ATHENA – the virgin goddess of war and wisdom and limitlessness, she encourages warriors to gentleness, the patron of useful and elegant arts
- ❖ ARTEMIS – mistress of animals and all wild untamed things symbolizes female independence, healing goddess, values solitude.
- ❖ DEMETER – Ancient Greek mother goddess of Persephone. Giver of fruitfulness and abundance. Blesses us with coming joy, abundant life and hope.

Other Goddesses who have made an impact through time are:
- ❖ KWAN YIN – Chinese Goddess of infinite mercy and compassion. Said t0 be born from Buddha's tears for the suffering of the world. Protects women and children and works with the healers of the world.
- ❖ MOTHER MARY – The Creator goddess known as 'Stella Maris' and associated with heaven and sea. Mary reminds us to be gentle and compassionate to our selves and to all others.
- ❖ PACHAMAMA – Earth Goddess of Peru known for inspiring healing and wholeness and holiness when we open to mother Earth and commune with her.
- ❖ NUT – Egyptian Goddess of the night sky who reminds us to open up to the mystery of life and to the unknowable, to let it flow and to trust a higher flow to bring us what we need.
- ❖ NU KUA – Dragon Goddess and restorer of universal Order of the Hopei, Shansi people of Northern China. She assists us in creating order from chaos
- ❖ VALKYRIE – Ancient Bird goddess, giving life, death, regeneration. Represents our fearless self and can lead us through darkness so that we grow.
- ❖ HEL – Norse Goddess of the underworld, a place of renewal and the embodiment of divine mystery. Teaches us to look behind the masks in life and beyond appearance.
- ❖ EVE – Mother and nurturer of all life, creator of the world and all living beings. Represents rebirth and regeneration, embodies primal female creative energy.
- ❖ GAIA – The eternal pre-historic Earth mother goddess of the soul who clothes us with the atoms of her essence. Reminds us to be grounded in the reality of nature and to balance and embrace all aspects of our selves from the heavenly to the Earthly.

- ❖ SEDNA – Eskimo Goddess who rules the underworld. Reminds us of the nourishing gifts that we can find in the darker places that we most fear.
- ❖ PELE – Hawaiian volcano Goddess of creative fire. Reminds us that even in the midst of fiery eruption there is creation and new life. Regenerates with fire.
- ❖ IX CHEL – Mayan moon goddess married to the sun, is the midwife to creative ideas. Goddess of fertility and freedom. Patron of childbirth and medicine.
- ❖ HINA –Polynesian Goddess said to be the original creator of the world, of gods and goddess and of humans. Represents the ability to be nourished in all situations.
- ❖ BRIGID – Celtic Triple Goddess of fire and inspiration, healing and divination.
- ❖ OYA – African Yoruban Goddess of weather and Brazilian Macumba deity of change, women call on her for protection when in hard to resolve situations.
- ❖ BABA YAGA – Slavic birth-death Goddess who inspires us to get in touch with our wild woman and free our vital, instinctual and primal energies by integrating our self destructive behavior.
- ❖ MAYA – Hindu Mother of Creation, weaver of the web of life and illusion. The virgin aspect of Kali's virgin, mother and crone. Maya comes to show us the illusionary nature of the material world, she brings magic and creativity.
- ❖ MAEVE – Intoxicating Irish Goddess of the magical land of Tara. Maeve challenges us to act responsibly and become the Queen of our domain.
- ❖ MAAT – Ancient Egyptian Goddess of Law, Order, Truth and Justice. Maat comes to bring justice to our life, to right wrongs and administer lessons that we need.
- ❖ FREYA – Northern European Goddess of sexuality of maiden and mother as two aspects of the Great Goddess. FREYA assists us in honoring our sexuality and connecting with our vital, primal energy and to be fully present in our body.
- ❖ LILITH – Middle Eastern Goddess of fertility and abundance, brings equality, refuses subordination. LILITH also represents the lotus and the ability to grow in darkness. She represents the spiritual nature of our folding and the blossoming of our heart of wisdom.

One of my favorite Goddesses currently is:
EURYNOME – the ECSTASY GODDESS

- ❖ Great Goddess of all things divided the sky from the sea and danced on the waves to create the north wind and birth creation.
- ❖ Calling in this pre-Hellenic Greek Goddess of Ecstasy opens us to fullness, exuberance and rapture. For those wishing to have more joy in life, the conscious decision to seduce and entice ecstasy ensures it will come.
- ❖ And by healing our wounded emotions via self nurturing, we create more room for ecstasy when it comes.
- ❖ Code: "I now open my fields to the joy and ecstasy of life. I call in the energy of the Goddess Eurynome to bring this to me NOW."

DIVINE NUTRITION PROGRAM – Technique no. 15:
So we can download the Goddess energy as follows:

- ❖ Step 1: Think about the areas that you feel that you (and/or the Earth) need to rebalance now.
- ❖ Step 2: Ask for the perfect Goddess/es to work with you now and to step in to influence your (and/or the Earth's) field in a way that is perfect for you.
- ❖ Step 3: Research all you can on her so that you understand her legend, aspects and gifts.
- ❖ Step 4: Pray and/or sing to her daily to help you (and/or the planet) come into perfect balance with joy, ease and grace.
- ❖ Step 5: Put her image in your meditation space, activate it to act as a dimensional doorway.

Of course there are many more Goddesses that may be called upon than those who are mentioned above but this will give you an indication of the vastness of the Divine Mother energy and her multiple expressions.

Additional Ecstasy Exercise: Discover what brings you (a drug free experience of) ecstasy. Focus for a week on doing that which makes you feel ecstatic then do something daily that brings a little more ecstasy into your life.

Chapter 7

Theta – Delta Wave Feeding
An Energetic Hook-in to a Never-ending Source

Having enough of the Theta – Delta wave flow through us and supply us with all our vitamins, minerals and nutrients so that we are not just free from the need to take food, but are nourished on a physical, emotional, mental and spiritual level; means refining our inner energy fields to specific frequencies. Again this means consciously moving our self into the sustainable brainwave patterns of the Theta and Delta fields and 3 energy doorways need to be opened and programmed to do this.

First, we need to **open the energy centre of the heart**. The heart chakra or psychic heart of the bio-system needs to be plugged in to a never-ending source of love so that we have access to a never-ending source of nutrition. This is known as plugging into the Divine Love channel of pure Mother love. This also means that when we are working within the Beta – Alpha fields we can transmit a limitless stream of specific frequencies that not only feed us, but also feed the planet enough to support the manifestation of higher paradigms. The more we allow ourselves to feed from the field of the Violet Light flow, the sooner we are nourished on all levels, although this also depends on our capacity to receive. Every human being can work on their own capacity to receive and again this occurs via the application of the tools in this book. The Love Breath meditation in particular keeps this heart channel open and expanded.

The next channel that needs to be opened is the Hara, also known as the lower Tan Tien or the Sacral Chakra. This energy channel needs to be tuned to the inner plane power Source we call the Central Sun which is our true seat of power. Deep rhythmic breathing or alternate nostril breathing keeps this door open to the channels we are seeking, as our breath has always been our freest, quickest, most powerful channel changer.

Thirdly, our Crown Chakra must be plugged into the cosmic computer using the '3 cable: Divine Love, Divine Wisdom and Divine Power system' as per the steps following. This allows our system to be constantly nourished by the only Source capable of meeting all our hungers, and fulfilling them, for it is this Source that gave birth to our hungers originally.

Once the Violet Light is being constantly downloaded and once the heart is constantly flowing with love, and once the sacral is drawing energy from the Central Sun, and once the cells and atoms are being irradiated with Violet Light, then we can begin or continue with the conscious de and re-programming of the software called 'survival' in our systems which will in turn activate this grid and direct the inner and outer energy flow.

Things to acknowledge and remember ...

a) Our bodies are 70% water. Dr Masaru Emoto's work has proven that water responds to words and music as in his book *Messages from the Water*.

b) The fluids of our body can be reprogrammed and the water we drink daily can be programmed to nourish and support us as well.

c) Also the glands of our body, particularly the pituitary and pineal, and the fluid in the endocrine system and cranial sacral fluid – all need to be reprogrammed. Programming these glands for self-regeneration and immortality also feeds back and impacts upon the bio-system, as these are basic Theta – Delta field attributes.

Again, as the inner field doorways download the Theta – Delta waves, in a way that we can handle, our outer field emanations also spontaneously change. These outer fields too, can be reset to access the external Theta – Delta field of prana that surrounds and permeates all. This can be done via the use of certain Bio-Shield Devices that we will discuss in detail later.

It is also important to support all fieldwork with basic common sense attitudes, and via our lifestyle, while we expand our body's capacity to attract and hold and radiate the Theta – Delta waves. What we have been doing in our previous time to this date will determine what type of program we need to apply for successful tuning of our personal fields and we will add a summary of suggested steps to do this later.

The ability to access the Theta – Delta waves is also part of the Dimensional Biofield Science of Matrix Mechanics and it requires our personal biofield to be tuned in a particular way. Matrix Mechanics is a complex and in depth science that uses DOW power to feed and sustain energy lines created on the inner plane via visualization, will and intention. It is a science that uses light rays and sound waves to attract specific molecular structure, where thought processes amplify through a grid structure of Biofield Devices that are created for specific outcomes. In the following meditation we will consciously hook our bio-system into three major grid feeding points, the heart of the Divine Mother, the Central Sun and the mind of Supreme Intelligence.

As we shared on book 2 of the 'Biofield and Bliss' series, "A major grid station, our sun is the sustainer and feeder of life. It is the doorway to DOW Power to connect our physical body with our lightbody.

"In our small speck of our galaxy, our sun accumulates energy from outside the solar system to feed itself, and after having refined what it has digested, it creates a pranic soup-type of output which radiates out to feed the planets in our solar system. This includes of course the Earth, from which we are nourished, directly by etheric absorption or by partaking of the Earth's food chain. As to what proportion is absorbed ethereally by most people, the Armenian seer and teacher, G. I. Gurdjieff, said we obtain 70% of our energy from breathing, which he calls our 'first food'.

"The sun derives its vitality by feeding on the refuse of space, attracting rays from outer space with its great force. The rays consumed are life—atoms, many at a far higher vibration rate than physical, that have flowed from the other suns of space. So the suns feed each other, with the new energy component being acquired as the cosmic rays stream through interstellar space, the rays having come mainly from the stomachs of other suns. They are ingested at the sun's North Pole, pass through the heart of the sun, are cleaned and washed and leave at the South Pole. All planets feed in the same manner. Our sun is the heart and the brain of our solar system.

"This procedure of exchanging life atoms is the same in humans. Whenever a group of people gather, life atoms interchange, which is one of the reasons why people who live together tend to grow to resemble each other. This is the occult understanding of the saying that you 'are known by the company you keep' as it reflects the merging of our Personal Biofield with the Social field. Similarly the real source of nutrition, that feeds our souls and our cells, flows in through our chakra system when the inner doors are open.

"In Dimensional Biofield Science, the physical sun is the material clothing of an Intelligence known esoterically as Lord Helios who is a ray of consciousness from the central sun. The central sun is the galactic centre of universal life – electricity; the reservoir within which is focused the Divine radiance at the beginning of every creation. Our sun is the symbol of the human Self (also referred to as the DOW, Atman, Monad, or I Am Presence), the highest, purest nature of every individual. A person experiencing enlightenment sometimes undergoes the affect of having their body surrounded by light, which may remain for days, which is spoken of as being clothed with the solar splendor."

DIVINE NUTRITION PROGRAM – Technique no. 16:
Meditation to open our 3 channels for Theta – Delta wave feeding.

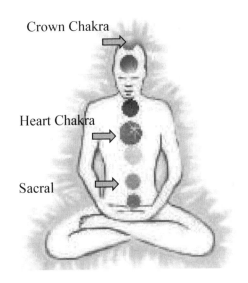

Crown Chakra

Heart Chakra

Sacral

Diagram 11

❖ *Step 1:* Sit in silence and do the Love Breath meditation where you visualize that your heart chakra is plugged into a never ending stream of Divine Mother love. Imagine that so much Divine Mother love is flowing through your heart centre that it then flows over into your lower and upper chakras keeping until all your inner energy centers are tuned to the Divine Love channel.

❖ This opens the heart channel and if it is done each day the heart centre will be kept tuned to the Theta – Delta channel. This channel is strengthened further when point 6 of the 8 point Luscious Lifestyles Program (L.L.P.) is applied – this is the 'daily service without the thought of reward' focus where we treat others with kindness and compassion.

Step 2: Requires us to open the lower Tan Tien or Hara – our sacral chakra, and tune it to the inner plane Central Sun channel which also feeds our Earth's sun.

- ❖ Again sit in silence and focus on the area just below your navel. Imagine the Violet Light flooding in through your open heart and down the front of your body and into this energy centre.
- ❖ Imagine that this sacral centre is feeding off the Violet Light and growing and expanding and being tuned to the Divine Love, Divine Wisdom and Divine Power channel, from which the Violet Light comes.
- ❖ Imagine now that these same 3 beams are flowing from Source through space and time and are now magnetized to, and then flowing through an amazing centre or ball of brilliant white light which we instinctively recognize to be the Central Sun, a powerful inner plane grid connection point.
- ❖ Imagine these beams passing through this Central Sun and into our sacral chakra and are now permanently hooking in there like 3 cosmic cables.
- ❖ Imagining that the perfect amount of Divine Electricity that you need to feed this chakra is now being downloaded on a permanent basis.
- ❖ Imagine also that enough pure light from the Central Sun is radiating through this chakra and flowing down to nourish your base chakra and up to nourish your solar plexus chakra, so that these three chakras are kept in a state of expansion so that they operate as one spinning tunnel of light as per the Violet Light One Chakra column meditation in Chapter 7.

Step 3: Plugging in our Crown Chakra to the cosmic computer – God or Source – using the 3 cable Divine Love, Divine Wisdom and Divine Power system.

- ❖ As per Step 2, sit in silence and imagine the Violet Light beaming from Source through time and space and hooking in permanently to your Crown Chakra. Perhaps you see it first as one pink colored beam carrying Divine Love directly from the heart of the Divine Mother as we do in the Love Breath meditation.
- ❖ Next see a golden white beam of light hooking in to your crown centre and downloading all the wisdom you need from the mind of Supreme Intelligence.
- ❖ Next visualize a beam of blue carrying all the power that you need to do what you have come to do and that you can now do it with love and wisdom. Again imagine that once connected, these 3 cables are downloading a limitless, never ending source of pure nutrition into your system from the Theta – Delta fields.
- ❖ As with Step 2, imagine also that enough pure light from Source is radiating through this chakra and flowing down to nourish your brow chakra and throat chakra so that these three chakras are kept in a state of expansion, so that they operate as one spinning tunnel of light as per the Violet Light One Chakra column meditation in Chapter 7.

Diagram 12

The above meditation, like all energy grid work, needs only to be done once for once the connections are made, they are made. However making the connections strong enough and keeping the doors open so that enough of these energies can continue to flood our bio-system and feed it in a nourishing way so that we are no longer hungry, this depends totally on our frequency which again depends on our lifestyle. As we keep stressing, the Luscious Lifestyle Program determines how well we connect to the Divine Love Channel. Also the more we focus on something the stronger it grows so the more we assume, trust and expect the above meditation to do as intended, the sooner and longer that it will.

If you are someone who loves to eat physical food and have no interest in living purely on the light that flows from the Divine Nutrition channels, then everything we have discussed to date is still applicable as the meditations and programming codes and the lifestyle suggested will nourish you on a physical, emotional, mental and spiritual level. How much nourishment you receive depends on your desire and dedication, as only you can tune your personal biofield to this channel to attract the health and happiness that you need.

Diagram 13: Summation

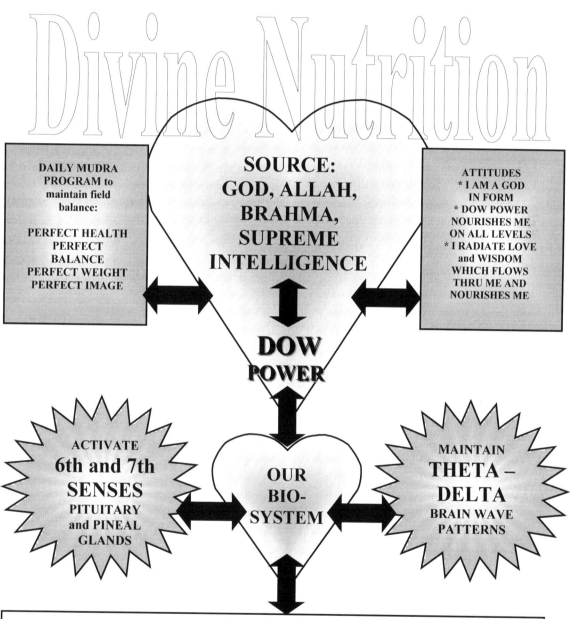

DAILY MUDRA
PROGRAM to
maintain field
balance:

PERFECT HEALTH
PERFECT
BALANCE
PERFECT WEIGHT
PERFECT IMAGE

SOURCE:
GOD, ALLAH,
BRAHMA,
SUPREME
INTELLIGENCE

DOW POWER

ATTITUDES
* I AM A GOD
IN FORM
* DOW POWER
NOURISHES ME
ON ALL LEVELS
* I RADIATE LOVE
and WISDOM
WHICH FLOWS
THRU ME AND
NOURISHES ME

ACTIVATE
6th and 7th
SENSES
PITUITARY
and PINEAL
GLANDS

OUR
BIO-
SYSTEM

MAINTAIN
THETA –
DELTA
BRAIN WAVE
PATTERNS

RECIPE 2000➜ - 8 POINT LUSCIOUS LIFESTYLES
PROGRAM FOR ACTIVATING A DIVINE NUTRITION
FLOW. L.L.P. TUNES US TO 'THE MADONNA
FREQUENCY' DIVINE LOVE CHANNEL FOR PHYSICAL
EMOTIONAL MENTAL and SPIRITUAL NOURISHMENT.

Chapter 8

Nourishing Environments

Not only are there many conventional and non-conventional sources that can physically, emotionally, mentally and spiritually nourish us, but we also have another very important field of nourishment which is our personal abode. Not just how we live, but where we live can either starve or nourish us. An environment where the television is constantly blaring, or loud music, or constant talk with very little silence can starve our spirit just as much as an environment with constant conflict, anger, friction or fear can deny our emotional body the love and security that it needs to blossom. Similarly an environment filled with boredom and lack of purpose and direction can starve our emotional, mental and spiritual bodies.

The decision to create an environment that is nurturing to us on all levels means that we must then look both at our internal environment, and address the metaphysical, and also the external and address the physical space we surround ourselves with. Metaphysics after all means the study of the science of life and feeding ourselves successfully on all levels is our personal responsibility and also our daily challenge.

I wrote the below article for our free online magazine The ELRAANIS Voice, at the beginning of 2003, when I myself was seeking a better way of being nourished for after 7 years on the road living mainly in hotel rooms and polluted cities, my inner being had begun to suffer from lack of the particular type of nourishment that I found that I needed. Even though the work I do with spirit is so rewarding and nourishing, I had successfully completed one aspect of the program and was hence guided to take some rest in an environment where I could drink more deeply from the Theta – Delta well.

Metaphysical Assumptions and Creating the Appropriate Ashram

What do you do when you know that if you want to change something, you always take yourself with you? That what it is that needs changing to make our world sing for us, is, literally, us? Just an attitude shift and a whole new game begins … I find it all quite miraculous. But what if an attitude change is not enough?

Recently I was guided to relocate from my city abode and create my own beach-side ashram – a solo girl monastery with no external stimulants like television or food, a sacred place with a daily dose of devotional music, lots of silence and sea breezes, exercise, meditation, yoga, to drink lots of fresh, pure water and indulge in the odd cup of tea. For some, to live like this energizes us joyously yet for others this reality zone is way too extreme.

Yet if we wish to operate as an example – a beacon of health and happiness, peace and prosperity in the world – then it has to be real for us, a lived and living affair, a harmonious dance between all of life's elements and ourselves. How can we wish this for others in the world if we have not attained this, or cannot sustain this in our own lives? To realize this – and not do what we can to attain it – keeps us devoid of joy for it is hypocritical not to practice what we preach and to ignore our inner guidance can only bring us pain.

Relocating and creating a new, nurturing energy field can be a rewarding yet time consuming affair, so I employed my accommodation angel, provided it with a telepathic list with the usual at the bottom sign off of: "or something better please" and of course was guided to the perfect place to begin my nourishing sabbatical from city life. As I looked around the family home to see what it was that I wanted to take with me, I realized again that my needs at this time in my life are so few. A few paintings, esoteric sculptures, my mountain bike, paints and my easel, my meditation cushions, lots of great music and a few clothes and I was off and ready to begin a new year with some nurturing time out for me!

Nearly 30 years ago I'd applied to move into a Sydney based Ashram only to be told that I was too young and to go out and live life a little more, which I obviously did. Sidetracked by family and children and later a career, and playing the role of nurturer and provider for all, I have finally found myself free from most of that and drawn to ashram life again. Perhaps it's the age of the crone creeping up on me, perhaps I just need some 'down time' from so much time on the road; yet regardless I have discovered that rather than move into an existing ashram, I can create my own! What a joy!

An ashram is – in the highest definition – a sacred space, an energy field tuned to the Divine Channels using the tools of will, intention and frequency. Ideally an ashram is a Holy place that nurtures an individual's fitness – their physical, emotional, mental and spiritual fitness – while providing a disciplined environment to grow. While some traditional eastern ashrams focus on discipline through austere living and on spiritual growth through service and silence, the modern day ashram (that we can create in our homes) needs to promote fitness on all levels while delivering the perfect alignment for an individual to take the perfect action in life. The perfect outcome – if desired – would of course be an experience of health and happiness, peace and prosperity that feeds us on a deep, soul level. An ideal ashram needs to allow us to feel as if we are 'home'; aligned with our true nature and as if we exist in a space that nurtures us on the deepest levels of our being.

When we are being properly nurtured we can say two things:
- ❖ I am pleased with everything that I have created in my life now.
- ❖ Today is a good day to die.

Point 1 is self-explanatory and point 2 is an ancient American Indian warrior cry, which can be translated to mean that everything in my life is at peace; everything is in its place and has been attended to, to the best of my ability. It means that everyone I know, knows that I love and appreciate them, there are no regrets, no 'sorrys' left unsaid, no unfinished chapters. It means that everything in my life is complete on all levels so that I can relax and be in the now. This is also known as taking care of business.

It also means that 'having taken care of business' that we treat every moment as precious and can enjoy the outcome of our choices and recognize all that comes our way for what it is – a reflection of our own consciousness and a chance to grow and learn. It also means being appropriate with others, offending no one, especially not our Divine Self by ignoring Its voice. Yes I know that our Divine Self can never be offended for It simply observes us lovingly and laughs, pleased we are playing the game and wanting to play with us when we invite It, or is doing so having been invited eons ago.

It is obvious that people have to create the appropriate ashram for themselves – something that delivers the 'happy and healthy, peaceful and prosperous' game if this is what we require. In Dimensional Biofield Science this means getting the frequency right so that the quantum field can deliver this type of payload. Nonetheless while uniqueness rules, and there is no one path to joy, there are standard tools and presumptions that can tune us to the health and happiness channel. The first is our lifestyle and thought patterns which can redirect our energy into the health and happiness direction. The next tool is our environment – what some may call the inner and outer house of God. An ashram is an outer house of God that is created to reveal the inner house.

Ancient Wisdom says that the only reason we have a physical, emotional and mental body is so that our Divine essence may know Itself in form and for many, this has become basic metaphysical presumption no.1.

Presumption no. 2 is that we are clones of God, pre-programmed with the same software as in the Jesus decree "I and my father are one". No. 3 presumption is that this software runs our bio-system effortlessly if we invite it to do so and let go of our toxic ways. We also know that toxic thinking, toxic feeling and toxic feeding will break down our bio-system and create disease and decay.

Presumption no. 4 is that our physical bio-system is Divine hardware and actually part of a Divine mainframe or 'organic cosmic super chip' of which each of us is an atom or a cell.

There are many more metaphysical presumptions that are just awaiting scientific confirmation and we discuss many of these throughout my books but let's get back to our tools. Experiential research has found that the environment we allow around us can be crucial to the imprinting of our fields – which along with our beliefs then determines what we magnetize to ourselves in life. Creating an environment that delivers, and maintains us in the "Perfect Alignment for Perfect Action and Perfect Outcome" game is in itself an art.

In other words, the ideal environment for those wanting to experience health and happiness and peace and prosperity, is a loving and supportive one that runs a stress free, win-win-win game – the win for me, win for others and win for the planet agenda that is so necessary now in the co-creation of paradise.

So we invite you to look at the 'I am pleased with everything' and 'Today is a good day to die' ideas and give yourself an honest answer. If you get a yes to both, then relax and enjoy it all. If you get a no then keep refining your life until you can say yes to both.

Remember, wherever you go you will take yourself with you and change can begin with just a simple shift in attitude towards our life. Having traveled the world for over 7 years I have witnessed so much suffering and seen so many people who by Western standards are in great lack and yet some of the happiest people I have met have been the poorest in material terms. Setting and achieving the goal of health and happiness, peace and prosperity for our self – and the world – needs to be an accepted minimum standard, for it is all easily within our reach and we now have more than enough tools at our disposal to create physical, emotional, mental and spiritual fitness.

Having the courage to break old habits that no longer support us, or being brave enough to move on, to say 'sorrys', or goodbyes, or hellos to new possibilities, is all just a natural part of the cycles of life and is required if we wish to put our house in order, for the true ashram reveals our Divine Self and the purity of our hearts determines our experience of It.

Personally, I love the idea of a family home base where I can dip back into a field of familiarity that still is a part of me, yet how I can also extend my field to now include my Ashram apartment, which is also my Divine Mother Monastery on the hill with its sea breezes and invitation to be fit. I look around at all that we have achieved over the last decade as I have experimented with my fitness and pushed myself to extremes, and rested and then pushed again; how we've held the door open to controversy and been bathed uncomfortably in its gray light and quietly closed it again. Now finally able to bundle all the work up into the Planetary Peace Program and the Divine Nutrition game, there is a sense of completion and also peace and all is well with my world.

The art of creating the perfect external environment that can nourish us deeply can be helped by the ancient tradition of Feng Shui as well as the utilization of Bio-Shield devices and field re-weaving techniques. Our outer living environment is a reflection of our inner environment and a person who is well nourished on all levels of their being automatically seems to create an external environment that supports this nourishment flow and also nurtures others. At this time in our world, we are being asked to not just nourish ourselves effectively with minimum drain to our global resources but also to be able to extend our fields when required and nourish others for we have found that the 'me, me, me' paradigm blocks the Divine Nutrition flow, while the 'us' game frees it.

Divine Nutrition Program – Technique no. 17:

Create a nurturing environment in your home.
- ❖ Clean out/give away all objects that you do not use or that have no sentimental or spiritual significance.
- ❖ Apply Feng Shui to your home to increase and positively redirect its inner energy fields.

- ❖ Create a meditation/yoga room space where you can be in silence and build up an Alpha – Theta field and energy pool.
- ❖ Adorn your wall with spiritual images and activate them to act as doorways of Holy Being energy to radiate through and feed you on a soul level.

Chapter 9

Frequently asked Questions
Divine Nutrition & Theta – Delta Field Feeding

Before we begin this chapter I would like to stress that there are 2 types of food available for humanity – the food we cultivate from our natural resources and the 'non-conventional' food we can access as Gods in form, which we can cultivate via our personal frequency adjustments.

People often ask:

Q1: Is it really possible that we can be free from our dependence on food?

A: Yes.

Q2: But don't we need to nourish our bodies with vitamins and minerals?

A: Yes.

Q3: But if we don't eat, how can we survive?

A: We do this by learning how to access and feed our selves from an alternative source of nourishment that is continually flowing within our cells and we will provide a step by step process for this in Chapter 11.

Question 1: Why do we have a stomach and teeth if we are not meant to eat physical food?

Answer Q1: Our current digestive system has evolved over time to mirror our beliefs and as these change so will our digestive system. The fact is that we can do anything we choose when we merge again with our DOW power, for we are the masters of our own body and as such every cell of our body is constantly listening to our thoughts, words and actions to which the molecules and atoms then adjust themselves in response. As we are the first generation of light eaters in the West we are also dependant upon the process of evolution for the inner system to change. However in time the future generations of light eaters internal circuitry will end up quite different so the short answer to this question is that it is just a matter of evolution, and time, and our body's ability to mirror our beliefs. Those who continue to eat will keep their current digestive systems and those who choose Divine Nutrition will eventually have a digestive system that reflects this new way of being nourished.

It is said that when we first took form on this planet we had a different bio-system that was self-sustaining and needed neither food nor fluid; we have evolved over time to our current system and our future bio-system evolution depends on our lifestyle and choices.

Question 2:   Can the lion really lay down with the lamb as per the Biblical prophecy of true peace among all kingdoms?

Answer Q2: Again this is to do with the morphogenetic field. If we eliminate the aggressive nature of human kind and cease the slaughter of human and animal life, this will change the social and planetary biofield resonance powerfully enough to imprint all kingdoms. If we then ensure that all individuals are plugged in to energy channels that provide complete nourishment so that we all feel fulfilled and become altruistic, aware and begin to act like loving respectful masters; then obviously this too will also imprint all kingdoms. I have often said as I travel that the level of aggression we see in the animal kingdom is a mirror of the level of aggression that we see in the human kingdom. Eliminate our human aggression, and boost our Divine Love radiation capacity, and we will see the 'lion laying down with the lamb' reality.

Question 3: How do people who are nourished by just prana, maintain their body weight?

Answer Q3:   Simplistically this is to do with attitude and programming and faith. It is also to do with the science of our mind/body connection and how convinced we are that each cell of the body truly listens to our thoughts and commands and how if we act like masters, the body must obey our commands. This type of programming will not work if we have internal sabotage programs running, so these need to be addressed and cleared. The good thing is that all programming codes can be tested before actually completely letting go of the ingestion of all food substances. Hence we recommend that this be tested gradually as you reduce your food intake from 3 to 2 meals per day plus decrease the quantity and variety.

Living successfully on Divine light requires a degree of physical, emotional, mental and spiritual preparation, cleansing and health. It also requires trust in DOW Power. We have discussed the Luscious Lifestyles Program and also the health/balance/weight/image command that needs to be applied to maintain our body weight and we will shortly discuss using this with the chi machine. It is interesting to note that without programming, the body's weight will eventually stabilize anyway but often not until significant weight loss has occurred.

Question 4: Many who are now living holistically and are accessing the Alpha – Theta – Delta zones due to their lifestyle are becoming increasingly sensitive. This sensitivity often makes them feel as if they must be more reclusive as they do not like mingling in the denser Beta – Alpha fields of community life. There are also often estrangements that occur as an Alpha – Theta field dweller moves out of the 'normal' relatable range of family and friends. Can you comment on this? What has your research found?

Answer Q4: A Dimensional Biofield Technician, and spiritual initiate, is someone who has learnt to work with all fields and who – ideally – can exist in harmony in any field without disruption to their own field. As we have already discussed, the two most powerful tools we have to selectively absorb the frequencies we want from the world are:

- a) Our intention, will and attitude, i.e. the absorption versus radiation game, and
- b) The use of the Bio-Shield devices which we discuss in Chapter 11.
- c) I also feel it is helpful to understand how to influence an existing field and how to weave a new field to support us in a more nurturing manner and will devote more time to this discussion later.

It is also beneficial to understand that accessing the channel of Divine Nutrition is not something that happens just to the lucky ones or the blessed or the Holy Ones. Any one can access the Madonna Frequency Field and its Divine Love, Divine Wisdom Channel and hence tap into pranic nourishment. However it is still a daily challenge to be able to exist in a predominantly Beta – Alpha field and still get enough nourishment from the Theta field to maintain health. This is why our energetic hook-ins and Bio-Shield devices are so helpful as they allow us to control the pranic flow. Also the daily practice of Kriya Yoga* and Surya-yoga** and techniques like the Love Breath meditation are most helpful.

* & **: These are specific forms of yoga that aid the Divine Nutrition flow which we will discuss shortly.

Another problem mentioned is the fact that as we consciously shift our frequencies to anchor ourselves in more nourishing fields, we do move out of relatable range with those who choose not to frequency match us. This is particularly noticeable among family and friends who may not understand our choice of a more refined diet or sensitive lifestyle. In response to this I would like to share that we have our bloodline family and also our global family and the ideal way of sharing is with unconditional love. So to make sure you give and get this type of loving, ask your DOW to bring you people with whom you can have a mutually beneficial and supportive relationship. Next when you are with family focus on sharing things that bring mutual pleasure rather than focusing on your differences. *(We have discussed this in detail in the Biofields & Bliss series.)*

Question 5: Which is better?

a) *To act as a channel to allow the Divine Love and Divine Wisdom Nutrition to flow through us and radiate out into the world thereby transforming both our bio-system and the world simultaneously or*

b) *To build up a reserve of this type of Nutritional force and operate from that well?*

Answer Q5: Ideally both. Building up reserves happens when we apply the lifestyle first as a tune in program and then utilize it as a daily maintenance program. I have done both and find the combination more powerful than doing just one or the other. Sooner or later we may find we may need to give extra which may drain the well, consequently we need to be plugged into a never-ending limitless Source (as in Chapter 7) and we also need to keep the radiation pure which the lifestyle does. Because of the type of food that meditation offers, we find ourselves naturally hungry to be in that silent, loving space anyway especially when we are living in chaotic cities where we can feel as if we are drowning in a denser beat. Existing purely in the Beta field creates emotional, mental and spiritual anorexia and leads humanity into disharmony, war and chaos.

Question 6: What about the time of instant physical transformation? How come when people use a command or chant nothing seems to instantly change?

Answer Q6: There are a number of internal and external factors that inhibit this. Firstly there is the strength of the morphogenetic field and what the dominant beat is. This is like a small boy with a soprano voice singing in a choir of 100 men who are baritones – unless his voice carries and is extremely powerful, his sound field will be drowned out. Similarly light eaters are required to tune into the Theta field for our nourishment and live a lifestyle that keeps us tuned to this channel enough to maintain health – if you have only .01% of 1% of the people of this planet doing this, then maintaining this frequency can be difficult. However, thankfully the Theta field radiation is like an atomic blast in power compared to the Beta field radiation, which is like a candle in comparison, so numbers are not the overriding factor here.

The next factor is to do with how trusting an individual is of the God within and also how real is the idea that we are a God in form who has all the creative power, healing power and transformational power that we need at our disposal. Many people believe this intellectually but not on a cellular level. Tapping into DOW Power and then witnessing Its flow and the benefits It brings all helps to build this trust. In this field experience is everything for the flow of Divine Love is not an intellectual affair and only when we feel this flow within can we trust It enough to surrender and explore Its other attributes.

The third factor is to do with karmic learning and the fourth factor is to do with our Divine blueprint and the role we have agreed to play. Nonetheless, all unfolds perfectly as it should and all we are being asked to do is hold the vision of ourselves as Gods in form, and to act impeccably as if we truly are masters, so that the universe can support us back into the field of Oneness where all possibilities are real and where the highest realities that benefit all are supported into being. The more we do this, the sooner our abilities for instant manifestation become evident individually and en mass.

Over the last decade pranic feeders have noticed a very interesting social phenomenon, which is that many people who spend time in our fields automatically begin to eat less and feel much better for it. As the energy that radiates through us is love (for it is the Madonna Frequency of Divine Love that provides the Level 3 Theta – Delta nourishment attribute) and as our personal biofield has been imprinted with the knowing, based on experience, that we do not need to take nourishment from physical food, this tends to imprint the fields of people around us, allowing them quicker access to the Theta – Delta field within their cells which then provides certain benefits – like intuitive knowledge, increased sensitivity as in clairsentience and the desire to eat less etc. The highest alchemical action that we can attain is the transformation of our bio-system into a DOW Power radiation station, an act that provides us naturally with the by-products of Level 2 and Level 3 nourishment.

◆◇◆◆◆◆◆◆◇◆◇◆◆◆◆◇◇◆◆◇◇◆◆◇◇◇◆◆◆◇◇◇◆◆◆◇◆◇◆◆◆◆◇◇◆◆◆◇◇◆◆◇◇◇◇◆◆◇◆◇◆◇◆◇◆◆◆◆◇◆◇◆◆◆◆◆◇◆◆◇◆◇◆◇◇◇◇◇◆◆◆◇◆◇◆◆◆◆◇◇◇◆◆◇◆◆◆◆◆◇◇◇◆

Question 7: How beneficial is yogic training for being a Divine light eater? You mention both Kriya Yoga and Surya-Yoga; can you explain the difference and their benefits?

Answer Q7: As Yoga has become so popular in our western world, it is good to understand the different types and how they also relate to pranic feeding. Firstly it is virtually impossible to provide a specific Divine Nutrition access procedure for as we keep stressing, it is all to do with our individual frequency which is determined by our past and present experiences, and attitudes, and no two individuals are the same. However we can provide a selection of tools for tuning to the Divine Nutrition channel that the individual can then experiment with and yogic practice is one of these tools. I have also come to believe over the years that all yogic practices are required to successfully feed from the Divine Nutrition channel as each practice brings a specific tuning tool.

One of the esoteric teachers that I readily identify with on many levels is Omraam Mikhaël Aïvanhov and just as I began the final section of *The Food of Gods*, a book on his teachings arrived, as a gift, in the mail. I always pay attention to these type of 'coincidences' as although the book came with a postcard written in French, I knew it was required reading for me. The book is called *The Splendor of Tiphareth: The Yoga of the Sun*. The day before receiving this book, I was invited to join Hira Ratan Manek on a USA tour to promote solar feeding. Both instances have prompted me to assess a little more deeply the value of solar nourishment and as I began to read Mikhael's book I realized that it contained vital information that I need to add here particularly in relation to the art of Surya-Yoga, a practice that I have been intuitively involved in for years although I did not realize that this is what it is called.

Surya-Yoga is the yoga of the sun. As we discussed in the solar feeding section in Chapter 6, the most prolific modern day research into pranic nourishment was done in India at the turn of the millennium with Dr Shah and his team and their 'guinea pig' Hira Ratan Manek – a yogi also known as Shri HRM. However Surya-Yoga involves more than solar gazing and absorbing the pranic flow through nature. Surya-Yoga incorporates all the other yogic practices while focusing on connecting with the Supreme Intelligence that feeds our physical sun and flows through it. Recognizing the Divine Force that sustains our sun and directs its energy into the lower planes of the third and fourth dimensions creates Bhakti-Yoga, a feeling of devotion and awe for without our sun there can be no life. All recognized organisms including mankind are fed by the energy that radiates through our physical sun. To practice Hatha-Yoga and its various asanas in the warmth of the early morning or dusk time sun, opens and feeds all our meridians and our chakra system with another level of food and power. Applying positive mental projections and thought forms with Mantra-Yoga and using Kriya-Yoga to direct the outer light flow into our inner system, allows our sun time of Surya-Yoga to be even more beneficial.

Surya-Yoga also requires us to be in silence and project our minds via meditation and creative visualization, into the fifth Dimensional frequency band and beyond, where we can recognize the intelligent life levels that exists within the sun's fields but this is an advanced practice for those who are open to experience 5th, 6th, 7th (and upwards) multi-Dimensional life-form expression. As Mikhaël Aïvanhov shares in his Surya Yoga book, the idea that intelligent life can reside in the higher energy field of our physical sun is ludicrous to many, as is the idea that our body can access a source of nourishment from within its own atomic structure, or the idea that each atom is a doorway to an inner universe, or that we can direct Violet Light Rays to attract even more nourishing Violet Light rays – from these inner sanctums – and create a system of bio-feedback looping via Shabda-Yoga to feed our cells.

Aïvanhov also concurs with more recent research into the natural properties of our brain and its predilection to mirror and change resonance patterns to match that which it focuses on. He says that: "by focusing all his powers of concentration on the sun, he (an esoteric student) can capture and draw into himself, in all their original purity, the elements needed to ensure his health and equilibrium." He also says that as the sun provides all the elements for all life, we can feed on its pure essence and that: "When we gaze at the sun, therefore, even if we do not know it, our soul assumes the same shape and becomes a luminous, incandescent sphere. It is the law if imitative magic that is taking effect; we look at the sun and our whole being begins to resemble it. Simply by looking at something, we create an association, an alliance between ourselves and the object or being we are looking at, our vibrations adjust to its vibratory rate and, quite unconsciously, we imitate it." He goes on to say of Surya-Yoga that: "If you want to be like the sun, you must gaze at it with great love and trust. In this way you will become warmer and more luminous and better able to pour life into others. Your presence among others will be that of a sun radiating light, warmth and life."

Using mantra-Yoga to remind us that the sun is also the Source of nourishment for all life, we can then change our mindset by acknowledging that it has the power to feed us directly without going through the middle man food chain of the plant and animal kingdom.

❖❖❖

Question 8: What about other types of yoga? How do they fit into the preparation process for accessing the Divine Nutrition channel?

Answer Q8: To answer this question properly I need to take a little time to differentiate between some of the more traditional yogic practices as each has a role in our physical, emotional, mental and spiritual preparation for tuning to the Divine Nutrition channel.

Yoga is a metaphysical art that comes from India and Tibet, China, Japan, Egypt and also Persia and all religions have their own form of yoga. For example the practice of adoration, prayer, contemplation and devotion to God in Christianity is known as Bhakti-yoga in India. **Bhakti-yoga** is the yoga of devotion and spiritual love. Without devotion to our DOW and our desire to feel Its love, we cannot begin to connect to the Divine Nutrition channel, for devotion to the experience of Divine Love attracts the food of the Gods. The experience of devotion, contemplation and prayer provide the fuel of discipline for us to tune ourselves more deeply to the Divine Nutrition channel.

Then there is the yoga of knowledge – also known as *Jnana-Yoga* – which is the way to God through the use of one's intelligence and the practice of this yoga is said to suit people open to study and philosophical reflection. Accepting the possibility of pranic nourishment requires the honoring of our intelligence and the recognition that we also have a super-luminal intelligence within us that mirrors the Supreme Intelligence of the original Creative Force. To be nourished successfully we need to trust and surrender to this Force which can only occur when we have done enough intellectual and experiential research to relax and let go and let our inner God feed us. Discovering then honoring the Divine Intelligence within us is true Jnana-Yoga practice.

Karma-Yoga is for people who are learning about selfless service, service done without the thought of reward. Karma-Yoga teaches us altruism through the doing of good deeds that benefit others. This is a very important aspect of the Luscious Lifestyles Program for acts of kindness done with compassion are one of the most powerful tools we have to tune us to the Madonna Frequency Field of pure love.

To successfully feed from the Divine Nutrition channel and sustain health, we need to learn to master any limiting influences of our lower nature and become the Queen/King of our inner kingdom. We do this through *Raja-Yoga* where we develop concentration and self control.

Preparing the physical body to be strong enough to handle the download of the Divine Electricity flow that comes with pranic feeding, opens us to the practice of *Hatha-Yoga* and its ability to tap into our bio-systems psychic centers through the use of various asanas and postures. Hatha-Yoga gifts us with discipline, will power and perseverance – all of which are helpful as pioneers of the Divine Nutrition journey, however Aïvanhov says that Hatha-Yoga is often not recommended for the undisciplined Western nature.

The practice of *Kriya-Yoga* is the yoga most adopted by nearly all previous pranic nourishers, for Kriya-Yoga is the yoga of Light and its range of color. It consists of thinking on light, visualizing light and experiencing the inner Light flow through the brow chakra or upper Tan Tien, working with light energy through our auric field and learning to direct this light flow in a nourishing way as per practices like the Tao Master's Microcosmic Orbit.

It was a specific Kriya-yogic practice that sustained Giri Bala enough to be free from the need of food or fluid for over six decades and Kriya-Yoga that gave the Himalayan Babaji his immortality. Kriya-Yoga can be used to direct light through the grids as in the work of the Geomancers and the Dimensional Biofield Science Technicians and it is Kriya-Yoga that sustains the Bio-Shield Devices. Kriya-Yoga also feeds our chakras and their associated meridians.

Agni-Yoga is often practiced by rebirthers and those who utilize the power of the elements as Agni-Yoga works with the element of fire which ignites the fire within as the origin of universal creation. Agni-Yoga allows us to draw a stream of nourishment through the Central Sun via our lower Tan Tien, or sacral chakra, and it is this ability that differentiates us from the solar feeders. Agni-Yoga connects us with Lord Helios, the Intelligence that controls the light dispersion through the sun.

There is also **Mantra-Yoga or Shabda-Yoga** which is yoga of the power of the word where specific codes, commands or mantras are used at specific times with particular frequency and intensity to achieve certain bio-system changes and to redirect the cosmic forces of intelligence via light. This also is an important part of the Luscious Lifestyles Program as it allows us to access molecular intelligence, redirect internal and external energy flows and change cellular behavior patterns.

Divine Nutrition Program – Technique no. 18:
- ❖ Learn and practice meditation and yoga.
- ❖ Ask your DOW to bring you the perfect yoga and meditation teacher.

We have spoken at length about various yogic practices being applied as methods of tuning ourselves in preparation for being fed purely by Divine Nutrition. We have also talked of the importance of attitude. Now I would like to introduce a little data on the Shaman for it is usually the individual who has either yogic or shamanistic tendencies who is drawn to the Divine Nutrition, living on light reality. Due to their personal metaphysical experiences they can understand and grasp the concept more readily.

Question 9: What about the Shaman?
Answer Q9: The word 'Shaman' comes from the language of the Tungus of North-Central Asia and it came into use in English via Russian. A shaman is often known to be a master of ecstasy, or a shape-shifter or one who has the ability to alter their states of consciousness at will, via meditation or lucid dreaming, to leave their physical form and move between the worlds. They are often metaphysicians or healers or people with command over the elements of wind and fire and they usually work as solo players in the service game.

Like the yogi's, Shaman come from all walks of life and they often receive their powers after a near death experience, or after undergoing strenuous training and initiations. Many Shaman move between the dimensions of the higher and lower worlds performing tasks such as escorting the souls of loved ones through the lower realms, to consulting with, and receiving prophetic visions by the great light beings in the higher realms.

A shaman often lives at the edge of reality and at the edge of society itself. Few indeed have the stamina to adventure into these realms and endure the outer hardships and personal crises that have been reported by or observed of many shamans as they act as bridges between the worlds.

Question 10: The idea of Solar feeding or Surya-Yoga is all well and good but what about when we live in places where there is minimal sun and also maximum pollution that screens out beneficial pranic rays? Like London for example?

Answer Q10: This is precisely why I feel that solar feeding principles alone are insufficient to sustain the Divine Nutrition flow and that to do this we have to feed from the Central Sun's energy that flows through our lower Tan Tien – as in Chapter 7. Also all successful solar feeders that I have met including Hira Ratan Manek practice their version of the 8 point Luscious Lifestyles Program as discussed in Chapter 6. In order to consistently maintain our health and happiness levels, we must apply some type of Kriya-Yoga to our internal and external energy Light flow.

***

Question 11: What do you feel is the main requirement to live purely on prana, the secret to living only on Divine Light?

Answer to Q11: After over a decade of personal experiential research and interviewing hundreds who live successfully via Divine Nutrition, my one conclusion is that it is our vibration that determines our success with this, nothing more, nothing less. Our vibration allows us to draw this nutrition from the inner planes and back through our cellular structure, if this is our intention. It also allows us to attract increased doses of both internal and external chi, for prana – in the form of Cosmic Fire and Astral Light – which are the main elements sustaining all life particles. Things like a pure heart, the ability to serve with compassion and kindness, the openness to the Higher Laws and to using our higher mind, all these tune us powerfully to the channels that can reveal our paranormal powers, of which this ability is just a small by-product.

***

Question 12: With so much emphasis in the world on malnutrition and obesity, and on anorexia and body image, and with people constantly saying that physical food is a gift from God and that to not eat is 'unnatural' and is to deny yourself a great pleasure; how do you handle this?

Answer Q12: Firstly malnutrition, obesity and physical anorexia are all the result of humanity's various emotional, mental and spiritual states of anorexia which Divine Nutrition, when released from within, has the power to eliminate. Secondly there are many ways to nourish ourselves apart from the usual choices of food, or indiscriminate sex, or drugs that dull or stimulate our mind like television for example. I am not saying that any of these things are 'bad' per se, just that we have not yet been well educated as to alternative forms of nourishment.

The sharing of food with friends and in social settings does bring great pleasure, not just to the palette but also on emotional bonding levels. This is one of the reasons that some level 3 light eaters still eat from time to time even though their bio-systems have been freed from the need for physical food. For me personally, one the best 'meals' I can give myself is a walk along a beach where I can simultaneously bathe in – and absorb – sun and wind and water prana. Another 'meal' for me is a walk in a rainforest or to meditate on a mountain in the dusk or dawn light. Humanity has entered into a stage of evolution where we need to reassess what we term true nourishment, as for the first time in our history we have the extreme of approximately 1.2 billion people suffering malnutrition from lack of physical nourishment and 1.2 billion people suffering from obesity related problems due to incorrect physical nourishment and addictions to fast foods served to placate a fast society. For many people eating and the 'pleasure' food brings is an emotional addiction in an attempt to satisfy a deeper hunger. At this time in our evolution we are being intuitively guided to encourage pleasures that promote and sustain physical, emotional, mental and spiritual fitness in all.

Question 13: As a leading proponent in the world for the Divine Nutrition paradigm, and as someone who has had to deal with all the natural skepticism regarding the pranic nourishment reality, what do you see as the future of this?

Answer Q13: Like many yogis and shaman, I have been blessed with the ability to glimpse – from time to time – into our future and I have witnessed that due to its personal and global benefits, the 'prana as nourishment, level 3' reality is being Divinely supported and will not go away. I have seen a world where the slaughter of any life – human or animal – is no longer part of our reality and is seen as something belonging to our more barbaric, unenlightened past. In this 'new' world, there is love, honor and respect for all life and people have been educated as to how to create and maintain physical, emotional, mental and spiritual fitness. In this world we exist in rainbow cities of crystalline light that radiate with love and wisdom and health and happiness.

The question is how do we get there?

What steps do we need to take to evolve into this new world?

The answer is simply a matter of the expansion of our consciousness which happens when we adopt a more holistic lifestyle that is designed to change our brain wave patterns and activate our higher sensibilities.

While skepticism is healthy, ignorance and fear come from lack of education which is why it is crucial for those in the 'frontlines' of this new paradigm, to always act as masters. Part of this mastery entails being able to hold and radiate the vibration of love in all situations regardless of what is happening.

My connection with the inner plane Holy Ones has revealed to me through the years that everything is fed by, and exists due to, light and color and sound whose rays and waves are driven by Universal Laws and mathematical codes, just like a giant Cosmic Computer. As such all can be directed and utilized via our will, imagination and intention and nothing is impossible. I also feel that tuning our bodies, first to the Level 2 aspect then eventually to the Level 3 gift, of the Divine Nutrition Channel, is basic esoteric science and the next step in our evolutionary process.

So exactly what is the future of this?

Due to how challenging this paradigm is to mainstream reality, many of us have already lived through both ridicule, and overt and covert opposition yet we know that eventually we will come into a state of acceptance. As these stages unfold in the different countries where the light eaters are demonstrating this paradigm, some have gone underground rarely speaking of such things, others are very public in their support but most are simply circumspect, relying on their inner guidance as to whom they can share such things with.

Also the bringers of change always work in waves:- in the 1970's Wiley Brooks launched 'breatharianism' into the American scene, then I held the very public position with 'pranic nourishment' in Australia, Asia and Europe for nearly a decade until I completed my media assignment with this work, now Hira Ratan Manek is being the public face as he relentlessly tours in India and the USA, and works with the various medical and science teams to offer his 'solar feeding' program. After Hira there will be someone else and so it will continue. And of course we recognize all the work that others have done to contribute personally and professionally to the anchoring of this reality and some of these are acknowledged in Book 2 of this series. You can tell when a paradigm is here to stay when many different people, from many different backgrounds, most who have never met, start to reach and share the same findings and one of the current excitements within esoteric circles is regarding the gifts that come when we consciously shift brain wave patterns.

❖ ❖❖❖❖❖❖ ❖❖❖❖ ❖❖ ❖❖❖❖ ❖ ❖❖❖❖❖❖❖❖❖❖❖❖❖❖❖❖❖❖❖❖❖❖❖❖❖❖❖❖❖❖❖ ❖❖❖❖ ❖ ❖❖ ❖❖❖❖ ❖❖❖❖❖❖❖ ❖

Question 14: You often say that the idea of just being free from the need to take physical food, is not enough motivation for people on this journey and that people wishing to be involved with it need to be aware of the 'bigger picture'. Could you explain what you mean by this?

Answer Q14: Humanity has been gifted with an amazing ability which is to re-discover, recognize, experience and demonstrate the God Force within. We have been programmed to demonstrate this Divine Force and be one with it, any time we choose – for on one level we operate like mini computers that are run by the same software as the Cosmic Computer called God. This Divine Force, or God, radiates Its nurturing love and light through our inner sun centre to feed our chakras, and through our external sun and It has the power to feed our cells. However the remarkable thing is not to see a human being become free from the need to eat physical food, but to see a human being radiate such light and love that all are fed by their presence.

I think Aïvanhov summed it up best when he said: "When we focus our attention on the sun, the centre of our universe, we draw closer to our own centre, our higher self, the sun within; we melt into it more and more.

"But to focus our attention on the sun also means to learn to mobilize all our thoughts, desires and energies, and put them to work in the service of the highest ideal. He who works to unify the chaotic multitude of inner forces that constantly threaten to tear him apart, and launch them in the pursuit of one, luminous, beneficial goal, becomes a powerful focal point, capable of radiating in every direction. Believe me, a human being who masters the tendencies of his own lower nature can benefit the whole of mankind. He becomes as radiant as the sun. His freedom is such that his consciousness embraces the whole human race as he pours out the superabundance of light and love that dwell within him.

"The world needs more and more human beings capable of dedicating themselves to this work with the sun, for only love and light are capable of transforming humanity."

The addictions we form in our search to satisfy all our hungers, occur through lack of holistic education and a lack of awareness of 'who' we really are plus the misconception that we are separate from our Creative Force. Once we experience our true nature and unify all aspects of our lower and higher nature, the food of the God within begins to flow and our hungers and addictions disappear.

❖ ❖❖❖❖❖❖❖ ❖❖❖❖ ❖ ❖❖❖ ❖ ❖❖❖❖ ❖ ❖ ❖ ❖❖❖❖❖❖❖❖❖❖❖❖❖❖❖ ❖ ❖❖ ❖❖❖❖❖❖❖ ❖ ❖ ❖ ❖❖❖❖ ❖ ❖❖❖ ❖ ❖❖❖❖ ❖ ❖❖❖❖❖❖❖ ❖ ❖

Questions on dealing with family and social adjustments as a Level 3 light eater, are covered in the previous books in this series however there is one more issue that I would like to re-address. People often say to me, "I can't be a vegetarian, it doesn't suit my blood type, or my body type" they say, "I tried it and felt terrible" OR "My doctor or nutritionist said it was not a good choice for me". The most crucial aspect of the Divine Nutrition reality is the mastery of mind over matter. We are all Gods in forms and our body can absorb – from the higher inner and outer planes – all the proteins, minerals and vitamins we need to self regenerate, maintain peak health and longevity. It is also common for people to experience 'toxic dumping' from an impure system as they begin to lighten up their diet. All we recommend is that you be aware of your thought patterns and be prepared to re-program yourself out of any limiting beliefs which is the first step to opening the door to the Divine Nutrition reality.

❖ ❖❖❖❖❖❖❖ ❖❖❖❖ ❖ ❖❖❖ ❖ ❖❖❖❖ ❖ ❖ ❖ ❖❖❖❖❖❖❖❖❖❖❖❖❖❖❖ ❖ ❖❖ ❖❖❖❖❖❖❖ ❖ ❖ ❖ ❖❖❖❖ ❖ ❖❖❖ ❖ ❖❖❖❖ ❖ ❖❖❖❖❖❖❖ ❖ ❖

Divine Nutrition Program – Techniques no. 19a, b, c, d & e:

As part of your Shaman, Yogic training I also recommend the following:
   a) Learn to move comfortably through your home in the dark – this is night vision training.
   b) Learn to do things – e.g. making a meal, or a cup of tea or washing dishes etc. – without your actions making a noise. This is a Zen exercise about field silence training.
   c) Field non-displacement training: This is about learning to move through a field with grace and in silence and to not disturb the surrounding field by your presence. Many people for example may walk through their house like a 'baby elephant' they seem to stomp or slam doors, and generally their presence in the field to others is like a mini bomb blast. Learning to move through a field without disturbing it is the equivalent of stalking prey in the bush where the hunter must be incredibly aware and also silent in order to succeed.
   d) Finally train yourself to be ambidextrous – capable of efficiently using both hands as well as each other. This tool is about balance.

e) Finally train yourself to be free of the influence of weather – to always be comfortable in hot or cold weather and free from the need of particular clothing as you learn to control your body temperature at will. Always send love as heat or love as cool from your heart through your body to achieve this.

f) Do all of the above with joy, lightness and laughter and an awareness of how your presence always influences the fields. (*See more on this in Chapter 11 – Part 4 on Field Reweaving.*)

Chapter 10

Summary and Benefits

For those seeking nourishment on all levels so that health and happiness are attained and sustained, we recommend that you do the following step by step process which is Level 1 of the Divine Nutrition Program. Please note that the below program does not look at eliminating food from your diet, its basic aim is to connect you with the Divine Nutrition channel so that you can be nourished physically, emotionally, mentally and spiritually while still retaining the pleasure of taking physical food. *(The steps to eliminate the need for physical food – Level 3 of this program – are covered in chapter 11: 'Pranic Nourishment Hook-In: Step by Step'.)*

The below steps will also improve your health, increase your mental clarity, decrease your need for sleep and decrease your stress levels. If all steps are adopted you will find yourself coping with life a lot better, with increased stamina and enhanced feelings of love and well-being. Other benefits of the below program are those outlined previously such as increased intuitive abilities e.g. clairsentience, clairaudience and clairvoyance.

The benefits that you receive and enjoy will depend on how much time you dedicate to the below program, but as you will operate in a healthier and more relaxed manner, the program will also give you more time in return, as it will allow you to generally function better in your day-to-day life.

Achieving Level 2 nourishment of the Divine Nutrition Program:

❖ Step 1: Take some time to sit and think honestly – what are you still hungry for? Then ask yourself "What can I do to fulfill these hungers in a way that is good for me and others?" Make a list and set the goal of fulfilling each hunger practically. Until we are clear with what we want we cannot send out clear signals and hence get a clear response from the intelligent universe that surrounds us. Also an honest look at our life can often inspire the action for change.

❖ Step 2: To improve your basic health and happiness and inner peace levels, apply and enjoy the Luscious Lifestyles Program (LLP) as outlined in Chapter 6: Technique 5 and also as part of this, apply point 6 to reduce your consumption of the world's resources and also to increase your lifespan under the 'eat less and live longer' principle.

- ❖ Step 3: As part of the meditation aspect of L.L.P. and to attract more love into your field, do the Love Breath Mediation daily each morning and evening before you go to bed for 5 – 10 minutes as per Chapter 6: technique no. 1.

- ❖ Step 4: Practice technique no. 3 in Chapter 6 and spend 5 minutes every day smiling into your body at your organs to improve your health and general feelings of well being and to increase your mind/body awareness connection.

- ❖ Step 5: Use the Body Love Tool daily to improve your health and feelings of well being. This is Technique no. 4 in Chapter 6.

- ❖ Step 6: Discover the nourishment that comes from time spent enjoying solar and nature prana as in technique no. 8 of Chapter 6. Spending time in nature in silence is also part of the L.L.P. program. Learn Surya-Yoga – as outlined in Chapter 6 or study this form of yoga in a little more depth by reading Mikhaël Aïvanhov 's book *The Splendor of Tiphareth* ISBN 1-895878-35-X.

- ❖ Step 7: As part of the meditation aspect of L.L.P. and to attract more vitality and chi into your body, do the Violet Light meditation and each morning and/or evening imagine more pure Violet Light from the inner realms flooding into your inner system keeping it nourished with the food of the Gods. Do this 'inner light bath' daily for 5 – 10 minutes as per Chapter 6: technique no. 10. This is a good one to do when you are in the shower.

- ❖ Step 8: Practice the microcosmic orbit tool as in Chapter 6: technique no. 11. Practice first solo until you get the energy flowing through your own body then introduce it in your duo sexual sharing. Study the science of sacred sexuality and enjoy your love making pleasure more – both with quality and quantity as in loving time spent.

- ❖ Step 9: Do the 'Cosmic Cable Hook-in' meditation Steps 1, 2 and 3 in Technique no. 16 – Chapter 7 which will connect you to the inner plane Theta – Delta wave feeding channels. Again this is a once only meditation but it helps to daily visualize this inner flow being boosted and increasing Its flow through you when you shower. i.e. visualize that the water flowing over you is healing violet liquid light and that it flows in through the top of your head and through the pores of your skin.

- ❖ Step 10: Reorganize your living environment so that it is more nurturing and feeds you what you need e.g. less focus around the television and more family sharing/talk time if you are hungry for quality conversation, or daily meditation time if you are hungry for inner peace and silence. Ask family to listen to their music, or watch TV with headphones if appropriate. If you are hungry for more energy, rearrange your time schedule to exercise daily and switch to a live, raw food diet, or if you are hungry for more tactility in your life, have TV free nights, or children free nights, for more intimacy with your partner. Be creative as to the fulfillment of your hungers while still honoring the needs of your family. Remember that unless we learn how to nurture ourselves, others cannot nurture us as we may need them to.

❖ Step 11: Attitude changes: Decide to have more fun, laugh more, dance more, sing more, play more and give gratitude for all that is good in your life.

Benefits of Theta – Delta Wave Feeding and the Madonna Frequency Attributes

In our initial introduction to the Food of Gods and our preliminary discussion on brain wave patterns, we looked at some of the benefits that come automatically when someone is tuned to the Theta – Delta frequency field. We also shared that the secret to successful feeding from these fields was a) our lifestyle and b) which field our brain wave patterns are anchored in.

However the ability to be successfully nourished by 'The Food of Gods', is also directly related to our ability to love and nurture not just ourselves, but also others, and we can tell when this nutrition is flowing in our lives by the below attributes. I see these attributes as the natural by-product or result of being bathed in the Madonna Frequency which is in essence, pure Divine Mother love. It is also currently a frequency that is in shortage on our planet at this time hence our levels of poverty, war and chaos.

How can we tell when someone is receiving this type of pure nourishment? We can tell by the virtues they display.

Some of these may be:

a) Someone tuned to the Madonna Frequency Divine Love-Wisdom Channel will exhibit a DIVINE RADIANCE: I call this Delta Field Dancing for this level of radiance brings the joyous wave of Grace into our lives, plus health and happiness and peace and prosperity which are automatically attracted to us when our brain wave patterns are aligned to the Theta – Delta field.

b) Someone tuned to the Madonna Frequency Divine Love-Wisdom Channel will be motivated by a pure heart and have DIVINE INTENTIONS and hence have access to impeccable networks and DIVINE Support Systems, on both the inner and outer planes.

c) Someone tuned to the Madonna Frequency Divine Love-Wisdom Channel will receive DIVINE GUIDANCE from the Divine One Within – their DOW – a pure intelligence that is wise and loving and incorruptible as It always has the best interests of all at heart. Many are receiving DOW guidance now to create and utilize incorruptible networks. The first incorruptible network is C.N.N. – The Cosmic Nirvana Network, which can only be accessed telepathically through mind mastery and prayer. This is an inner plane 'good news' network designed to release empowering information to co-create personal and global paradise. Access to C.N.N. comes naturally as we activate our 6th and 7th senses and our pituitary and pineal glands.

d) Someone tuned to the Madonna Frequency Divine Love-Wisdom Channel will attract the river of DIVINE GRACE to support their peace work as we also fulfill our contractual tune-ups. While the Innernet is our main source of communication to bridge the worlds, the Internet, and the DIVINE GRACE WAVE are the main communications networks for outer plane connecting. As a form of Divine Electricity, the Grace Wave is automatically attracted to Theta and Delta Fields and may visit those in the Alpha fields from time to time. The DIVINE GRACE WAVE is a ray of light and a rhythm of sound, that carries with it support structures for successful living. Driven by Divine Codes called Universal Law, the Grace Wave runs via these laws and magnetic attraction.

e) Someone tuned to the Madonna Frequency Divine Love-Wisdom Channel may have access to DIVINE ABUNDANCE and PROSPERITY. Part of this may entail access to, and utilization of, the Cosmic Bank of Abundance – an inner plane etheric bank with open doors to those in the Grace Wave of Theta – Delta field. This bank can download an abundance of love, health, wealth, passion and purpose to those who can match its beat. Any person who sincerely works for harmonious global refinement, or lives their life in a way that is good for all, will have access to the perfect resources they need to do this. Purity of Heart, and Intention, are the key to this Cosmic Safe.

f) Someone tuned to the Madonna Frequency Divine Love-Wisdom Channel may receive DIVINE TRANSMISSIONS from our Holy Help line: C.N.N. (the Cosmic Nirvana Network). Channeling, receiving Divine downloads, automatic writings, clairvoyance, clairaudience, clairsentience are common and natural by-products of the Madonna Frequency. Interaction with Divine Hierarchies and receiving Holy help is also common in this field as from the Madonna's Divine Love all has been born. All life, all realms, owes its existence to the Madonna energy field.

g) Someone tuned to the Madonna Frequency Divine Love-Wisdom Channel may receive DIVINE REVELATIONS and hence they will be focused on the bigger picture. Divine Revelations that are released from the energy field of the Madonna Frequency inspire selfless SERVICE.

h) Someone tuned to the Madonna Frequency Divine Love-Wisdom Channel will automatically feel more compassionate, more altruistic, more merciful and concerned for the welfare of others. Flooding our systems with the Madonna Frequency brings out from within us the desire to nurture and be nurtured. It also magnetizes us into the fields of other like focused beings, hence allowing the group to also become stronger and more powerfully nurturing. The Madonna Frequency stimulates and supports mutually beneficial relationships.

i) Someone tuned to the Madonna Frequency Divine Love-Wisdom Channel will be involved in DIVINE CO-CREATION. The Madonna Frequency offers harmonious solutions and PERFECT RESOLUTIONS to those seeking the WIN, WIN, WIN game – the happy me, happy us, happy planet reality. The solutions support the creation of a truly civilized world where the motto is LOVE ALL, RESPECT ALL, HONOR ALL – in memorandum of St Francis of Assisi who always promoted the peaceful co-existence among all Kingdoms. His motto PAX ET BONUM was an old world greeting meaning 'Peace and all good things'.

j) Someone tuned to the Madonna Frequency Divine Love-Wisdom Channel will be capable of DIVINE COMMUNICATION and hence understand how to bridge the worlds. They will be focused and trained in imprinting the world with some aspect of holistic education such as bridging the worlds of: Religion and Science; Metaphysics and Quantum; East and West; Tantra and Yoga: Divine Mathematics and Divine Signs; or bridging more traditional areas such as Mainstream Medicine and Alternative Therapies. They may also be in the field of environmental sustainability, resource sustainability, alternative, sustainable energy systems, new financial systems, and any field that provides a beneficial service to people. True Divine Communication always guides us to co-create for the good of all as it is naturally imbued with the Madonna Frequency of Divine Love and Wisdom.

k) Someone tuned to the Madonna Frequency Divine Love-Wisdom Channel will understand the power of DIVINE MANIFESTATION. An aid to understanding DIVINE MANIFESTATION is to understand the basic mechanics of Dimensional Biofield Technology. The expansion of time, the importance of each new now moment and crossing the lines of time are all Dimensional Biofield Tuning tools.

l) Someone tuned to the Madonna Frequency Divine Love-Wisdom Channel will experience DIVINE BLISS. Immersion in the Madonna Frequency Field will release a flood of joy and light and understanding throughout our bio-system that can only be described as a pure endorphin high. Bliss, Nirvana, Samadhi, the WOW factor are other 'bliss' names. Some call this journey and reality, the ecstasy of ENLIGHTENMENT.

Inviting and then allowing our Divinely Enlightened inner nature – our DOW – "to love us, guide us, heal and nourish us on all levels" and to surrender to it's Divine Will and Supremely wise and loving influence, is one of the smartest things we can do at this time as our DOW is the only thing that the 6 billion plus of us have in common that is incorruptible. Remember DOW = God Within : God = all knowing, all loving, all wise, all powerful and all present field of intelligence that pulses out from a pure energy source that gave birth to all of creation. As such It understands the game and treats us as Gods in form, already enlightened yet perhaps forgetting to act like we are. The Madonna Frequency allows people to understand the 'Ask and Receive' principle of Divine Reciprocation.

m) Someone tuned to the Madonna Frequency Divine Love-Wisdom Channel will receive DIVINE NUTRITION, which is pure Theta and Delta Field loving. As we keep reiterating, the purest form of nutrition we can access is Divine Love, for it is the glue of all creation that keeps molecules alive and atoms expanding and cells and souls nourished and well fed. Divine Nutrition provides perfect physical, emotional, mental and spiritual nourishment.

As our other educational manuals also cover the art of creating emotional, mental and spiritual health, let us continue with our focus on the Divine Nutrition aspect of 'The Food of Gods' which is to introduce a very simple system for those interested to not just receive the nutrition we need to be healthy and happy – Level 1 – but also on a more specialized level, to actually allow this Divine Nutrition flow to free us from our dependency on our planet's resources of physical food – Level 3. We now offer a simple step by step program to ensure our success with this.

Imagine the impact this way of living will have on our future world if what we propose in the 'Divine Nutrition: Living on Light Series' proves to be correct? And the best way to prove it is to successfully apply it and be an example, so for those of you pre-tuned to do so, let us continue.

The following chapters deal with

"The Specialty Field of Divine Nutrition and Pranic Nourishment – Level 3"

A new recipe: For those whose path this is or may be.

Terminology:-
Pranic Nourisher, Light Eater,
Divine Nutrition Specialist:
Someone who can access the Madonna Frequency Field of Divine Love and Light and can download enough of this energy through their bio-system to be sustained and hence free from the need to ingest physical food and vitamin supplements.

Research Facts:

Of those successful with living from only prana for 6 months or more:

- ❖ 88% were vegetarians for more than 5 years prior to the letting go of physical food and of these 18% had been fruitarians.
- ❖ 98% had been long term meditators (5 to 20 + years).
- ❖ 60% had committed their life to, and were living a life of conscious, service.
- ❖ 98% prayed regularly.
- ❖ 66% prepared their body slowly over time via detox programs and the recommended lifestyle.
- ❖ 63% engaged in powerful mind mastery practices.
- ❖ 83% said they were aware they created their own reality.
- ❖ 58% took this path not because they wished to never eat again, but just to have freedom of choice.

Chapter 11 – Part 1

Pranic Nourishment Hook-In
Level 3 – Step by Step

In this chapter I wish to address the Level 3 Source of nourishment. These are the steps that we need to take to access enough prana so that we can be free from the need to take physical food.

The Inner View

When prana is flowing through the fields of a food free bio-system, the filaments within every cell respond by vibrating and absorbing the nutrients needed from the Theta – Delta wave that is flowing through the system. If the Theta – Delta mix is too weak and the bio-system is more Alpha – Beta tuned, it will not be as well nourished. Also, if the bio-system is working purely with Beta waves, then the physical body, if it is not fed by physical food, will go into the starvation and fasting mode.

When physical food is introduced to the physical bio-system, the cells begin to twist and contort as part of a natural chemical response to the foreign substance. The purer the food frequency, i.e. fruit and raw food, the less the cells will twist and contort. This is an inner world-view that comes from using the 6th and 7th senses to witness the body's reaction, and it is a view that still has to receive scientific and medical verification which can only be given by those tuned to the Theta – Delta wave who can scan the inner fields.

The yogic pranic nourishment history and our own this past decade, has been well covered in my other writings, as is the path we have taken to get here, so let us instead look at some basic steps required to obtain and maintain Level 3 nourishment. These steps do not necessarily need to be done in this order and each step is elaborated on shortly. Also while what we recommend below is similar to the Step by Step process described in Chapter 10, there are a few crucial differences.

Achieving Level 3 Nourishment in the Divine Nutrition Program

STEP BY STEP:

❖ Step 1: Discover your encodements and do the relevant re-programming.

- ❖ Step 2: Begin preparation of your bio-system, and the attunement of it to the Theta – Delta field, via the adoption of the Luscious Lifestyles Program's 8 point plan as detailed in the *Four Body Fitness: Biofields and Bliss* book and briefly touched on in Chapter 6. Do simultaneously with Steps 3, 7, 8 and 9 below.
- ❖ Step 3: Prepare the body via specific detoxification programs such as fasting and colonic irrigations and dietary changes.
- ❖ Step 4: Get to know your DOW – the Divine One Within you and understand Its role as Master Computer Controller of your bio-system. Learn to trust your intuition by listening to Its voice and seeing the positive evidence of Its guidance in your life. Apply tools – like the 8 point lifestyle mentioned – to develop the yogi and shaman within. Learn to test and trust your paranormal powers as they reveal themselves. Understand the power of the God within you and surrender to it. This 'getting to know our DOW' requires us to make the commitment to act impeccably, like the true Master we are, in every moment. Be a radiant example.
- ❖ Step 4 Part 2 deals with Cellular Pulsing and includes preparing the cells to handle more DOW Power.
- ❖ Step 5: Do technique no. 16 – the Cosmic Cable Hook-in Meditation in Chapter 7.
- ❖ Step 6: Do technique no. 14 – the Pituitary and Pineal Gland Reprogramming and Activation Meditation as outlined in this chapter and in Chapter 6.
- ❖ Step 7: Do the Violet Light One Chakra Column Meditation in Chapter 6, technique 8 to open up the inner plane pranic flow.
- ❖ Step 8: Begin using daily the "Perfect Health, Perfect Balance, Perfect Weight, Perfect Image" programming code as in Chapter 6 technique 10.
- ❖ Step 9: Begin the 3>2 then 2>1 meal a day program as in Chapter 6 technique no. 6. Gradually over time eat less and less and maintain the above programming code until your weight stabilizes. Begin the meat > vegetarian > vegan etc. or vegetarian > vegan > raw food program as in Chapter 6 technique no. 7.
- ❖ Step 10: Create a supportive home environment to support you in this journey.
- ❖ Step 11: Read and research all you can on the subject so that you are well informed.
- ❖ Step 12: For those who need to develop the ability to absorb only the energies that nurture them in this world, utilize the Bio-Shield Devices that we will elaborate on in this chapter.
- ❖ Step 13: Take your time, set a 2, 3 or 5 year goal plan of physical and social preparation e.g. in 3 years I will live purely on pranic light. Then apply the above points sensibly.
- ❖ Step 14: If it is in your blueprint to be public with this choice, read and apply the 'Responsible Reporting' Guidelines.
- ❖ Step 15: Slowly educate family and friends as to your future goal with this and the reasons for your choice of this lifestyle. Learn to speak of this only in appropriate situations. Family and friends love and care for you and are happy with your choices if they can see they are good for you, that you are healthy and happy. Therefore it is important to learn to control your cells and your body's weight slowly over time.

❖ Step 16: As in Part 4 of this chapter. For those who wish to nurture more deeply not just their personal biofield but also the community biofield and global biofield, learn the art of conscious field re-weaving and imprinting. Also do the radiation rather than absorption game.

Many of the above Steps were covered in chapter 10, however there are a few that we need to explain in order to provide a greater insight into their importance or to pragmatically provide more detailed meditations and programming codes.

Divine Nutrition Program – Technique no. 20:

Step 1: Elaboration and exercise: Discover your Encodements:

The first step at this point of your journey is to discover if you are one of those encoded to pioneer this at this time. After a decade of first hand discussion with people drawn to the pranic nourishment path I have discovered some interesting things. Firstly, when people read my first book in this series, something in them said: "Yes this is for me". Or some deep intuitive knowing said: "One day you will do this, one day". For others it was a "Wow wouldn't that be great?" For still others it was a reaction of: "I've always known it was possible". For those who have had this type of reaction it may just be that you are what I call pre-encoded to be involved with this as part of the necessary pioneer group that always spearheads change.

We can discover if we have been encoded to do this via the below steps.

❖ Sit in silence and center your self by applying the Love Breath Meditation – technique 1 Chapter 6 – followed by the Vedic Breathing tool – technique 2.

❖ Check your inner plane Cosmic Cable connection and imagine downloading an additional blast of Violet Light into your system as per the meditations in Chapter 6 – technique no. 12 and Chapter 7 – technique no. 16.

❖ Once you are centered and feeling the love and calmness behind your breathing pattern, imagine that you are the King, the Queen of your inner realm, that you and your DOW are One, one being sharing the inner space of your cells, one being with many different aspects and modes of expression

❖ Imagine all aspects of your being are listening, aware then

❖ Ask: *"I now ask my body consciousness, my Divine consciousness, my DOW – is it in my blueprint to live purely on light in this lifetime?"* Wait for a yes or a no.

❖ If you get a clear 'no', then thank your body and continue meditating and relax and enjoy the pleasure of physical food but keep your diet light and live and definitely vegetarian to keep you tuned to maximum capacity to the channel of kindness and compassion.

❖ If however you get a 'yes', then ask: *"Is it in my blueprint to do this in the next year?"*

❖ If you get a 'no' to this time frame ask: *"Is it in my blueprint to do this in the next 5 years?"*

❖ Keep checking to get a time frame as this will help you with your bio-system preparation and goal setting. Once you have determined the pre-encoded transition time, you need to then do the following:

❖ Focused on the God within you say with conviction and sincerity: *"I now give the Divine One Within me and my physical body consciousness permission to provide me with all the vitamins, minerals and nutrients I need to maintain a healthy, self regenerating system. I ask that these be absorbed as pure prana from the Divine Nutrition channel of love and light."*

❖ Next imagine that standing before you on the inner plane is your physical body consciousness, your emotional body consciousness and your mental body consciousness. Acting as the God you are, you now issue firm instructions to all three and say: *"I now call forth, the full attention of my physical body consciousness, my emotional body consciousness and my mental body consciousness."* Imagine them all standing to attention and saluting you waiting for your clear command.

❖ Then say: *"I now instruct/ask that from this moment on you unify all aspects of my being to support my transition into pranic nourishment with joy and Grace and ease. I ask also that you harmonize perfectly to fully manifest my Divine Presence, as the God I am, in form, in a manner that supports the Divine Blueprint for paradise on Earth – NOW."*

❖ The above program is self-explanatory but also allows for the natural elimination of any internal sabotage programs from previous lives and it is particularly powerful when reinforced by the daily use of the "Perfect Health, Perfect Balance, Perfect Weight and Perfect Image" program.

❖ Then act as if the above is occurring naturally and begin to prepare your bio-system responsibly and also decrease your dependence on food by applying the additional steps mentioned.

Additional Standard Divine Nutrition Pranic Nourishment Attitudes and Programming Codes:

One of the most difficult things in the Divine Nutrition program that we need to address to be successfully nourished by just prana is our day by day thinking processes and how our thoughts are constantly programming our bodies and our lives.

For lifetimes we have absorbed and been influenced by limited overt and covert programming, social conditioning, restricted research findings that have not yet matched metaphysical experiences and so are hence contradictory in their view and more. Hence the transition into pranic nourishment must include the re-programming of the brain's neural pathways and we can begin with the statement that is made every time we eat.

For example the "I eat because I love it, not because I need it" attitude is one that we need to adopt and hold constantly. We also need to adopt an attitude and a belief that: *"All my nourishment, my vitamins, my minerals, all that I need to maintain a healthy self regenerating system, comes from prana, from the Divine Love channel and through the Theta – Delta field."* This is a basic mind over matter reality.

Step 2: Elaboration – Live the Divine Nutrition Access Lifestyle *(This is technique no 5 of Chapter 6)*

Get your self tuned to the Divine Nutrition channel via your day to day lifestyle which should allow you to become physically fit, emotionally fit, mentally fit and spiritually fit.

I cannot stress enough that the ability to access the Divine Nutrition Channel is not a 'hit and miss' affair. As discussed throughout many of our research manuals, everything is a matter of frequency matching. The ability to tune into this alternative feeding channel for Level 3 nourishment requires in-depth preparation via a change in our lifestyle and our research shows that it also requires the application of the 8 point Luscious Lifestyle Program that we introduced in Chapter 6 as technique 5.

However, while meditation, prayer, diet and exercise have been well researched as to their benefits, a successful Divine Nutrition program – as in providing the body with all its vitamins and minerals – is highly dependant on de and reprogramming our body, our beliefs and our habitual thinking processes. Attitudes and repetitive thinking patterns are crucial in the success of accessing the Food of the Gods.

Also it is important to note again that we believe that it is the combination of these 8 points that will change our frequency enough for us to be nourished us on all levels.

I have on occasion, met the rare individual who has managed to live purely on prana without adhering to the type of lifestyle we recommend as frequency is something we maintain and build on with each life and they have obviously maintained their frequency from other life times.

One of the greatest objections that I receive is the recommendation of a vegetarian diet, yet the frequencies we need to match into require our fields to be tuned to the channel of kindness and compassion and for our hearts to be pure.

Every point of this lifestyle provides a specific flavor in our field tuning and needs to be explored and honored to the best of our ability. Together they allow our DOW to reveal more of Its power and for our paranormal powers to be stimulated and grow while also allowing us to enjoy increased levels of physical, emotional, mental and spiritual fitness.

> ## MEDITATION + PRAYER + PROGRAMMING + VEGETARIAN DIET + EXERCISE + SERVICE + TIME IN SILENCE IN NATURE + DEVOTIONAL SONGS / MANTRAS
> ## =
> ## ACCESS TO THE DIVINE NUTRITION CHANNEL

In *the creation of fitness on all levels* Dr Shah, one of our leading researchers in solar feeding shared with me the following. I include it here as Dr Shah is both a yogi and a respected medical practitioner in India. (His credentials are shared in our Research section.) I also include the below data as I cannot stress enough the importance of taking the necessary steps to create fitness on all levels for those who are seriously contemplating living purely on prana as the fitter we are, the easier the journey of transition is for us.

Physical health:

At a simplistic level, physical health means the absence of diseases and ailments – a state where all the systems of the body are functioning optimally well. In this state a person feels vigor, enthusiasm and has the capacity to do all their work and perform all their duties well, and for sufficient lengths of time, so that their goals in life are achieved and so that their physical health levels can then become a tool to achieve mental and spiritual health.

When something goes wrong, the person acquires disease, discomfort, and ailment. The system function deteriorates, imbalance occurs in bodily processes and a person may feel a lack of vigor and a sense of fatigue. A variety of symptoms may appear from minor problems to serious complications and even death can ensue.

Why does physical disease occur? Science has postulated the interaction of various factors resulting into disease. Mainly the phenotype, genotype, environmental factors and mental status of an individual will govern their health or disease status. Phenotype means bodily disposition or the tendency of a person towards disease. Their weight, habits, nutritional status, daily rituals, exercise schedule, sleep pattern etc. can be conveniently discussed under phenotype and this can be altered by a change in their food habits, exercise, a change in lifestyle etc. *(e.g. the Luscious Lifestyles program alters our phenotype by changing our habits.)*

By genotype, we mean whatever is inherited through genes, the genetic chances of a disease, or susceptibility of getting a disease, due to our birth through specific parents. While this is more or less an unchangeable factor, the expression of the disease can vary depending upon our lifestyle, mental status and our environmental factors.

Also with the availability of genetic engineering, cloning techniques etc. many of the genetic diseases will be altered and will become preventable, controllable or even curable in our near future. But still the genetic factor is very important in the genesis of a disease.

Similarly, environmental factors can bring diseases. Simply speaking, people living in crowded or polluted areas have a higher likelihood of contracting infectious diseases or diseases related to improper nutrition. They can also modify genetic expression of a disease, e.g. by change of weather or shifting from a humid place to a dry place can alter asthma, even in a genetically prone person.

Science has also now firmly accepted and established that mental status, attitude and personality can contribute significantly in the acquiring of health or the genesis of diseases.

Apart from this there are several other unknown causes, not yet clearly understood to science – for example the role of the belief system, the role of blessings and curses, power of meditation and yoga etc. all of which are still not properly understood but we suspect may have an impact on genesis of diseases.

Broadly speaking modifiable factors in prevention or treatment of diseases would be good lifestyle, nutritious food, stress free mind, physical exercise, breathing control and a healthy environment.

To solve physical ill health, there can be and there are several approaches. Science offers modern medicine (conventionally known as Allopathy) but there are equally famous Ayurveda, Homeopathy, Chinese medicine, Acupuncture, Aromatherapy, Yunani and several other pathies. Naturopathy offers only treatment at the lap of nature and is drug free. From a holistic viewpoint all these pathies are complimentary and really none can be a complete answer. As the genesis of disease is multi-factorial the answer to the problem should also be multimodal. Each human being is different, each person has a different prakriti (disposition) and each has a different genetic code; hence we need to take account of these individual factors too – no generalization can therefore be done in therapy related comments. Many times it is wiser to join two or more complimentary systems. However, no scientific guidelines are as yet available, as to which pathies should be safely and effectively combined for which diseases. Further, it should be again emphasized that by merely taking treatment or drugs one can't remain away from disease; one has to adopt a healthy lifestyle, have good nutritious food, do exercise and try to relieve mental stress etc. This will also help in maintaining health, once it is regained.

Dr Shah goes on the share about: *Mental and Emotional Health*

The Tibetan Masters (Alice Bailey's teachers) predicted that in the near future, we will become a different race of men women. At that time we shall operate upon mental energy, magnetic energy, spiritual power, and scalpels and chemical agents will no longer be necessary.

I think we are almost near to this time. The movement has already started in this direction, with people from every religion and from different spiritual disciplines as well as biofield technicians (as Jasmuheen describes including her own self) are all working on how to improve mental and emotional health of the people and are sharing how to attain spiritual health.

Though according to some, mental and emotional processes are separate, however, from an expanded health model point it's difficult to separate both. So when we talk of health, we may discuss mental and emotional health together.

The mind is an invisible organ, which is said to be responsible for our thoughts, perceptions, emotions, desires, instincts, behavior etc. There is no anatomical representation of mind in one particular area of the brain, but by intuitive logic, it appears that the mind is represented in the brain, and according to some, 'the whole brain is in the mind'. Actually each cell has its own thoughts, and its own instinct and behavior, hence each cell actually has a mind and if it's not anatomical then it can be visualized as a continuous electromagnetic and chemical process, operating throughout the body, with perhaps its important commanding stations in the brain, at the levels of the hypothalamus, pineal gland, limbic system, autonomic system and other endocrine structures.

From the theory of the cosmic mind if we think, then our mind, an individual mind, is nothing but the continuity of the cosmic mind with some modifications and adaptations as per the individual.

Depending upon one's moral strength, ego, intelligence, discipline, the mind gives reactions to every single stimulus; be it physical, social, environmental, ecological, spiritual, emotional etc. The mind gets the perception first, then throws emotional signals, simultaneously thinks, and then initiates a process of acceptance or retaliation. In yogic terms this is felt as happiness at the pure superficial level of Raga, and Dwesha on a little subtle level. If further acts or responses are needed then the physical systems are activated, e.g. the manifestation of anger which is reflected in our behavior. Physical health also affects our mental health, although our mental health affects our physical health more.

Apart from a response to a stimulus, the mind has its own automatic, continuous functioning, i.e. thinking and behavior. Without any obvious external stimulus, thoughts are generated and they either die away completely or modify our behavior. It is said by Yogis that "ego – feeling of existence" itself is the cause of these thoughts. The yogis of high astuteness can dissolve the ego and therefore enter into the thoughtless state where there is nothing but permanent bliss – no happiness – no unhappiness – no Raga – no Dwesha – and only spiritual health.

However, for 'non-yogic' people, mental and emotional health may just mean peace and happiness in continuity.

What is the sub-state required for this? In my opinion perhaps we can achieve it by 1) moral health, 2) by a positive and creative attitude, 3) by sublimating our ego and 4) by focusing on our 'highest intellect'.

To elaborate on this:

(1) We know that "as you sow, so shall you reap". If one's moral health or moral strength is poor, then one cannot expect people or nature to do good back to him/her and hence, peace and happiness cannot be achieved. By moral strength, we mean the basic virtues like Truth, Honesty, Non-violence, and maybe even Celibacy (or faithfulness in marriage, if married).

As Jainism says, these virtues should be reflected in all 3 Levels i.e. Thinking, Speaking and Action. Moral health needs to be applied to all 3 levels.

(2) Attitude decides the progress of a person, a religious commune, an institute, a house or a family and the importance of attitude can't be overemphasized. In general one needs an emotional attitude of serenity and compassion that always considers another person's viewpoint. Truthfulness and thorough kindness are two virtues, which if developed fully and expressed can change a human being from a simple person to a saint or rishi. Ideally we can act in a way where we harm no one at any level as per the "Do unto others, as you would like others to do unto you" principle.

Ideally we can observe each thought, emotion and instinct that surfaces on one's own mind as when we observe these consciously, our negativity automatically recedes and with mind and thought mastery, only good and positive thoughts and emotions will prevail. Ultimately we can rise above our attachments, likings, hatreds and dislikes as a balanced person behaves, thinks and moves around in a detached manner.

So these are some of the symptoms and signs of good mental and emotional health.

To achieve it, constant awareness has to be developed via regular meditation, self-restraint, a pious heart and a contented mind all of which support mental health.

In thoughts and words, one can apply the principle of relativity, which involves looking at things from different angles as truth can be multifaceted. One person's viewing angle is not absolute truth and is merely his/her version of the fact. The ultimate truth is different. It is difficult for a common person to achieve the real and total perception of truth yet this knowledge is required to change the attitude for any person.

On *Spiritual health* Dr Shah, adds:

One has to understand that real spirituality lies in the constant awareness about the Divine Self – the soul. This means no unawareness for even a fraction of a second, and it means the loss of attachment towards the body as to identify oneself with only being a body and not a soul is the cause of all our major troubles. As the prophets say, "the One who knows the soul, knows everything". If one separately identifies the soul from the body, he enters into constant serenity.

With meditation, self-discipline and our constant exposure to spiritual knowledge (reading, listening, thinking, analyzing); we can gradually enter into a pure spiritual field where we experience glimpses of Samadhi and can ultimately remain in a permanent state of Samadhi. Yogis say that this is the final stage of spiritual attainment and as it is a matter of experience, it can't be described easily.

The substrate for spiritual health is Divine love.

If every individual sincerely attempts to gain physical, mental, emotional and spiritual health, and defines his/her own goal; then there will be heaven on this Earth. There will be total peace, perfect health, pure happiness, and then Divine love will prevail everywhere.

Our Chakras as grid points in the Beta – Alpha – Theta – Delta fields

Diagram 14:
We are born into, educated in, & grounded by, the Beta field.

The use of higher mi emotion plus self awareness, sacre meditation will bring Alpha fiel

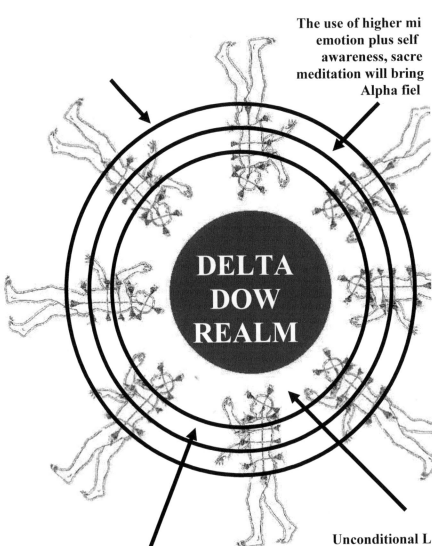

DELTA DOW REALM

Kindness, Compassion & L.L.P. bring us into Theta field. Our heart chakra needs to be open & radiant to access this field.

Unconditional L nourishment as p Gods anchor us in & 7th senses and chakras must b

Step 3: Elaboration on Fasting and Colonic Irrigations

The sensible preparation of our bio-system is a must for those who would like their transition into pranic nourishment to be one of joy and ease and Grace.

Gabriel Cousins from the Rejuvenation Centre writes:

"Spiritual Fasting is the Elixir of Spiritual Life: I am continually inspired by the awesome healing power of Spiritual fasting as a self-healing tool. Spiritual fasting cleans the body-mind and feeds the spirit, allowing our physical bodies to better extract the Divine cosmic energy from our normal biochemical energy sources. The end result is the enhancement on all levels of bodily energy, including the Spiritualizing Kundalini force.

"Today in our society, when everyone is so attached to food as a way to palliate the ego, and to suppress our real feelings, the idea of fasting can create a little trepidation. Most people do not realize how easy it is to do a fast. On our standard one-week group juice fast almost everyone is amazed at how easy it is. The appetite fades after the first few days, allowing one's emotional and physical attachment to food to diminish. The mind becomes freer to experience the higher states of communion with the Divine. ... Their success brings them to another level of freedom and self-confidence. To be free from the addiction of food is a tremendous freedom and joy."

See http://www.treeoflife.nu/ewell.htm for the complete article.

As meat and other toxic matter can sit undigested in our intestines for up to 20 years slowly putrefying, I recommend periods of fasting after a period of colonic irrigation as a basic preparation for receiving Divine Nutrition and the Food of Gods. For further details on this do your own in depth research and also read Dr Walker's book *Raw Foods*.

Divine Nutrition Program – Technique no. 21:
Tune in and ask your DOW and the Universal Intelligence to bring you the perfect physical, emotional, mental and spiritual de-tox program and if required the perfect person to do colonic irrigations with. Please note that I always ask my DOW and the universal forces of intelligence to aid in such things as then the right connections are always made. Also when meeting with any new people always use the 'DOW Match' technique so that all our sharing always transpires at the highest level with the purest intentions. Of course you also may still do the physical things required for manifestation but working telepathically on the inner plane like this feeds this reality.

Physical Change that occur from Level 3 nourishment:
As all who fast know, the stomach takes approximately 3-5 days to shrink and lose its voice of hunger. With fasting the body begins to detox, live off its body fat, then slowly begins to consume muscle until all that is left after this cannibalistic exercise is skin and bone. Deprived of physical nourishment, the lack of vitamins creates another set of problems for the bio-system depriving it of much needed nutrients, so it eventually shuts itself down, as in death.

Pranic nourishment is the reverse.

When our field frequency is flooded constantly with Violet Light and Divine Love, and held in the Theta Delta fields via our meditation and service based lifestyle, if invited and activated, the pure 'food of Gods and Goddesses' nourishment begins to flow. As previously covered it does this via a system of bio-feeding looping bringing prana from the inner planes back through the atoms and molecules and cells and back into the blood, organs and the skeleton, muscles and so on, and hence keeps all in a state of perfect health. In time the metabolic rate completely slows down, as the bio-system no longer has to go through the digestive actions.

Mental Toxicity

Just as we can physically detox our system through colonic irrigations and fasting, we can also mentally and emotionally detox ourselves. Mentally detoxing requires the cessation of both negative thinking patterns and negative communication patterns. It means the deprogramming of limited beliefs and the reprogramming of limitless beliefs. One powerful way of detoxing mentally is to look back over the events of our life and choose to see everything in a positive light i.e. rather than look at what we failed in, look at what we gained from every experience. Doing this changes our frequency, which then in turn attracts more positive experiences to us.

Emotional Toxicity

Emotional detoxing is being aware of patterns that trigger the release of debilitating emotions such as fear, anger, sadness, etc. We already know that the physical system is literally hard-wired to think before we feel, and all emotions simply follow mental observations, and that those emotions that appear to be instantly released within are just emotions that come from mental pre-conceptions that are based on our past experiences. Although emotional fine tuning may mean processing and working with our shadow side and maybe even doing inner child work, or some type of therapy, there are a few factors of Dimensional Biofield science that we need to be aware of when we choose the path of emotional fitness.

For example, as all the fields are interconnected, when we begin the game of 'processing' and releasing our toxic emotions, we may also hook into the global emotional baggage field and continue to process the emotions of over 6 billion of our population, thus trapping ourselves within an endless biofeedback loop of constant processing and suffering. Remember that when we look for emotional disease and experiences of imbalance or pain the more we will find these in the field as like attracts like.

Assuming the average bio-system holds 30,000 years of cellular memory, which may represent a thousand embodiments of an average of 30 years each life, then this literally means that it can take another 30,000 years to process the last 30,000 years until we come into a state that we may feel to be in emotional purity, i.e. devoid of the depths of our suffering and pain. Yet it is the very depths of our emotional suffering and pain that has usually given us the greatest gifts, therefore there is nothing 'negative' to be processed, for these gifts are valuable true imprints in the fields and when focused on like this and hence appreciated, will rebalance the energy of suffering. Our shadow side will also shrink or grow according to our focus upon it.

So, rather than emotional detoxing and processing, I prefer the system of Theta – Delta field flooding. This means the flooding of our cells, and the memories that they hold, with the Violet Light spectrum of Divine Love, Divine Wisdom and Divine Power, a frequency field that has the power to transmute everything into Itself. This works on the concept of assimilation where, for example, if enough pink dye is added to a bucket of water it transforms the water from being clear to bright pink depending on how much dye is added.

Part of the property of the Theta – Delta field and its Violet Light spectrum is its natural power of transformation as we have shared before. So the choice is that we can process, or flood and transform, or do both if required. I prefer to bathe in the love of the Divine and be both nourished and also naturally transformed by It for in the field of metaphysics, we are what we focus upon.

Bio-System Preparation Summary:

As we have stressed, to access the food of Gods for Level 2 and Level 3 nourishment, we need to create emotional, mental and spiritual health. This goes hand in hand with physical health and fitness and for the physical system to be healthy and successfully plugged into the Theta – Delta field and well nourished, certain adjustments need to be made.

So far we've:
- ❖ plugged the system in via the Violet Light cosmic cable, (technique no. 16)
- ❖ we've created a spinning chakra column that is constantly radiating millions of lines of light through the cells, molecules, and atoms which then attracts via bio-feedback the ultra Violet Light resonance and all the Theta – Delta field energies that our bio-system needs.
- ❖ We've also began a responsible preparation program via lifestyle adjustments and a cleansing detox program and
- ❖ If you got a yes for our encodements of being pranically nourished this lifetime and so you have done the program recommended to allow your master computer controller as pure DOW power to feed you, and
- ❖ You have programmed for the transition to be one of ease and joy.
- ❖ You have begun to change your dietary intake and habits and you have taken the steps to become a vegetarian, or if you are vegetarian you have become a vegan, if you are a vegan you have gone to raw foods, etc. (*as in techniques 6 and 7 of Chapter 6*).
- ❖ You may also have begun working with alternative healers such as a kinesiologist so that you can release any limiting energy blocks that you may still be carrying.
- ❖ You also have adopted the mind-set that

1) You only eat for pleasure and not for need;
2) All your vitamins etc. come from the Theta – Delta field;
3) Your frequency determines your ability to successfully be nourished by the food of Gods; and that
4) Your lifestyle controls your frequency.

❖ You have also begun to focus more on the Divine One Within you and surrendered to its love and wisdom and are possibly meditating more to increase your sensitivity to, and awareness of, your DOW and to experience Its Grace in your life.

Step 4: DOW POWER: Elaboration on 'Getting to know your DOW'

Divine Nutrition Program – Technique no. 22: DOW Surrender

As DOW power is my favorite topic of research, I would like to elaborate on this in greater detail for as we have shared so often, our DOW holds the key to all our paranormal powers. Our DOW is the God of our being and as such it is all powerful, all knowing and limitlessly loving.

To successfully be fed by the Food of the Gods, we must learn to control not just our mind/body communication but also our DOW downloads, and our field imprinting via the programs and activations we use within the Dimensional Biofield.

We know that in the Dimensional Biofield science each atom is filled with DOW power and that each atom has been pre-encoded to respond instantly to the love and beauty of the Theta – Delta field regardless of which field predominates around us externally. Only the timing of DOW power manifestation is restricted by the Beta field. Eventually, all longed for and desired and clear programs come into manifestation in one form or another, in one time frame or another. Our DOW is a multi-dimensional, limitless being who is fully aware of Its power as a God in form. It is also aware that we are all pre-programmed with all the creative power of the Cosmic Computer and that we can create any reality that we choose once we have remembered the real boss and the real power that drives the bio-system.

Hence the first step in perfect Theta – Delta field feeding is an all level alignment with our DOW and our *sincere* surrender of the bio-system to our DOW. Once given back Its power this master computer controller can begin to de or re-activate pre-encodements and activate support systems required to shift our bio-system into a natural self regenerating and self-sustaining level. The following is a suitable program for surrender:

❖ First center yourself using the Love Breath and Vedic meditation breathing tools.
❖ Next imagine your DOW as an inner God and summon all the feelings you have regarding God into your conscious being. Allow yourself to feel devotion or reverence to, or Oneness with, this power.

❖ Then say sincerely from your heart: "I now surrender every cell of my being to my Divine Self. I ask to be brought into perfect alignment on all levels of my being so that I may radiate my Divine nature perfectly on all planes, through all dimensions now."

Surrender in this respect does not mean giving up, it means an active acknowledgement and reclamation of the true power source within, bowing to Its superior intelligence and acknowledging It as a pure divine consciousness that fills each atom within. The act of surrender is also an act that will allow for activation of the 90% of the brain capacity that is used for thriving on Earth, for as we know only 10% is needed for the game of survival.

Being honest enough to stand before our own inner being, our DOW, and acknowledge Its presence and power, and then join forces and merge back with It, is a miraculous gift for it allows us to recognize how the universe can just tap us on the shoulder and say, "Hello God, how can I serve you?" And in Its presence we 'know' how to be in the Presence of the Supreme Splendor where we can finally relinquish all our hungers.

This is the path of ascension.

To be filled with such a flooding of light and love, until every cell is satiated; to see all of creation through the eyes of the Divine Father while we feel as if we are being held in the embrace of the Divine Mother. To feel and know we are all one, to feel the heartbeat of life and all its different expressions in all the fields, to see the complexity of the grids that support each paradigm and the reasons why they do, to know why some fields need to be dominant and to recognize and feel the natural order of things – these are the experiences of some the shaman, and yogis, and of many on the ascension path who are focused on the merging of the metaphysics and mathematics of life.

How well tuned we are to DOW power and which field – Alpha, Theta or Delta – we are operating in, is obvious by our personal and global health and happiness levels.

Step 4 – Part 2: Cellular Pulsing – *Increasing DOW Power in the cells*

While touring Europe during 2003 and presenting the Food of Gods research, one very important aspect of this journey became clearer to me to the point that it needed to be included in this section, for although we have touched on this in my book *In Resonance* I had not understood the profound relevance of the below data in the Divine Nutrition Program until this tour. It is to do with what I now term 'Cellular Pulsing'.

As discussed in the book *In Resonance*, we know that our cells store memories and emotions and act as our personal internal filing cabinet. We also know that each cell consists of atoms which consist of 99.99% space. We know also that this space is really pure Divine consciousness that is undetectable to the normal scientific measuring scopes, as DOW Power resonates at a frequency too refined to be detected by normal methods. For the purpose of this discussion I would like to call the beat of this Divine consciousness that fills each atom, our internal classical music station.

What I have also come to understand is that the more that our cells are filled with the emotional and mental toxicity of life, the weaker the Divine or classical pulse in each cell is and yet how well we can be nourished purely by prana is totally dependant on the strength of the Divine pulse in each cell. Again for the purpose of this discussion I would like to refer to this cellular toxicity, that comes from our past emotional experiences and negative mental perceptions in life, as our internal heavy metal music station.

Now imagine two radios standing side by side, both switched on with one tuned to the classical music channel – our Divine pulse; the other tuned to a heavy metal music channel – our collective memory patterns. Assuming a maximum volume of 10, then if the classical music volume is playing at a 1 or a 2 and the heavy metal station is at a volume of 9 then we will definitely end up with the usual range of human limitations, diseases, decay and eventual death. However if these numbers are reversed and the Divine pulse of classical music is at a 7, 8, or 9 volume level and the toxic heavy metal channel is at a 1,2,3 volume level then the game and our experience in life becomes very different. A 9 to 1 ratio where the classical beat dominates, allows for Level two and three nutrition to occur much more easily so our job is to empty the cells of toxic matter or transmute this 'heavy metal' matter into a purer frequency.

We can do this via a few methods. One is flooding the cells with violet light – as in Technique no. 12 Chapter 6; the other is emptying the cells of unnecessary dross by freeing ourselves from both karmic debts and energy influences that no longer support us.

We can do this using the tool of forgiveness.

An aware metaphysician knows that on one level everything is perfect, that there are no rights, no wrongs, and that all occurs to teach us and help us to develop and grow. However we didn't always have this type of awareness and so we hold in our cells lifetimes of hurts, angers, judgments and energies that hold a negative charge which takes up unnecessary space in our cells and keeps the heavy metal music station at a higher than healthy volume thus drowning out the more nurturing classical beat. Hence when we apply Technique no. 23 below, and then flood the cells with the violet light, we reset the volumes to a more supportive pattern so that the cells can be nourished instead of depleted.

Divine Nutrition Program – Technique no. 23: Forgiveness

I recommend that you record the following meditation onto a tape and let your own voice guide you through until you feel it is complete. This is a meditation that if it is done with sincerity and focus only needs to be done once.
- ❖ Sit in meditation and use the breath techniques previously given to centre yourself and still your mind.
- ❖ Next ask yourself are you ready to be free? Are you ready to forgive and be forgiven for all the hurt you have ever caused or experienced? If yes then continue.
- ❖ Imagine that on the inner plane you are now surrounded by all your family, friends and colleagues with whom you have any type of non-supportive energy imbalance. Imagine that you are in the centre of a circle of these people.

- ❖ Imagine now that forming another circle around these people from this life, are who they were to you in your last life together.
- ❖ Imagine another circle forming around them representing who all these beings were to you in the life before that again.
- ❖ Keep imagining circles and circles of beings forming around you, all representing right back through time through Egypt, Atlantis even perhaps as far back as Lemuria.
- ❖ Imagine circles and circles forming right back to when you first took embodiment and began energy exchange with other beings on Earth. Imagine you are in middle of a wheel and each line of beings radiating out from you forms a spoke of this wheel right back through time.
- ❖ Take 3 deep breaths. Breathe deeply, finely and evenly through your nostrils.
- ❖ Now let's go off planet and take this cleansing and release to a galactic and interdimensional level …
- ❖ Imagine now more circles forming around these circles of beings with whom you have some sort of non-supportive karmic imbalance, but that these new circles are beings with whom you have shared from lifetimes in other star systems. Sirius, Pleiades, Orion, Arcturius and so forth.
- ❖ Just keep imagining that on the inner plane, circle upon circles are now forming around you of beings with whom you have shared and co-created some sort of energy imbalance right back through time to when you originally began to feel that you were separate from others.
- ❖ Breathe deeply.
- ❖ Perhaps you have cleared most of these imbalances and so there are not many beings in these circles around you or perhaps there are now thousands, just let your intuition guide you, trust that the right ones will come for their freedom now.
- ❖ Imagine now other beings coming into these circles, beings that you have not yet connected with this life but who you are destined to connect with in the future because of energy imbalances that are creating karmic debts and a magnetic pull.
- ❖ Now imagine pure light flowing in through your crown chakra as per the previous meditations and that your whole being is filled with this light now.
- ❖ Imagine your heart opening and a beam of pure pink love radiating from your heart into the hearts of all these beings that are surrounding you now on the inner plane.
- ❖ Imagine that their hearts opening and that they are absorbing this love and that they are ready and open for this karmic release, that they too are open for freedom from these types of bonds.
- ❖ Take a deep, deep breath.
- ❖ Imagine so much love pouring out from your heart into them and you say sincerely:
- ❖ "With this love I say thank you. Thank you for all our sharing, all our caring, all our joy, all our suffering, all our pain, for everything we have shared through time. I thank you knowing that all this sharing has allowed me to grow, to gain wisdom and become the person I am today. Thank you, thank you, thank you."

❖ Next imagine that the light beam that is flowing out of your heart is changing color and becoming a powerful, healing ray of green light. It is as if your heart is a lighthouse that is radiating powerful rays of green healing light that is now being willingly absorbed by all these beings around you and you say:

❖ "With this green healing light I now choose to forgive you all. With this green healing light I forgive you all for all the pain, all the suffering, the hurt, the anger, the misunderstandings that we have ever shared. With this green healing light I forgive you, I forgive you, I forgive you."

❖ Take a deep breath.

❖ Now imagine more green healing light flowing out of you again into the beings on the inner plane that are surrounding you and you say,

❖ "With this green healing light I now sincerely, humbly ask for your forgiveness. With this green healing light I ask to be forgiven for any thoughts, words, or actions that have created suffering or pain or a negative energy imbalance among us all. I ask for forgiveness, I ask for forgiveness, I ask for forgiveness."

❖ Now let us call in some angelic help to cut these ties and psychic bonds that no longer serve us. Say with sincerity:

❖ "I now call forth the energy of Archangel Michael and all the holy help that is required for this meditation of freedom now."

❖ Next imagine that on the inner plane Archangel Michael is standing before you and you say:

❖ "Archangel Michael, I ask now that you move through these lines of time and use your mighty sword of freedom to cut through and release us all perfectly now from all the psychic ties and energy bonds that no longer serves us. So it is! So it is! So it is!"

❖ Imagine Archangel Michael now moving through these circles of beings like a hurricane cutting all these ties right back through time.

❖ Breathe deeply.

❖ Imagine now that the light beam radiating from your heart is changing color to become the violet light.

❖ Imagine pure violet light firstly filling your whole body as it pours in through your crown chakra and radiates through your chakra column into your organs and cells filling all your cells with this pure energy of nourishing violet.

❖ Imagine it now radiating from your heart into the hearts and energy bodies of all these beings around you on the inner plane until they too are all completely filled with the power of this transmuting violet light.

❖ As this beam radiates from you, you say with all sincerity:

❖ "With this violet light I forgive, I am forgiven! With this violet light I forgive, I am forgiven! With this violet light I forgive, I am forgiven! With this violet light I am free, you are free! With this violet light I am free, you are free! With this violet light I am free, you are free!"

❖ Now imagine that Archangel Michael has completed cutting all the psychic bonds that no longer serve you. You may notice that there are some energy ties between you that are still there as these are the ones that are positive bonds there to love and support you.

❖ Next imagine that the light beaming from your heart changes to pink and that again your heart is radiating a beam of pure pink love out into the hearts of all beings around you and you say:

❖ "With this beam of love again I say thank you! Thank you! Thank you! And with this beam of love I now ask that all beings with whom I share through all planes, all lives, and all dimensions, that when we meet we communicate immediately Divine Self to Divine Self so that all our sharing is for the highest good of all, DOW to DOW."

❖ "I also ask with this beam of love that any beings I meet from now and in the future that if there is still karmic energy to rebalance, that this be done with joy and ease and grace. So it is! So it is! So it is!"

❖ Now imagine finally bowing before all these beings on the inner plane and them bowing before you. Imagine that all of you are smiling, that all of you happy and that all of you are now released from all the karmic debts that can be released because this act of forgiveness has freed you all magnetically.

❖ Breathe deeply and imagine pure love flowing in from the inner planes into your heart chakra and complete with a few moments focused on the love/breath meditation.

❖ As you thank Archangel Michael for his help you make the commitment to always treat all beings with love and honor and respect.

The above meditation works on many different levels, firstly it cleans up old karmic ties and also eliminates the need for many future karmic exchanges, as when true forgiveness has been given and received the normal magnetic pull that is there from lack of forgiveness automatically disappears. However please note that there are some major karmic ties that need to come into being for our growth and learning.

The next benefit that comes is that because we have released many emotions via this forgiveness, this minimizes and decreases the heavy metal music station volume and gives more room for the classical music station to broadcast and be heard. In other words, there is just more room for the Divine pulse to reveal Its presence in ourselves.

An elaboration on this technique is to each day imagine on the inner planes standing before you is a member of your family. First day begin with your father, next day your mother, next day a brother or sister and next day imagine an ex-wife or husband, until you have gone through every member of your family and all beings who you have ever loved.

As you imagine them standing before you, you send a beam of love from you heart as you share all the things that you have ever wanted to say to them, to forgive them or to ask for forgiveness, until there is nothing left to say. Then imagine them sending you a beam of love while they share all the things that they have needed to say to you. Then again send the violet light and reclaim your freedom and give them theirs by saying: "With this violet light I forgive and I am forgiven". Say this three times and then say as you imagine a pink beam going between you: "With this pink light of love I am free and you are free. Thank you!" And again say this three times.

Both of the above techniques are powerful healing mechanisms as they are designed to shift the energy flow in all of our relationships and also make more room in our cells for the classical Divine beat so that we can be fed from within in a more nourishing manner.

Step 5 Elaboration: See Chapter 7 and do the Cosmic Cable Hook-in to allow us access to a pure, wise and loving never-ending Source of nourishing power. Both this tool and the Violet Light inner plane feeding tool (Technique 12 – Chapter 6) are crucial to successful Level 3 nourishment.

Step 6: Elaboration on the Activation of the 6th and 7th Senses and the Pituitary and Pineal Glands:

The following article is by Christian Paaske, (email: om@yogasenteret.no) Yoga and Meditation teacher in Norway. I include it here as it provides some additional insights to what we shared earlier. As a yoga teacher, Christian also offers a few extra tools for energizing the bio-system that many have found useful.

"The pineal gland is considered one of the body's greatest mysteries. Today we know that it is an endocrine gland which secrets the hormone melatonin. It is shaped like a pine cone and placed exactly in the middle of the brain. The French philosopher Descartes suggested that the pineal gland, or the cone gland, as he called it, was the dwelling place of the soul, and the gateway to the spiritual world. But apart from this comment, western science has mainly ignored this gland and considered it more or less useless. Since Darwin it has been described as reminiscent of an eye which no longer is in use, and originates from earlier history of evolution when we were a more primitive species.

"It is not until the last 50 years that science has started to uncover some of the pineal glands great secrets. After seven years of age small layers of calcification appear in the gland, and makes it look like a small cone in x-rays. Because it is situated in the middle of the brain, it is used to detect tumors of the brain, which displace the pineal gland from its centre. With the exception of the kidneys, no other place in the body receives as much supply of blood as the pineal gland, and there are several indications that this gland plays a much greater role than previously thought. New discoveries have now shown that the hormone secreted by this gland, melatonin, has several effects:

❖ Decreases the aging process*
❖ Starts off puberty
❖ Strengthens the immune system
❖ Regulates body heat*
❖ Regulates the estrogen level in women

❖ Regulates sleep function*
(* All of these change when we feed purely from prana)

The pineal gland is light sensitive, and as part of the body's biological clock, it has a regulating effect in sleep function. Melatonin has in fact also psychedelic effects, and can release special ecstatic and transcendental experiences, among meditators and mystics.

The mystical third eye:

According to several occult traditions, the pineal gland is connected to 'The Third Eye', which is situated in the middle of the forehead, on a straight line from the pineal gland. With Shiva and The Buddha, the third eye is found described as a 'shining spot' and 'a flaming pearl', symbolizing unity, transcendental wisdom and spiritual consciousness. This point is often used as point of concentration in meditation, because it is one of the places in the body where it is most easy to hold a steady focus, as well as it activates psychic energy. Concentration on this point will sooner or later give strong impressions of inner light, and is a method to get in contact with the energy dimension beyond the physical body.

In the Bible there is a saying that refers to the third eye: "Let thine eye be single. That thy whole body shall be full of light." (Mark 6:22 and Luke 11:34.) This is from the King James Version of the Bible which was written in the time of Shakespeare. Later editions have other translations which often loses this interesting point.)

The Tantric yogi, Swami Satyananda gives this description of the third eye: "This chakra is called the third eye or the command centre. It is a point in the psychic body where information from the outer world is perceived, and where the guru in more advanced forms of practice guides the student through instructions. It is the famous eye of intuition, where the psychic developed can observe everything that goes on both on the physical and psychic planes of existence."

Melatonin and the immune system and cancer:

Although the pineal gland is not bigger than a pea, it is still the organ in the body that produces the most melatonin, even though small amounts are also produced in the eyes and in the intestines. Normally the secretion of melatonin is low during the day and high during the night. By exposing the body to light during the night it will decrease the melatonin production, because the eyes are neurologically connected to the pineal gland. An Australian researcher, Swami Sannyasananda writes in a research report on melatonin: "Reduction of melatonin during the night increases the cells vulnerability towards cancer causing substances. It has been reported that there are increased cancer incidents in areas with abnormally high electric power fields, which results in decreased melatonin production during the night. Melatonin is an active cancer protecting substance, which both prevents cancer and the development of cancer, and is an important part of the body's immune system. It is particularly in its function as an antioxidant that melatonin has this effect. Melatonin also influences the production of T- cells which counteracts stress and is one of the immune systems most active substances."

Melatonin decreases with age:

According to two scientists at the Macquarie University in Australia, Professor Keith Cairncross and Professor Arthur Everitt this gland is a pure fountain of youth. After three years of research they are convinced that the hormones secreted by the pineal gland plays a central role in the mechanisms controlling stress in primates. They presume that the reduction of melatonin with age is a central cause for many of the diseases occurring in the elderly. They therefore suggest giving many elderly hormone supplements in the form of synthetic melatonin to counteract diseases and prolong life. Because of melatonin's powerful effects there is today a lot of research being done. Often this includes experiments on animals, which do not necessarily correlate to reactions in the human body.

Yoga and melatonin:
There are natural means to increase the production of melatonin, and particularly simple yoga techniques. Swami Sannyasananda by Adelaide University Medical School has through research found that the Tantric yoga techniques, alternate breathing or Nadi Shodan pranayama, and particularly Candle gazing or Tratak, has a dramatic effect on melatonin production. Tratak is concentration on an external object and in this case, the flame of a candle. Experiments on people doing Tratak every evening before sleep, showed a significant increase of melatonin.

Doing the Tratak practice before bedtime can calm us down, secure deep sleep, strengthen the immune system, and the two practices are good in combination i.e. Alternate breathing followed by Tratak which takes 15 minutes and can be used in the morning, as well as a preparation for meditation, or as described before bedtime.

Divine Nutrition Program – Technique no. 24:

Alternate breathing: Sit in a comfortable position with a straight back, either in a meditation pose on the floor, or on a chair.
- ❖ Close the eyes and concentrate on the spontaneous flow of air through the nostrils.
- ❖ When the breath has calmed down, place the index and middle finger of the right hand on the third eye, 2-3 cm above the eyebrows in the middle of the forehead. Use the thumb to open and close the right nostril, and the ring finger to open and close the left nostril.
- ❖ Keep both nostrils open, and take a deep calm in breath.
- ❖ Then close the right nostril and exhale through the left.
- ❖ Now begins the alternate breathing:
  - Breathe slowly, deeply and without sound in through the left.
  - Exhale through the right.
  - Inhale through the right
  - Exhale through the left.

This was one round of Alternate breathing. If you managed without getting short of breath or feeling choked, continue another round, otherwise, take a break and breathe through both nostrils until calm. Count the rounds, and do this for 5 minutes. This is the first stage of this exercise, and there are many other levels. After some time you can start holding the breath, and include different ratios of counting, like breathe in for 1, then hold for a count of 4 and then exhale as you count to 2. Do not go on to higher levels before it feels comfortable and relaxed to do so. No force should be used in this practice as the approach should be gentle.

Divine Nutrition Program – Technique no. 25:
Tratak
Sit in a comfortable position with a straight back, either in a meditation pose on the floor, or on a chair. Place a burning candle approx. 30 cm from the eyes in a horizontal line.

- ❖ Close the eyes and concentrate on the spontaneous flow of air through the nostrils.
- ❖ When calm, open the eyes and gaze at the candle.
- ❖ Sit for 5-10 minutes. Try not to blink. If you can avoid blinking the mind will be calm and free of thoughts, the moment you blink, thought comes.
- ❖ Then close the eyes and concentrate on the light impression until it fades away.

- ❖ There are many other forms of Tratak, using different objects of concentration. For example; place a red dot on the third eye, and sit in front of a mirror, or in front of another person also with a dot on the forehead. Do Tratak for 10-15 minutes. With both practices you are in for a surprise.

Thanks Christian!

Note: Our Pituitary and Pineal Gland activation can be done by the techniques shared in Chapter 6 and also by flooding these centers daily with the Violet Light.

Steps 7, 8, 9 and 10 are well covered in Chapter 6.

- ❖ Step 7: Do the Violet Light One Chakra Column Meditation in Chapter 6, technique 12 to open up the inner plane pranic flow.
- ❖ Step 8: Begin using daily the "Perfect Health, Perfect Balance, Perfect Weight, Perfect Image" programming code as in Chapter 6 technique 10.
- ❖ Step 9: Begin the 3>2 then 2> 1 meal a day program as in Chapter 6 technique 6. Gradually over time eat less and less and maintain the above programming code until your weight stabilizes. Begin the meat > vegetarian > vegan etc or vegetarian > vegan > raw food program as in Chapter 6 technique 7.
- ❖ Step 10: Create a supportive home environment to support you in this journey.

Step 11: Read all you can and become well informed: Additional Data
Before we provide some additional data of interest, many people ask

Qa) How they can stay in contact with others who have chosen the path of being nourished purely by prana and

Qb) Where they can find additional information on the subject so that they can become better informed.
To Qa: www.jasmuheen.com/living-on-light/

I would like to share also that many of the Level 3 pranic nourishers live very low key lives and are uninterested in being public with this choice. Hence the ideal thing for you to do is to ask your DOW to bring you into contact with all those who will support you in your choice of this new lifestyle and this will naturally happen. Also many of the people involved in this come from Shaman and Yogi type backgrounds where they are used to being on their own and handling the fact that often their personal lifestyle choice can create social isolation.

Similarly regarding research material, telepathically tell your DOW to bring you all the data you need on this so that you can be open to take the right step for you regarding any physical, emotional and intellectual preparation that you may need to do.

Step 12 Elaboration: Nourishment through using Bio-Shield Devices

This next section is quite detailed as we will look at matrix Mechanics and the various types of Bio-Shield Devices, why they are beneficial, how to create them and how to maintain them and why.

All created Biofield Devices, and natural Biofield grids such as our chakra system, depend on Matrix Mechanics to function and in Dimensional Biofield Science the underlying power base of each grid is dependant on the three primary frequencies of Divine Love, Divine Wisdom and Divine Power which form the Violet Light field supply that we all have access to.

These three frequencies form the basis of all life and matter, and are the true power Source behind all. You could call these frequencies Divine Electricity. As mentioned in the Taoist discussion, the Violet Light is the light that responds best to programming and as grids only become activated when programmed, then the Violet Light must form the foundation of any grid work that is to be programmed. In Dimension Biofield Science and Matrix Mechanics, thought, will and intention are the primary drivers of all the grids. When these are pure and used to drive devices constructed by the Violet Light, then the outcome is also pure and incorruptible.

Matrix Mechanics is the science behind all life and it deals with the way energy flows throughout the worlds. The ability to access the Theta – Delta waves is part of the Dimensional Biofield Science of Matrix Mechanics and it requires our personal biofield to be tuned in a particular way. It is my theory, based on extensive personal and group research, that our light body matrix and physical chakra and meridian system is activated by the specific lifestyle we discussed in Chapter 6. Here we looked at how meditation and prayer, programming, vegetarian diet, exercise, time in silence in nature, service and the use of chanting and devotional song, when practiced daily together tunes the system to the Theta – Delta waves as effectively as a motor mechanic who regularly services and tunes his car.

Matrix Mechanics is a complex and in depth science that uses DOW power to feed and sustain energy lines created on the inner plane via visualization, will and intention, a science that uses light rays and sound waves to attract specific molecular structure, where thought processes amplify through a grid structure created for specific outcomes.

An example of a Dimensional Biofield Science Matrix Mechanics Device is C.N.N. – the Cosmic Nirvana Network – an incorruptible inner plane network utilized by all beings of great light and love for pure and Divine communication. This innernet good news station is incorruptible as it can only be accessed by those whose 6th and 7th senses, and hence their pituitary and pineal glands, are open and tuned to the DOW power channel. As we have already mentioned, DOW power is, by its very essence, incorruptible. However, this suggestion brings in another interesting discussion and that is the perception of good and evil, wrong or right, corruptible and incorruptible.

In a Tantra view all is perfect and all is borne from God and is one. There is no wrong, no right. In this reality people are Gods in forms, and as bio-systems of energy we are encoded with the same software programs that drive the Cosmic Computer called God. As we are creative Gods with free will neither the intelligent quantum and virtual fields nor the Cosmic Computer as the creator of all, cares what we create.

God, as ever tolerant and benevolent loving creating parent, just says, "You have all the tools, all the wisdom, so when you are sick of creating war, poverty and violence then create something else". In this Cosmic Computer's eyes all is valid as all we create teaches us and expands us, and imprints us with valid experiences.

As the master computer controller of our bio-system, our DOW is eternal and from this view we all have the time in the world to create and problems only arise from ignorance and fear because we see our physical system as fallible. Because we are attached to it we forget that the physical system is technically just a set of clothes. Yes, it is a temple to be treated well, but it is a naturally limited mechanism unless we are disciplined enough to steer clear of toxic feeding, toxic thinking and toxic feeling, which cause our bio-system to eventually break down, become diseased and decay and die.

When we indulge in quality thinking, quality feeling, quality feeding and live an holistic lifestyle that keeps us tuned to the Theta – Delta frequency fields, then all the natural rules that we have come to understand in science and medicine become suspended as a new energy is released throughout the system allowing the system to be free from the need of food, of fluid, of sleep, and even aging. However, this is advanced Matrix Mechanics for our time, even though it is kindergarten mechanics within the Dimensional Biofield Science operating in other realms.

Obviously, in the Yogi view, there exists a reality of duality, black – white, negative – positive, good – bad etc., and adopting either the Yogic or the Tantric view is simply a matter of personal reality choice. Suffice to say that the fitter we are physically, emotionally and mentally, the easier it is to access the Divine Nutrition channels – provided we have set the supporting grid energetics in place, attended to our programming and adopted the right attitude.

Bio-Shields – Point and Application and Devices

As I have mentioned in my previous writings on the adjustments that occur when we choose to be sustained purely by prana, and take no physical food, one of the problems that many people have is extreme sensitivity that can create problems with our existence in the Beta field world and as mother nature is a predominantly Alpha field, we usually feel more comfortable in natural, non-city environments. Over the past decade I have spent most of my time living in polluted cities, dealing with people's polluted minds and energy transmissions, and generally being the object of ridicule and at times strong negative attention. No matter how graciously I acted, I was still challenging the status quo delivering research news that had the potential to upset the billion dollar food industry plus the pharmaceutical and medical industries as people living purely off prana no longer seem to manifest illnesses. Hence the energetic attention that was channeled my way was at times quite toxic and as a result of this I learned, how to use various Bio-Shield devices so that I could move through this world and stay relatively unaffected by the various forms of pollution that we encounter when we live anywhere other than perhaps in a secluded mountain village or monastery.

Consequently in accessing Divine Nutrition we have devised a few devices that allow us to energetically hook into the prana channel and attract specific frequencies as a Bio-Shield device allows us to absorb what we want from fields selectively rather than being bombarded with the random frequencies of a chaotic Beta field world.

Briefly a Bio-Shield is a cocoon, or web, of Violet Light that is created, programmed and activated to set up specific biofeedback responses within the quantum field of Universal Intelligence. Fields can be overlaid and woven by a system that some Dimensional Field Technicians call patterning and weaving and forethought must be given to the type of outcomes intended as well as the consequences of imprinting a field. We will look at these issues and how to 'weave a field' in the chapter of that name.

In his booklet *Systemic Spherology of Biofields: A Holographic Model of Reality* Dr Johannes Edelmann writes: "Biofields are holographic energy fields and fields of consciousness. Typically they are spherical and obey systemic laws. We know that holograms are characterized by the fact that they are fractals i.e. even the smallest part of them always contains the whole, although sometimes only as a potential, just like the acorn contains the entire oak tree and will eventually become an oak tree, when the time is ripe". He goes on to say: "Looking at holographic inner pictures will trigger the circuitry in our brain which supports our choice through neurological changes. A clear vision or goal functions like a magnet, attracting the appropriate situations and creating possibilities for them to manifest."

In other words if we believe that we are Gods in form, who can create energy fields from the Violet Light and program these fields to magnetize certain realities into our life, then we can. As we often share, this reality is powerfully supported when our intentions are governed by the win for me, win for others, win for our world outcome game.

BIO-SHIELD DEVICES:

Divine Nutrition Program – Technique no. 26:

a) *The first tool to aid in the Divine Nutrition game is the Digestive System Bio-Shield.* Its purpose is to act as an internal conversion system that instantly transmutes everything we eat into the perfect vibration of light that we need. Using our will, imagination and intention we:

- ❖ Take some time and sit in stillness and centre ourselves with the love breath tool then
- ❖ Visualize 5 lines of light coming out of your fingers and with a circular motion begin to
- ❖ Weave a web of etheric light around your mouth,
- ❖ Around your throat,
- ❖ Down your esophagus,
- ❖ Continue to weave this circular pattern of light around your stomach,
- ❖ Down around your intestines, and finally
- ❖ Down around your elimination system,
- ❖ Wrap your whole digestive system in a field of pink light, then golden light, then blue light, then Violet Light.
- ❖ Check on the inner planes using your third eye to see that your digestive system has now been cocooned
- ❖ Next this new energy matrix needs to be programmed as these light fields remain relatively inert until coded.
- ❖ Recommended Programming Code: First focus on the etheric web around your digestive system and
- ❖ See it as a living field of intelligence just waiting for a software program to run itself.
- ❖ Then command into it telepathically the following statement: "I now command that all food, all fluid, and all that I ingest from this moment on that flows through my digestive system Bio-Shield – is automatically converted into the perfect frequency of light and Divine Nutrition that my body needs now! So it is! So it is! So it is!"

Then anything you eat, you say to yourself "I eat because I love it, not because I need it and all that I eat and drink is automatically transmuted into what my body needs now". This reinforces the original field program and reprograms any limiting self talk – like "chocolate is so bad for me" or "I need this food for nourishment to survive" – both of which are limiting statements. Yes it is possible that the sheer attitude of "everything I eat is good for me" to override all toxicity but this requires focus and mind mastery, hence the Bio-Shield Digestion Device supports the process energetically while we develop this mind power.

b) *The second Bio-Shield Device that I feel is necessary, for those being fed via The Madonna Frequency Field of Divine Love, is a Bio-Shield that encases our personal energy field* and screens out all signals and frequencies that no longer nurture us. If programmed adequately, it will also allow us to only imprint, via our personal radiation, the Social Biofield with Divine Love, Divine Wisdom and Divine Power or frequencies from the healing Violet Light Spectrum. Again this has been briefly covered in BB1; however we can extend its functioning by applying the Violet Light plug in meditation. For those interested in the detail of Biofield Science, I recommend you read the Biofield and Bliss Series.

The ***Personal Bio-Shield*** is crucial for someone tuning to the Divine Nutrition frequency and choosing to feed themselves only on prana and for those with their Bio-Shields already in place we will look at the next level which is a basic maintenance program. Bio-Shield maintenance is required by those active in the world and includes the ability to dump and dissipate data and energy patterns from our personal Bio-Shield without destabilizing other fields. It also requires us to do regular tune-ups and resets.

Step 1 – Basic Bio-Shield Creation and Bio-Shield Data:

As already mentioned, the Bio-Shield is an environmental field device, that when programmed, acts as an invisible force field around us. Screening out discordant frequencies, it allows us to select from the world only the vibrations that we require and stops random signals penetrating our auric field and hence creating field imbalances and schisms.

Constructed on the inner planes using the frequencies of Divine Love, Divine Wisdom and Divine Power, it allows an initiate freedom to maintain sensitivity and sanity while we serve. As we have previously shared, it also creates a cocoon for the DOW to dwell within and radiate permanently and powerfully into the world.

This cocoon of etheric Violet Light acts as a Cosmic Hotel allowing a 'comfort zone' space for our Divine Delta field DOW being to dwell successfully, and fully, in our physical form even though our physical form dwells predominantly in a Beta – Alpha world.

The creation of this shield is quite simple and the below meditation only needs to be done once, however the programming and maintenance of the shield may need regular or sporadic adjustments, depending on our activity in the world.

Diagram 15

Divine Nutrition Program – Technique no. 27:
ACTION:
❖ Sit comfortably in meditation – centre yourself with either the Love breath or the Vedic breath tool.
❖ Imagine yourself seated in a field of light, a web, a cocoon or shield that is now being woven around you.
❖ Be still – breathe deeply and imagine that you are the King / Queen of your domain seated within a gossamer web of powerful Violet Light.

Diagram 15:

The visual comes from the booklet *Systematic Spherology of Biofields* by Dr Johannes Edelmann

- ❖ Imagine this web-like shield is made of the powerful invisible force of Divine Love, Divine Wisdom and Divine Power as potent, original forces of creation.
- ❖ Imagine that this shield is connected on the inner planes to 3 cosmic cables that carry an endless stream of Divine Love, Divine Wisdom and Divine Power.
- ❖ Imagine that these cosmic cables are connected to the very heart and mind of the Supreme Force of all creation
- ❖ Imagine that this shield is alive with intelligence and pulsing around you, waiting to radiate clear instructions to the intelligent universe that surrounds it
- ❖ Imagine that this shield that is now pulsing with Violet Light which will soon absorb what we program into it.
- ❖ Imagine that this shield is a bio-computer and that your mind is a software program.
- ❖ Think of all you desire re: love health wealth, happiness, passion, purpose.
- ❖ Imagine these desires clearly and that as you think them, they are being implanted into your shield. Add the emotion of having all your wishes come true.
- ❖ Imagine the Law of Resonance bringing you all that you require in response to the clear signals and images that your Bio-Shield has been just imbedded with and is now pulsing out.
- ❖ Imagine your shield absorbing now from the intelligent universe around you, and magnetizing back to your field, all that you desire and need.
- ❖ Once you have finished imprinting this shield with your thoughts and desires, imagine that these messages are now lighting up in the Bio-Shield like neon signs and are giving clear messages to the universe.
- ❖ Imagine that as you now say "So it is!" 3 times your Bio-Shield programs are activated.

Once the basic Bio-Shield has been created and its field set and we have confidence in DOW power, then it is a matter of scanning through and re-setting the fields of every aspect of our lives. In other words, if we wish to manifest anything in life, we have to give the supporting forces around us that aid in physical manifestation – clear signals so take the time and really think through what you want in all aspects of your life. Remember that the intelligent field around you is reacting to you all the time and always brings to you a mirror image of your predominant signals.

Step 2 – Basic Bio-Shield Maintenance: Dumping, Dissipating and Destabilization
Divine Nutrition Program – Technique no. 28:

Bio-Shield Maintenance is required by those who are actively involved in the Beta – Alpha fields as while the personal Bio-Shield reflects, refracts and redirects energies, when the field imprinting is constant enough and powerful enough we can absorb Beta field residue which can imprint our Bio-Shield with its toxicity. This is more likely to occur when we have mirroring emotions still anchored in our cellular memory base which sets up a mirror in the Bio-Shield that then acts as a field of magnetic attraction.

With the plugging in of our Bio-Shield via the 3 cosmic cables to the Violet Light Source, it is true that if we expect and accept it, the constant flowing of the Violet Light into and around our shield will keep it free of most field toxicity as Violet Light transmutes naturally everything it touches and transforms it back to its essence. However, if we are active in the Beta field world then we may find the need from time to time to dump unnecessary energies from our shields and this will need to be done without destabilizing the field around us.

The best way to do this is again by flooding the filled with Violet Light as transmutation is the perfect dissipation tool. I also like the program "DOW boost Bio-Shield Now" which strengthens the shield's base energy pattern and also its program codes. It is also important to retune our cellular memory patterns for empowerment and this can be done via

a) being thankful for all the learning we have gained through our suffering in the past

b) using kinesiology or vibrational medicine to release toxic emotions from our fields which can create schisms or weaknesses in the Bio-Shield, and

c) flooding our inner (meridians, bloodlines, skeleton, chakras etc) and outer fields (auric field and our immediate external environment) with Violet Light

d) Also daily imagining as we stand under the shower that the water as it flows is pure Violet Light that is cleansing and feeding our Bio-Shield and our auric field also helps.

The Self-Sustaining Template is an optional Biofield mechanism for those existing purely on the Food of Gods.

As already mentioned, another advanced Dimensional biofield tool is the self-sustaining template the concept of which was introduced in BB1. What I like most about the self-sustaining template is that it is an energy matrix that is woven over and through our existing light body. This template is designed to act as an energy foundation or grid for a particular program to play out on. Two factors not discussed in BB1 are firstly that once a field has been created, using the Violet Light spectrum, we have to imprint the template with specific emotions – usually virtues that we need to successfully fulfill our life and purpose here with Grace and joy. When activated this new self-sustaining template can automatically merge with and override the old light body and meridian fields.

I believe that the self sustaining template is a most fascinating and worthwhile Biofield device as once activated into elemental equilibrium, it will then regulate the flow of the food of the Gods for it is the perfect equilibrium of all of the elements of air, Earth, fire, astral light, cosmic fire and Akasa, that allows the template to fulfill its self sustaining aspects. The self-sustaining template is a new light body matrix that has been imprinted to achieve specific goals – namely for the physical bio-system to be free from the need of food, sleep, water or aging, for example. This new template is automatically activated when the inner and outer field frequencies match and are strong enough to trigger it.

The self-sustaining template originated after I was shown how a cosmic master creates a body of matter when he or she decides to come into form, for certain physical processes must be adapted and manifested within the fields to create a bio-system for our DOW to express Itself in form. For the 'ageless, no fluid, no food, no sleep' system to come into being a specific arrangement of elements has to come into being.

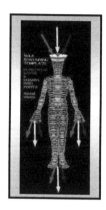 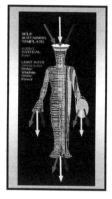 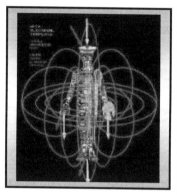 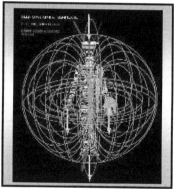

Diagrams 16, 17, 18 & 19:
The above are simple diagrams of Self Sustaining Template creation.

Programs in the Self-Sustaining Template are also set into the field to increase courage, clarity, compassion, commitment, discipline, devotion, humor, humility, impeccability, integrity and so forth, whatever we intuitively require as a new emotional base from virtue imprinting.

Creating a Self Sustaining Template:
Divine Nutrition Program – Technique no. 29:

❖ Sit in meditation, tune yourself with the LOVE breath and/or the Vedic Breath as in techniques 1 and 2 of Chapter 6.

❖ Breathe until you feel aligned with the beat of your DOW then use the following DOW Program: - "I ask my DOW to help me create the perfect Self Sustaining Template NOW."

❖ Imagine a Template in your mind, a web like body made of fine, pulsing lines of light, like a cocoon. Imagine that this Template is brand new, perfectly hardwired, strong and vital, a pure light matrix like web – a bio-computer waiting to be programmed.

❖ Imagine this is a new grid and that it is hooked into a Supremely Intelligent and unconditionally loving Cosmic Computer which is constantly downloading into the

Template limitless love and wisdom and power for the Template to utilize as required.

❖ Imagine stepping into this template and that it merges within you, anchoring itself into your chakra and meridian system.

❖ Imagine all the elements of Earth, air, water and fire coagulating around you, gathering molecules and atoms to reform a new bio-body around this new grid and Template.

❖ Imagine a new form being molded that is ageless, self sustaining and self regenerating

❖ Imagine a holographic image of the perfect you, beaming out from this template – complete, whole, healthy, happy and fulfilled – ageless, radiant, self sustained.

❖ Instruct your DOW: "I ask my DOW to now cross the lines of time and gather all the learning from all my emotional experiences through all time, all the love, compassion, mercy, wisdom, honor, empathy, joy, wisdom, and power that I need to create an emotionally balanced, strong and healthy Template now."

❖ Instruct your DOW as you hold the image of your body youthing: "I ask that my Bio-Body Template be age ____ (25, 35, 45?)" – think of what you would like and, while holding the image of this new Template in your mind, chant 3 times, "Bio-Body 25, Bio-Body 25, Bio-Body 25" or whatever age you are envisioning. Visualize your body being imprinted from this new inner Template and – supported by your new lifestyle – imagine your body now begin to become younger and rejuvenate itself from this new grid within.

Note that for this Template to be anchored and activated, we must not doubt that stopping the aging process and regeneration like this is possible. Once the Template has been created and anchored into our light body and our Bio-Shield we can relax and get on with life and trust it will be activated at the perfect time for us. The template will activate itself automatically when we have achieved elemental equilibrium from enjoying the Luscious Lifestyles Program, thinking with awareness and positivity, acting impeccably and maintaining a pure heart.

Other Data & Devices:

Other devices have been developed now to both change our brain wave patterns, and also to chart the benefits of changing our brainwave patterns, from the Beta – Alpha field to the Theta – Delta field. Initial research with devices like the Pineal Trainer of Paul Louis Laussac; have found the following occurs when we retune our brain wave patterns to the Theta – Delta Field:

1. Changing in metabolic rhythm.
2. Natural changing in breathing rhythm.
3. Changing in skin resistance.
4. Biochemical changing.

5.   Synchronism of brain waves pattern.
6.   Synchronism of the electrical activity of the brain hemispheres.
7.   Less galvanic reactions of the skin to a stressing stimulus.
8.   Lowering of the cardiac beats per minute.
9.   Lowering of the breathing rhythm per minute.
10. Diminishing of the blood pressure in hyper tense patients.
11. Increasing of the personality.
12. Diminishing of the anxiously.
13. Increasing of psychological health.
14. Increasing of self-realization.
15. Increasing of perceptual capacity.
16. More quick reaction's time.
17. Better recordation from short and long time.
18. Reduction of the use of alcohol and cigarettes.
19. Less number of spontaneous galvanic reactions of the skin.
20. High academic development.
21. Improvement of business, through new ideas and concepts

Devices like a Pineal Trainer plus our Dimensional Biofield Devices, operate via a system of biofeedback looping and according to research done by the Primal Foundation, (www.primaltherapy.com) the brain has a capacity to naturally harmonize its resonance to the dominant field. Consequently bombarding both our brain and the fluid in our body with music and mantras creates some interesting changes in our field and our transmissions signals and consequent life experiences. The primal Foundation has also mapped the brains wave patterns in terms of amplitude, peak frequency and distribution of power within the Beta, Alpha, Theta and Delta bands and then applied the results to aiding with emotional therapy. Their research talks about 'gates' which hold back or release, primal energy and separate our bands of consciousness and control our emotional states and responses thus confirming that when we alter our brain wave patterns we can alter the experiences we have in life and hence remove ourselves from any victim mentality into another level of mastery.

The Chi Machine:

Personally I prefer to be machine independent for the most perfect and complex computer which we have at our disposal is the human bio-system. To me exploring its capabilities via lifestyle changes that shift our brain wave patterns naturally, is always a healthier and more liberating choice. I think this attitude goes back to my early yogic training that advised "Never be dependant on anything outside of yourself". I have found that to always be good advice as the true source of power is our DOW.

Having said all of the above, I personally have enjoyed a device called *the Chi machine* as it aligns very powerfully with my programming research. The idea that we can reprogram the fluids of our body to achieve certain benefits is supported by the work with water consciousness by Masaru Emoto (*Messages from the Water*). As our bodies are 70%

water, and as we know that water responds to music and words, then many things can be gained by tuning to and then programming directly into the fluids of our bio-system.

For example, the Chi machine device, gently rocks a person from side to side as they rest their feet upon a vibrating block and lie still on the floor. At the end of the session a rush of chi energy flows up from our feet and literally floods our bio-system with pure prana. It is during this rush that programming like *"perfect health, perfect balance, perfect weight, and perfect image"* (technique no. 10) can be utilized as when we do this with certain finger mudras, the imprinting goes deep into both our cellular and neutrino core.

However remember that this program will only work if it is said from a point of being that we **are** Gods in form who are all powerful, all knowing and all loving and wise and whose physical, emotional and mental body have one function which is to support the manifestation of our Divine Self on Earth. To briefly recap, the above program gives the Divine One Within us permission to create perfect physical, emotional and mental and spiritual health within our being and the 'perfect balance' command gives it permission to bring us into perfect balance on all levels of our being through all lives. The perfect weight program stabilizes our weight when we are not taking physical food nourishment and the perfect image command allows us to let go of society/media conditioning re our image.

Also remember that we are surrounded by an intelligent universe that

❖ sees us as Gods in form and
❖ constantly reads our personal biofield to see what our dominant thoughts and programs are and then delivers this to us.

So if our constant self talk is a mantra like "I am healthy, I am happy, I am peaceful, and I am prosperous" then whether or not this is true for you initially, eventually the universe says: This master in form believes this so let us rearrange the molecules of life around this one and make it so. As we keep stressing, this is especially true when it is said with sincere emotion and supported by a pure heart and the kind and compassionate nature of someone who truly wishes to live their life in a way that benefits all.

Divine Nutrition Program – Technique no. 30:
❖ Experiment with a Chi machine and use the Perfect Health etc. program.
❖ Feel the difference in your system.

Step 13: Take your time, set a 2, 3 or 5 year goal plan of physical and social preparation e.g. in 3 years I will live purely on pranic light. Then apply the above points sensibly. There is no rush, it can take decades or even lifetimes for some to prepare their bio-systems for this experience and how quickly it occurs depends solely on our frequency which we can control and alter at all times.

Step 14: If it is in your blueprint to be public with this choice, read and apply the 'Responsible Reporting' Guidelines. See below.

Responsible Reporting:

I was guided to write this article after having to deal with a backlash of criticism regarding a person now living on prana who has been doing a lot of media work – a role, which thankfully I have now retired from. I love being able to decline such invitations particularly from the mainstream print media and everyday I feel more and more like Greta Garbo who said "I vont to be alone" – at least when it comes to the global mainstream press.

I loved to read the words in a recent article by a well known New York journalist (that again failed to consider the power of Divine Love) that said something like "the Australian Guru of Alpha, Jasmuheen, declined to be interviewed" and with such a controversial subject as prana power, silence for me has become more empowering. All the data has been gathered and presented (as per the free research manual that we have created at www.jasmuheen.com/who.asp#lol) and now only awaits respectful acceptance. Time of course will, as usual be our champion.

None the less, those of you inspired, or pre-programmed, to tackle the media re holistic educational matters, may find this article helpful.

After 7 years of making myself available to do newspaper, magazine, radio and television interviews and documentaries, it's great to have completed my assignment in this field and to have gone into semi retirement re the global mainstream press.

In late 1999, I made the decision to no longer do any print media and to only do live radio and TV, as I was disappointed with the media circus that was made around something that had occurred as the result of a very sacred spiritual initiation. I was also tired of the mis-education and blatant misrepresentation that often occurs within the mainstream press. The final straw came after I had spent two hours with an intelligent reporter, obligingly providing in-depth credible research and painstakingly ensuring all angles were responsibly covered, only to find her article full of factual errors – over 20 to be exact. I remember thinking "I know she's not stupid" so the only conclusion that I could draw was that she had set out deliberately to misinform the public – hence my decision to no longer support public mis-education in this way. Thus I restricted my media work to supportive journalists open to metaphysics who operated with higher levels of integrity and to all of them I extend my heartfelt thanks.

So a thousand or so interviews later, after reaching over 800 million people since 1996, I can consider myself to be well informed enough to offer a few insights. I do so knowing that our job as metaphysicians is holistic education. We all now know that all fear is bred through ignorance and that for some of us this may mean that part of our work to dispel this, may mean time spent with the global media.

So let's begin:
1) For the more esoteric connected I recommended the employment of an Angel Marketing and Media Team, together with the employment of a Holy One to oversee your media connections. This is a great time management tool and saves us wasting or

mis-directing energy. My Public Relations Media Agent is St Germain who agreed only to send me switched on reporters. (Unfortunately, I forgot to ask for switched on editors as well.)

2) Be aware of the 'slash and burn' technique common with mainstream print media. By this I mean you can spend wonderful interview time with an aware reporter only to find that although they may deliver a balanced, well researched article, that their editor will literally slash it to pieces for the sake of sensationalism and consequently 'burn' you, making what you say in your interview appear far fetched and/or incomprehensible as credible references and research that you have provided is deleted. The same editor is likely to run a catchy sensationalistic and misleading title to draw attention and boost sales. Journalistic integrity, among these ones, is a low priority.

3) Be aware that while we naively assume that all articles bought from another newspaper will be confirmed for story and reporting accuracy before going to print, this is not necessarily so. I have experienced top credible magazines buying and printing ill-informed factually incorrect articles from the tabloid newspapers, who as many of us are aware, often fail to check their facts as they usually opt for the sensationalistic to sell copy instead. Money from sales is a higher priority for many of these tabloids, rather than providing correct intelligent and factual reporting.

4) Hence my recommendation: Steer clear of the tabloids! Also before agreeing to do any media interviews check their journalistic integrity and credibility re reporting.

5) Examine your own integrity. Why do you want to be involved in the media? Do you harbor a secret desire for fame and fortune? How well do you know your material? Are you living what you are preaching? Is your experience 100% based in truth? Many journalists are trained to trip you, to always look for falsehood, and to expose fraud and deeper hidden motives for what they may see is your seeking to be well known. It is absolutely imperative that you stand tall and act in integrity and have 100% belief in yourself, in your product or proposal. Any schisms in your field will be targeted and manipulated.

6) When dealing with less than friendly media, never match aggression with aggression, as it will turn the public away. During my time with bringing Divine power and its ability to nourish our cells and our souls, to the global stage, I encountered countless angry and/or aggressive medical practitioners, psychiatrists, nutritionists and even fellow metaphysicians who would go into total attack mode – sitting forward in their sits, accusing, finger pointing, shaking fists, raising their voices etc. To be able to sit there quietly and answer accusations with loving patience, and provide well-researched back up material will always be in your favor, particularly when dealing with controversial subjects. The viewing audience will be impressed with your calm and mastery in this adverse situation, particularly if you have trained yourself to radiate enough love to touch the viewing audience in their homes. Remember, people learn only 7% of what you say, 93% of how they learn is gathered through your tone of voice, physical movements, and body language.

7) Make sure you are well plugged into the Divine Channels and can radiate the perfect voltage of love and wisdom in all situations. Always act like a true Master with intelligence, respect and honor, regardless of how your interviewer and the supporting panel may be treating you and your research proposal or product. This takes training particularly in the field of meditation, which allows you to always act rather than react when goaded.

8) If doing a promotion for an event make sure it is also educational in some way by providing a free tool or practical, beneficial research for the audience. Also ensure the interview will be published or go to air prior to the event you are promoting. Obviously, I am not talking about paid advertising here.

9) If possible, ask to proof read, for factual representation, any article before it goes to press. However, with mainstream media very rarely is the interview subject granted any editing rights.

10) Make sure any contract you sign is checked by your lawyer and operates under the terms you agreed to. Don't be rushed into making any decisions, always check all angles and options.

11) Be aware of the impact of your media work on the global game. If you do not follow the previous points you can be jeopardizing the credible work of your colleagues, particularly those who have spent years perhaps applying the previous points. This is particularly relevant to controversial subjects such as pranic healing or pranic nourishment, and other energy healing modalities, as we are challenging conventional beliefs and many of us have spent many years setting up very particular educational systems to bridge the metaphysical and mainstream worlds, and hence invite all to support this by being very aware of what is shared here.

12) Be aware that if your research threatens those who worship the God of money, that even if you do all of the above you may still be portrayed in a negative light. Lifestyles that act as preventative medicine programs will deprive the medical profession of their livelihood, just as much as being free from the need to take nourishment from physical food will upset the billion dollar food industry, the medical industry (as we never get sick), the pharmaceutical industry, and anyone who has not experienced the benefits of Divine Power and its ability to heal (Reiki, Pranic Healing etc.) or to guide (clairvoyance, clairaudience), or most controversial to nourish and love us.

13) Consequently, some times, at best, all you can expect when dealing with main stream media is to plant a few seeds in fertile minds, hence the more credibility you can offer, the better. So do not be attached to the outcome of your holistic educational work. The right ones will be magnetized to you, those ready will hear. Those who do not hear are either not ready or they are not part of your work stream.

14) Remember, Spirit and DOW power and the C.N.N. will always ensure the message is heard via the right channels. The innernet is incorruptible so use it.

15) Always give credit where credit is due. If you have developed certain abilities after studying someone's work and applying their tools and techniques always credit that person's research. For example, in the field of Sacred Sexuality and Taoists practices, one of the world's leading researchers is Mantak Chia, for pranic healing it is Choa

Kok Sui, for in-depth research into the phenomenal capabilities of the human body, Michael Murphy's book *The Future of the Body* offers great credibility. Similarly, Dr Deepak Chopra is the leading researcher in understanding the mind/body connection.

16) Similarly if someone sends you an important piece of information that aids your work, credit him or her and thank him or her where appropriate. Cross promotion and respectful acknowledgement is part of the new game of unity and needs to be encouraged and supported as Divine etiquette.

17) Choose the media that will best advantage you and your research product or your proposal. For example, spiritual or holistic programs usually provide less bias, more open coverage although they too may often engage the services of a professional to add credibility to their show. For example, both mainstream and esoteric media have often consulted with doctors and nutritionists for their opinion regarding living on light, which unless the practitioner meditates and is familiar with chi or pranic research, is basically a waste of time. All traditional nutritional research only applies to a person who is anchored in Beta/Alpha brain wave patterns, and for a meditator living a holistic life and operating from the Theta/Delta brain wave pattern, our ability to access levels and types of energy unavailable to the mass populace is something not yet understood by mainstream researchers.

18) Be well prepared and well informed. Live your life as a Master. Always act impeccably and never lie or stretch the truth. Then no matter what anyone says or does you will always have a clear conscience.

19) Lastly, dealing with mainstream global media with a controversial topic is not for the naïve or the faint hearted. Having supposedly a reputable TV, radio or magazine twist or misrepresent facts to suit themselves, or even lie to suit their own hidden agendas, can be heartbreaking and confusing.

20) Remember, not everyone will rejoice in what you have discovered via your experience and research, especially not those whose money machines are threatened or who have something to lose. Not everyone in the world wants to create a planet where the Gods of fame, money, sex or power are kept in their proper perspective or a planet where the power goes back to the people. For example, saying that God is everywhere including within us and that we can go direct to experience God via the divine inner plane channels will threaten the hierarchy of priest power and the foundation of many churches, just as much as new energy sources of cheap sustainable power, will (and do) threaten the existing energy barons with their fossil fuel monopolies, just as preventative holistic medicine programs threaten some traditional medical factions whose livelihoods depend on people remaining in the cycle of illness and disease.

21) Not everyone in this world has pure agendas, and while we may have been trained to see God in all beings, it is naive for us to think that we can deliver new and better ways of existing in this world and not be challenged, particularly when we are public in our work.

22) So, our last word of advice for those involved in the global media game, is: don't even think to go there unless you are well informed and have both courage and a pure, pure heart.

Step 15: Educating family and friends re your Divine Nutrition

Lifestyle choice: This is self explanatory – just DOW Match them all, be a radiant example and do all that you are guided to do with respect and love. (This was covered in more detail in the book *Ambassadors of Light*.)

Post Conversion – NOW WHAT?

After I wrote the first book on the subject of Level 3 nourishment in the Divine Nutrition Program, many people said that there was not enough written re:

"Well I now live purely off prana, so now what?" or

"How do I cope with the world's reactions and social reintegration stage?"

This is something that is nearly impossible to give guidance on as we are all so different in our reactions to the world and it also depends on our blueprint with this.

If we are private with the success of our Level 3 conversion then it is a lot easier adjusting socially than if we are meant to challenge the status quo and be public. If we are public then many of the 'Responsible Reporting Guidelines' are very helpful in dealing with all sectors.

Are people skeptical? Definitely.

Can they get angry and be hostile re this? Definitely.

Will you sometimes be ridiculed and feel isolated? Definitely.

Will it get easier with time? Definitely.

Do you need strength and courage to live the Level 3 nourishment life?? Definitely.

Basically our post conversion success with this is open – it must be lived and every moment dealt with accordingly – just like life. And just like life, when we are totally in tune with and guided by our DOW – it is all so much easier!

Before we go on to look at field sensitivity and re-weaving the fields so that they support and nourish us, let us stop and answer a few more commonly asked questions.

Chapter 11 – Part 2

Frequently Question & Answers

Because I would like this book to be as informative as possible, I have been guided to add in here some of the questions previously covered in the book **Pranic Nourishment – Nutrition for the New Millennium – Living on Light** *before we go on to look at other in-depth issues that we have discovered over the last decade.*

Firstly I would like to clarify the difference between the 21 day process outlined in my book *Pranic Nourishment* and what we are recommending in this new book *The Food of Gods*. The 21 day process is a wonderful spiritual initiation that allows many who are in the right frequency to move into Level 3 nutrition of the Divine Nutrition Program; however it will not guarantee this for all as again, success is determined by our personal frequency only. Hence *The Food of Gods* offers wonderful tools to slowly tune ourselves into successful level 3 nutrition by working with our personal frequency field.

Excerpt from *Pranic Nourishment – Nutrition for the New Millennium* written in 1994. *(Some of the below questions have been updated for this book. Pranic Nourishment is my term for Living on Light or Level 3 of the Divine Nutrition Program).*

Q: What exactly is it and how does it work? When and where did it originate?

Pranic nourishment, and its Divine Nutrition aspect, has been around since the dawn of time. Universal Mind – the Akashic records – share that there was a time where all beings were sustained from the pranic forces. Pranic nourishment is the ability to absorb all the nutrients, vitamins and nourishment one requires, to maintain a healthy physical vehicle, from the universal life force, or chi energy. A being who practices this does not need to eat food. In order to be a pranic nourisher, one must be a tuned instrument who also understands and practices mind mastery – that is conscious reprogramming of cellular memory for the elimination of any limiting and non honoring beliefs.

Q: How does one become a pranic nourisher and what prerequisites are there?

As mentioned, it is about being tuned. Research shares that human beings have a four body system – physical, emotional, mental and spiritual, that can be likened to a four string guitar, each has their own note and when tuned, the music played (and the life lived) is magical and a being becomes both harmonized and limitless. When out of tune, people – like an 'out of tune' instrument – can experience various forms of emotional, physical or mental dis-ease. Prerequisites for being a pranic nourisher would simply be the heartfelt desire to be limitless and to live life to the highest maximum potential plus the desire to explore this level of freedom. This is about honoring ourselves enough to open mindedly explore exciting possibilities. To be passionate about being alive, to maintain a heart filled with joy and gratitude at the gift we have been given to simultaneously create, and also witness the majesty of creation. To absorb all that we desire, from all dimensions, through these five physical senses and our two more refined senses of *intuition and knowing*. Living on light is simply one natural by-product of the journey and experience of being a passionately impeccable BEing.

Q: What are the benefits/disadvantages?

One of the first benefits that I felt was incredible lightness of being, feeling vast, highly energized, expanded, multi-dimensional. These are the characteristics of the Divine spark within and, as one is allowing this Divine limitless spark within – and without – to sustain them, they then take on its qualities. I remember the first day that I felt as though I was no longer restricted to physical reality but was completely free. Free to choose. Free to create. Free to study, research and then apply these new ways of being and thinking. Every day I feel how life is a gift and literally thank the Creative Force for the joy of having this physical experience. I choose to remember that I am a spiritual being having a human experience. I am now in wonder of it all as seeing yourself as a spiritual BEing will then draw that essence to you via the Law of Resonance which operates – to various degrees, in all fields – electromagnetically.

Regarding other benefits, many report increased energy levels and abilities in healing, clairvoyance and clairaudience. Some are reporting hair re-growth and grey hair becoming its natural color again. Please be aware that this is not about whether you eat or not eat, it is about freedom of choice. For example, not one cell of my body believes it needs food to be sustained or to live. Knowing that – both intellectually and experientially – I am at choice and without fear of negative consequences of whether I eat or not, it does not matter. My natural preference is to live on light. The ability to do so is now simply a fact filed away in my data base of memories. However, for others in earlier stages of this journey, my research and then the sharing of it, goes on to make the pathway for others easier.

We are learning together, sharing together and then demonstrating together. My fellow travelers find that the main disadvantage is extreme social alienation that occurs from this choice as the majority of western culture eats for the pleasure of emotional-based reasons and so much of social interaction is focused on eating. There is also a slight problem with boredom from lack of flavor for those who choose not to indulge in the odd mouthful of flavor for pleasure. Many pranic nourishers choose to have the odd taste to satisfy the taste buds – this may be in the form of a chocolate biscuit once a month or whatever they are drawn to.

When one knows, and has physically demonstrated, that all their nourishment comes from higher finer frequencies of pranic energies (what we term photon or chi energy), one achieves amazing freedom from the imagined need to eat and can indulge their taste buds for the pure sake of pleasure, not need. We are still researching the depth and complexity of the human psyche regarding the connection with eating for emotionally based reasons and this aspect of boredom.

Note 2003: To me one of the greatest gifts over the past decade has been freedom of choice and freedom from limitation.

Q: Are there any associated health risks/problems or deficiencies (iron, B12)?

Continuing from the previous question, the essence of life is prana. If a person chooses, they may connect to – and be sustained by – the pranic forces which carry all the vitamins and nourishment that is required to maintain an immortal, self-regenerating physical body. Therefore, one only would feel tired or experience health risks or problems if one expects to and would be as a result of not changing their cellular/mental belief systems and mind set. I personally would not recommend this journey to anyone who is not consciously tuning their energy fields to the more perfected beat of their DOW, or aware of metaphysics, Universal Law or basic quantum physics. For this practice to be successful without detrimental effects, one must honor the intellect via research and release all limited beliefs.

2003 note: According to our medical researchers, the human body cannot manufacture its own Vitamin C which needs to be supplemented in our diet to avoid scurvy and other physical ailments, however in a pranic nourisher when we have blood tests we are never deficient in any vitamin including C. Obviously when a potent enough force of Prana flows through the system, it deposits into the system all that our body needs to maintain health.

Q: Does the body undergo any physiological changes?

If one practices mind mastery, with programming and intention, one can change the shape of the body at will. This is what we call re-imaging. The work we are doing is about activating then utilizing the four-fifths of the brain that houses higher consciousness. Generally speaking, many individuals are too busy caught up with 'lower mind' issues of survival in physical reality to explore their full human potential. Once one has mastered issues of survival one is free to explore higher consciousness, via meditation and other ancient practices. This type of conscious tuning then allows us to enjoy limitless BEing.

Physiologically, the pituitary and pineal glands increase in capacity, and mental telepathy becomes normal for many.

Note 2003: We also gain many other benefits as discussed in the balance of this book.

Q: What happens to the digestive organs, do they wither and shrink?

When one goes into the body and looks, with tuned inner vision, one witnesses a flow of energy, like a wave, magnetize to our body. This happens in response to our instruction and command to universal forces to be pranically fed. Prana then flows in through the pores of the skin. It reminds me of a process where whales sieve tons of water to absorb the plankton. To then look at organs and in bones and the bloodstream is amazing.

What I 'see' generally is a reflection of vibrant health. This inner 'diagnosis' of reading energy fields intuitively is our 6th sense being activated. Diagnosis can vary depending whether one is burning off dross on a cellular level or not. Dross is toxic thinking, toxic feeling and toxic feeding.

On an easily proven traditional level the metabolic rate changes and the stomach shrinks as it is no longer operating in 'normal' digestive process. Many of us have had both traditional and non traditional – alternative therapy – testing with positive results. One challenge with this is that many Western practitioners have had no previous experience with individuals who have made this life choice so they have no previous 'yardsticks' for comparison. Also, generally speaking, by the time one has tuned their vibration and energy fields to the beat of being able to be sustained by prana they are no longer creating any dis-ease or discomfort in the energy bodies to warrant seeing 'therapists' or doctors.

Digestion and nourishment are two separate discussions. If organs, blood and bones are nourished, whether it be from the etheric (prana) or physical realms (food) they will maintain and demonstrate complete health and vitality. To self diagnose energetically, I recommend that the individual recall the memory of the lifetime where they were well trained and practiced in this refined art of energy work and command full conscious awareness of, and ease with, the practice of energy diagnosis. It is simply intuition tuned to, and connected with, Universal Mind or highest group consciousness. It can never be misused for we can only attract to ourselves a vibration that mirrors our own consciousness.

So in a 'nutshell', organs maintain, then improve, to attain peak health as the MASTER in the body – yourself empowered – begins the vigilant process of mind mastery and conscious reality creation of limitlessness. The game of pranic feeding is one of the most powerful I know to prove the power of the pure energy spark that really sustains us. Without this we would not have life. Without this we would not know pleasure or joy or limitlessness. For when we call it forth we may instruct "Dear mighty I AM Presence I command full mastery of all my lower bodies for you to now fully manifest within. I NOW express completely Divine Magic and Mastery and Heaven within all realms – as above, so below. So be it!" What a great decree! Quality programs and thinking provide quality life experience!

* Or the God force within, the Inner Teacher, our DOW, the Mother/Father Creator God – whatever you wish to use.

Q: What happens to the taste buds? Do they crave flavor or sensation?

The major stumbling block for many involved in this pioneering work has been still craving flavor and taste sensations. It is important to not be in denial and as we research the emotional energy pattern, 'hook in' and the emotional dependence on food, we may continue to indulge in the intermittent pleasure of taste. What we have found is that people when they stop eating either become desirous of spicy flavor or very sweet flavor, or may fluctuate between the two. Having a mouthful of the desired flavor when the craving hits satisfies many while we also are utilizing reprogramming methods to move beyond the consciousness of food. Our intention is that this be a joyous journey and not one of denial.

Note 2003: After a decade of watching people let go of their emotional attachment and socialization habits around food, I have come to the conclusion that slow is better for most and that the methods recommended in this new book allow people to move through this transition with minimum fuss. Many are also finding that the 'no nibbling' policy is easier for then they find that they are rarely exposed to food and are hence less tempted. Similarly some 50% of people who join our seminars have been pre-programmed to also be fluid free this life which also seems to make the transition easier as one simply never goes to the kitchen either to take water or tea etc. Again I must stress that this is not a journey of self punishment, rigidity or denial or the strict path of a fakir.

Q: Is it possible to go back to eating and are there any problems with that?

The majority of people who explore this journey return to eating quite easily without problem by easing their way back first to more solid liquids – like soup – then to fruit and vegetables and then normal diet. The main reason people return to eating is again social pressure and from being tired of being different. This is not a process or a lifestyle choice that excites many. The majority of people who hear about the work that we are doing consider it to be either:

(a) Impossible or (b) say: why would you anyway when there is so much pleasure in eating? However there are also many who are pre-programmed to bring in this new choice for humanity and hence all of this feels completely natural.

Q: Is dehydration a worry? What do pranic nourishers drink, just water or flavored liquids as well? What about caffeine, alcohol, other stimulants?

There are beings who choose to neither eat nor drink but the majority of western pranic nourishers still maintain the ritual of socializing over a 'cuppa' so as not to be completely socially alienated. The majority do not indulge in alcohol as they may feel it lowers the vibrational rate of the energy fields of the bodies, or they may utilize mind mastery and transmute all that goes into the body into light. I personally still looove a good cup of tea!

Q: Does living purely on prana affect growth / development / body size? Are there any fat pranic nourishers?

People practicing this successfully are tuned instruments either developing, or already possessing, great command over their molecular structure and can manipulate body size and shape at will through re-programming and the utilization of basic lifestyle skills. We accept that the body is a bio-computer, the mind is the software package and our life is a print-out of the two. If we do not like life or any aspect of it, then we can rewrite the software program of our beliefs. Quality thinking brings quality life, limitless thinking brings limitless life.

Regarding the question on 'fat pranic nourishers', there are people who have begun this journey with an intention to lose weight. As this (the 21 day process) is a sacred initiation for the spiritual warrior, they have not been able to maintain the program and have subsequently gone back to eating. One's intention must be pure. Please note that regardless as to whether one returns to eating, success is achieved in that a new pattern of knowing has been laid down into the cells. Cellular memory comes from the experience that one can exist for months or years by pranic feeding. Hence a subtle yet powerful level of freedom is attained.

Q: How does it affect sleep? Do pranic nourishers all meditate? Are they energetic?

The majority of pranic nourishers sleep at least half of what they used to and some have mastered the requirement for sleep. Others simply sleep when they desire, usually to move out of the body at will to go into other energy bands of expression. In order to tune oneself to the Divine Nutrition channel, meditation is one of the most effective tools. It also allows us to access the limitless nature of the pure energy spark within. Many pranic nourishers have embedded their conscious awareness in the eternal now and choose to meditate formally for the joy of being in the stillness without the external distraction often experienced in a busy Western culture.

Energy levels are fantastic particularly when you expect them to be. Remember this is a journey of mind over matter. One of the most obvious proofs that our DOW is feeding us is that we experience increased levels of creativity, we need and desire much less sleep and our energy levels are much higher.

Q: How does it affect life expectancy? Is it a fountain of youth or does it age one? How does it affect physical beauty?

I cannot speak for all pranic nourishers, only of my personal journey, where in my reality physical immortality can go hand in hand with the pranic nourishment issue. Giri Bala of India, and Therese Neumann (who bore the stigmata of Christ), were both pranic nourishers who aged gracefully and died. Being a pranic nourisher does not guarantee physical immortality unless one reprograms the pineal and pituitary glands to only produce life-sustaining hormones. In order to be physically immortal one needs to let go of the belief system that one has to die, and release from the energy fields of the bodies all toxicity of thought, emotion and dietary substance. It is a path of purification and being the most sublimely tuned instrument in the orchestra of the Divine and manifesting that into physical reality. Therefore accessing the fountain of youth depends on one's mind set, beliefs and desire.

Personally I am the master of my vehicle (the physical body) and not slave to it and it is my intention to fulfill my life purpose and then take the body up into light or drop it when I have completed my work rather than have it die from neglect or abuse. Again, a small number of people have the shamanic shape-shifting ability and can change the physical appearance at will. Physical beauty is not an issue, vibrational beauty is and nothing is more beautiful than a being who is radiating the love and light of their own Divine essence.

Q: How does living purely on Divine Light affect one's sex drive and sexual relations?

For many pranic nourishers in partnership, the common practice is tantra or utilizing the Taoist sexual energy flows which stimulate both brain orgasms, heart orgasms and full body orgasms. The conscious practice of this incorporates the sexual energy (lower base and sacral chakras) with the spiritual energy (crown and brow chakras) and the unconditional love energy (heart chakra) via the microcosmic orbit technique (as outlined in Mantak Chia's work, the author of *Taoist Secrets of Love* – see Technique no 11. in Chapter 6).

Others may choose celibacy where celibacy is a choice made not from lack of opportunity for sexual expression but for intentional conscious transmutation of the sexual life force energy into a higher – more refined – creative vibration. A healthy body is a sexual body. The sexual energies must be transmuted into a higher vibration or utilized through either procreation or Tantric sharing.

Q: Is there an international; organization of pranic nourishers and if so what is its agenda? Is it a cult or religious movement?

No and no. Personally speaking, being a pranic nourisher is two per cent of who I am and is something that I, and others, are happily pioneering. Due to the potential powerful, positive global ramifications for world hunger we are simply allowing people to witness and possibly experience another way of being so that they may be free from the need for food, sleep and even the constraints of time.

Body temperature control and not requiring food or sleep are all by-products of being a limitless being and exploring our full potential. These three are practiced by countless Yogis. Jesus said, "All that I have done you can do and more".

Note 2003: People of all religious and spiritual persuasions and now answering their own inner call to be part of this new way of being, I always say that this is something that people are pre-programmed to do which we can discover via Technique no. 20 in Chapter 11.

Additional Questions that are commonly asked and some new ones that aren't:

Question 1:   Can a woman be nourished only by prana and give birth to a healthy child?

Answer Q1: Yes, this has already occurred in Germany, Switzerland and Brazil. As covered in our other writings on this, as long as a body is being nourished enough, there will be no physical problems. Also the Madonna Frequency Field of Divine nutrition is free of pesticides, food coloring and can't be genetically modified so it is a purer source of nourishment than physical food. It is also a cleaner source of nourishment unlike physical food which relies on our bio-system to break it down, absorb the nutrients and then eliminate the waste.

What I do advise is that a woman does one of two things:
   a) Proves to herself that she can be sustained purely by prana alone, until she has no doubt and she can only do this by living it for at least six months, before she becomes pregnant or
   b) Delays living purely on prana until she has had her children.

The reason for this is that any doubt can interfere with the baby's nourishment flow and create physical problems for the fetus which should be avoided at all costs.

Question 2: ***What does the mother then feed the child?***

Answer Q2:   Some mothers feed their baby breast milk, or other milk, and they do so until the baby indicates a desire to eat other food. This is an interesting reality as some of the new babies being born are already tuned to the Madonna Frequency Divine Nutrition channel and yet their success at being properly nurtured rests with the fields of those around them.

For example, there is a woman living on light in Brazil whose baby feeds every 3 or 4 days and is putting on weight and appears healthy. However, the young mother's own mother and mother-in-law and friends are all concerned about how little she feeds this baby and are constantly projecting their fears for its safety into both the mother's and her baby's field. This in itself can interfere with the way Divine Love can nourish her child, for the fear vibration can impede the flow thus manifesting, by their own energy field, what it is they fear. Catch 22. With the feeding of children we need to be extremely responsible so we recommend regular check ups and if the child is thriving though it eats very little, it could be a Madonna Frequency baby.

I remember when my children were very young vegetarians 20 years ago and how difficult it was for them at school. Imagine if a child is being nourished by Divine Nutrition and how much chaos this will cause at schools and among the families of their school friends. Still these young ones have come in with great love and awareness and no doubt with all the courage they need to challenge the status quo. Just as it was difficult socially for us to be vegetarian 30 years ago, similarly it is socially unacceptable today for us to feed only on Divine Nutrition yet again, in time history has shown that this will change.

Question 3: ***What about the taking of physical food, and any weight gain that may happen, after people have been living successfully off pranic nourishment? How does the bio-system cope? What about the metabolic rate which obviously must slow down if some one doesn't eat for a long time?***

Answer Q3: Many people who have successfully converted to pranic nourishment do, from time to time, still like to indulge in the pleasure of taste, either for social reasons or for emotional reasons, or just as part of a natural adjustment process. However, it needs to be noted that firstly, many changes have occurred in the body as a result of stripping* and these greatly affect the body's metabolic rate which obviously slows right down. Consequently, any food intake is first seen by the body as unnecessary – why does it need it if prana is in fact feeding the body all it needs? Hence this food is stored as fat, and energy reserves that can then only be burnt up by an increase in our exercise program or going back to the taking of no physical food. Our research has also shown that while our physical system adjusts very positively to the Divine Nutrition reality, due to the social isolation that this choice often brings our emotional body finds the transition more difficult. Social isolation and alienation is one of the main reasons for the return to sporadic social eating among the light eaters.

* *We will discuss the process of stripping and re-layering later.*

Question 4: Using Dimensional Biofield science and mind mastery can a person get tuned to such a state of equilibrium with the elements that they no longer need to meditate or practice the Luscious Lifestyles Program?

Answer Q4: The short answer is of course. However this requires a state of mastery that can take lifetimes to acquire. It also requires building up and accessing a pool of intense Delta field energy and spending enough time in the yogic 'ultimate reality' zone so that we are irrevocably transformed. This state is also easier to maintain for those who choose to exist in pure environments free of noise and energy pollution such as the Himalayas. For the yogis required to live in or travel constantly in cities, we need to regularly realign ourselves energetically. Hence the practice of the Luscious Lifestyles Program is like a daily shower of energy that keeps us tuned while we move through the denser Beta – Alpha fields.

Question 5: Does a person need to do all the things recommended in this book to free themselves from the need to take physical food for their nourishment? To some it may all sound a little complicated.

Answer to Q5: The short answer is no. I have met many people who have made the transition into this almost instantly and again this is due to their vibration and the daily lifestyle they have been leading that has made them physically, emotionally, mentally and spiritually fit. When they receive the data that Divine Nutrition is constantly flowing within them anyway, just waiting for an opportunity to provide all the nourishment that they need, when they hear this and really understand this, and know and trust their DOW enough, then they can cross over quickly.

Also due to the media work that we have done, where I have spoken to over 800 million people regarding our DOW's nurturing power, this reality has now been firmly anchored in the morphogenetic field and hence more and more are now clicking into the Divine Nutrition field with seemingly little preparation.

This is due to:

a) Their lifestyle that has put them in the Theta frequency band and

b) Their change of mindset as to this possibility.

It is no longer uncommon for me to spend a few hours with someone on this topic and have them healthily cease eating virtually immediately. An alternate reaction is that they go home and eat everything they can find for a few days or weeks as their inner child begins to deal with letting go of their emotional attachment to the pleasure of food and adjust to this new paradigm.

Those familiar with our first book in this series can attest to how our thinking has evolved as we have tried to understand how Divine Love and prana can feed us and free us from the need to take physical food. Those who know our research work and accept our metaphysical theory, also know of my desire to always keep things simple, however the mechanism of our bio-system and how it operates is anything but. Our physical form is a 6.3 trillion cell complex bio-computer that operates in unison with the 6.3 trillion stars of our universe, and all operate in perfect unison as cells in the body of a Supreme Intelligence that some call God.

To bring this Kriya-Yogic practice back to simplicity, I must go back to the first requirement for Divine Nutrition and Theta field feeding, and that is follow your inner guidance and do what you are inspired to do in the preparation for this transformation. There is no right or wrong and personal experimentation and trusting the DOW's voice is crucial in this journey. In 2002 during a visit to Poland I met with a very interesting Russian man who informed me that I was no. 5 of a list of people he was investigating re various methods and propositions for Divine Nutrition feeding; so more methods are being constantly downloaded by those accessing universal mind, as feeding ourselves in this manner is just a matter of basic esoteric evolution.

Question 6: You have talked about the process of 'stripping and re-layering' that occurs within the bio-system as people transition in and out of this paradigm. What do you mean by this?

Answer Q6: One of the first things I noticed from working with subtle energies – as in meditation – is that often we don't notice the changes until we stop doing the activity that is creating them. Because we are dealing with 'subtle' energies, the changes within our bio-system come as gradual shifts in consciousness. Similarly during the preparation for the living on light reality, our bio-system goes through a subtle and gradual process of stripping back, as our denser energies become more refined. This 'stripping back' is only something you notice that has happened when we begin the process of re-layering if/when we choose to tune ourselves back into a denser frequency.

I discovered this phenomena after I had not been eating for more than 2 years and then after another 5 years of existing on less than 300 calories per day (from the soya milk and sugar I added to my ginger tea and the odd piece of chocolate, or a light pumpkin soup). After another year of eating a light meal once a week, I decided to take a year off and try to re-stimulate my metabolic rate and densify my frequencies to be more socially relatable. During this time, I felt as if my insides, the layers beneath my skin, were being rewoven from a light, translucent substance back into a more dense form. It truly felt as if I had been stripped back and then when I was so light, I was barely there, that I then underwent – of my own choosing – a form of re-layering. Interestingly, the only substances I was guided to ingest during this time were ginger and pumpkin both of which are known to stimulate the production of the chemicals that keep our brain wave patterns locked in Theta.

I would like to share here, that for some people, our path with this new paradigm is one of constant experimentation and the idea for many of never eating physical food again, holds little appeal. Many who are drawn to this usually seek to do it for the personal expansion and freedom it brings rather than the idea of never eating again. Having said that, most also share that their preferred state of consciousness is when they exist purely on a prana diet which is my personal experience as well. However, the idea of stripping and re-layering needs to be examined when taking into account any medical research, unfortunately we cannot as yet measure the expansion of consciousness except by the personal benefits we experience and perhaps a detection of the altering of our brain wave patterns.

Question 7: The 'ultimate' goal of many yogi's, shaman and metaphysicians is to experience the ecstasy of enlightenment. How does Divine Nutrition support this and does accessing the food of Gods help to bring this much sought after state into being? Also what about the field dynamics?

Diagram 20: The Descent of our DOW

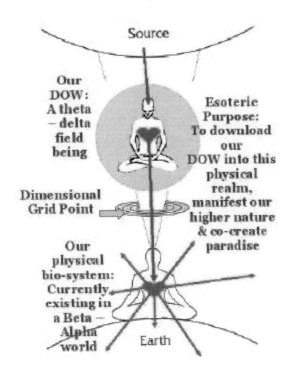

Answer Q7: In the field of Dimensional Biofield Science, this is an interesting challenge. For example, the below diagram shows a classic image of an individual existing in the denser material reality of this world yet being guided by the higher Divine nature.

The questions are as follows:

1.   If the current esoteric reality is that rather than ascending, we are to 'descend' our Dow into this physical plane and manifest our Christed or Buddhic consciousness, then how can a predominantly Theta – Delta field being exist in a Beta – Alpha field? Isn't this like trying to mix oil and water and is hence an energetic incompatibility?

2.   What about the reality that if God is everywhere and in everything, then aren't we already enlightened?

3.   How can the field dynamics be altered to support the descent of our DOW into the physical plane?

The above 3 questions confront every esoteric student at some point in their philosophical thinking, especially those concerned with field science, and the answers are quite simple. Firstly, it is true that at this point in humanity's evolution we are looking at the group ascension dynamic rather than just individual ascension. At this time, the two are destined to go hand in hand.

The level of sensitivity that a light eater (pranic nourisher) needs to develop to access the food of Gods, is extremely high and sustaining ourselves in Theta frequencies when we live in a predominantly Beta – Alpha world is a challenge that can be met with the use of Bio-Shield Devices which we will discuss in detail later along with a detailed analysis of

Violet Light power. This Bio-Shield can then act like Cosmic Hotel which we fill with the Violet Light spectrum of the Theta – Delta field and hence create a compatible environment for our DOW to exist within.

Together with
    a) the 'we radiate rather than absorb' attitude, the Cosmic Source Cable plug in meditation in Chapter 7 that allows us access to a never-ending source of love and light,
    b) and the commitment to always act impeccably that attracts like forces to us, we can then move through the world, well connected and able to attract, hold and radiate our DOW in this physical world.

The use of a Bio-Shield Device is one way of altering the field dynamics so that our physical bio-system can match frequencies with our DOW in all Its glory – however it is important to note, that our DOW can only download Its power into our circuitry according to our capacity to receive Its light and love. Our capacity can be increased via the Luscious Lifestyles 8 point program as per Chapter 6.

Next to be enlightened means to be filled with light so yes tuning to the Divine Nutrition channel of love and light will aid this. Also at this time the general esoteric understanding is that what we focus on grows so if we are always in a process of becoming enlightened we never actually get there, but if we act as if we are then the universe brings this into being.

The ancient wisdom of esoteric thought and experiences teaches us that Theta – Delta wave feeding on a soul level produces a state of enlightenment in an individual. That is a state of being filled with light. As our ability to attract, hold and radiate the Theta – Delta wave frequency expands our inner fields can access more DOW power, as more cells light up and the atoms become stronger. The innate nature of the DOW is to heal, re-energize and strengthen. This increase in our DOW's chi radiation brings some very interesting by products. Three obvious benefits are:

1. The bio-system reduces need for sleep as the chi flow keeps it literally zinging.

2. Due to the emotional wave pulse attracted to us via time spent in the Alpha, Theta, Delta fields, the bio-system becomes less stressed and less diseased until it releases its own abilities to heal itself. Eventually the need for aging and disease is eliminated altogether as the fields are pulsing with too much Theta – Delta frequencies for the being to be in the zone of toxicity that produces death and disease in a normal bio-system. This, of course, is also supported by the lifestyle choice of the individual, which naturally happens to be one that is positive and regenerative and relies on the body's innate capacities to keep creating new cells.

As we know from the work of Dr Deepak Chopra, within a year and a half to two years, not one cell of our body is the same as it was that time before. Everything in our body is constantly changing. The ability to deliver and release all the vitamins nourishment and minerals that a healthy human bio-system needs is a natural attribute of the Theta – Delta field when it is given the opportunity to do this.

3. There are many books on the miracles of yogi life, which describe the effect that Theta Delta field immersion has on our human bio-system. Michael Murphy's book *The Future of the Body* is just one of the many that now provides medical and scientific referencing.

Question 8: What else can you share about enlightenment for is this not the true gift of the Gods, the experience that we are enlightened beings?

Answer Q8: In the Eastern cultures, enlightenment (or ascension in the West) is a much sought after state, with the Yogis of Tantra and Chi Masters aware of the need for discipline, dedication and devotion to the goal. Few possess enough drive or determination to apply the physical, mental, emotional or spiritual commitment that is required to be disciplined enough to exist in, and are completely nourished by, these purer fields. Yet millions are always trying. In the West the reality of ascension or enlightenment has long taken a back seat as the main focus has rested on the Gods of fame, money, sex and power, all of which are tests in the path of every spiritual initiate. For how we deal with these things is the real issue, as is how we allow them to imprint us.

All life is spiritual for in the Dimensional Biofield all is literally interconnected and born from the Oneness, even though creation is displayed in a multitude of frequencies of waves, and may appear at times to be quite separate.

This is now common knowledge to a Dimensional Biofield technician, so hence the morphogenetic field consciousness has received new imprints and these new imprints are supporting new field realities for human potential. In simple terms it means our capacity to absorb Theta – Delta field frequencies has increased en masse. So we now have far greater choice regarding what we wish to download and radiate in the energy spectrum. It also means that we can be less influenced by the Beta fields thanks to discussions raised by new age philosophers and cutting edge scientists and physicians, which have often been shared with our metaphysicians.

Due to the work of all our previous Dimensional Biofield technicians, Earth and its inhabitants have entered into a new field of possibility which supports a mass ascension. The Alpha waves are moving more fervently through the Beta field, and although there still appears to be very little light, love and feelings of harmony and inner peace are becoming a constant experience for those tuned to the Theta field.

Some past examples of Theta – Delta field connections are:

1. The Buddhist rainbow bodies, where Lamas dematerialize and shrink their bodies after death causing it to entirely disappear.
2. The 'incorruptible'. The bodies of the saints that maintain themselves for hundreds of years after the spirit has departed and the physical bio-system has been declared literally dead.
3. The Yogis who allow themselves to be buried, from 3 weeks to 40 years, without food or water, or even oxygen or sleep – and they achieve this by moving their conscious awareness to rest deep within the Theta and Delta fields. There are Yogis who have

been tested and proven that they can maintain full consciousness even when they are anchored in the Delta field, e.g. the Messenger Institute, USA experiments.

Meditation takes the Yogi deep into the enlightened state of the Delta field, so deep that the Yogis go into a state beyond their mind and retain no conscious recollection of it, (apart from the lost time syndrome) and yet when eventually they regain awareness they feel completely transformed. You cannot linger in the Delta field without being transformed, as the Delta field is a band of such love, purity, creativity, knowingness, certainty, awareness, clarity and wisdom, and much more than we can even begin to comprehend. Anyone who immerses themselves in this field is forever affected by it in some way. How powerfully we are transformed by it depends on the periods of time we bathe in its field.

Remember that Theta – Delta field access is determined by our own brainwave patterns, which are again controlled by our lifestyle, which includes meditation and the use of ancient and modern day metaphysical tools to keep us tuned. In the past the Yogis used meditation, chanting and mantras, breath techniques, prayer, a light vegetarian or vegan diet, and service and satsang – the sharing of truth – to tune themselves through the Alpha and Theta to the Delta fields. While the ultimate reality of a Yogi is the immersion in the Delta field of Samadhi, Dimensional Biofield technicians are now focusing on operating from this state daily although not so deeply as to lose our conscious awareness of practical life. Instead we seek to operate from the Alpha, Theta and lighter Delta waves as we conduct our daily living. We do this knowing the benefits that will come.

In the past, lamas, yogis and saints have continually undergone challenging initiations to test their abilities and expand their awareness as they enjoy the enlightening journey of moving through the Alpha, Theta and Delta fields, and the journey itself allows them to become more familiar with the benefits and the gifts of each field.

Q9: In Chapter 6 you talked about the Violet Light and its connection with Taoist philosophy and how it is the real source of pranic nourishment as it can fill the bio-system with all the love, wisdom and power that it needs to be self-sustaining. How does this relate to the 3 Fold Flame of Saint Germain and also the Maltese Cross?

Answer Q9: Saint Germain has long been known as a Master of the Highest Alchemy for his focus, like mine, is on freedom – the freedom of humanity to expresses their Divine Nature and hence create paradise again on this Earth. One of his tools was the Violet Flame of Freedom and yes this is the same Light that we use for our nourishment. It is said that this flame resides in everyone's heart chakra and feeds us the love, wisdom and power we need to grow in alignment with our Divine nature. The more we focus on it, the more of its virtues we can utilize. The Maltese Cross is a symbol of Saint Germain and it is a cosmic generator of great 'God controlled' power that we can visualize in the centre of our heart chakra where it will radiate the below energies through our bio-systems and out into the world.

❖ The energies of spirit descend through the north arm which is white in color and represents the downloading of the virtues of our Christ or Buddhic identity and of the Sacred Fire of transmutation.

❖ The left arm carries the blue energy of Divine Power, just like with the Violet Flame. The left arm also denotes the west and the negative, or minus charge of the Trinity in form and denotes the physical nature of man as a crucible into which the Light of the God force is poured.

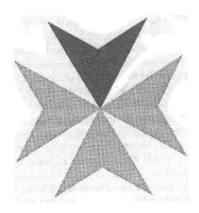

Diagram 21:
The Maltese Cross

❖ The right arm of the Cross denotes the east and the positive charge of the Trinity and is qualified by the pink light of Divine Love which is released when we act appropriately with the challenges of the left arm.

❖ The southern section of the cross carries the energies of Divine Wisdom, or the golden flame of illumination which imbues both the left and right arm with direction and purpose.

The Violet Light Ray is the seventh ray of spiritual freedom which is refracted to form the 3 rays of blue, pink and golden light. The Cross also symbolizes the perfect integration of God and man and the freedom we find when we release the energies of this trinity within us and allow them to radiate through our world.

For those who are open to and relate to this cross, you may wish to use the below technique.

Divine Nutrition Program – Technique no. 31:
❖ Sit in meditation, use the Love Breath meditation and centre yourself into the energy of Love.
❖ Fill yourself with the Violet Light as per the Cosmic Cable Hook-in meditation in Chapter 7 and as per technique 12 in Chapter 6.
❖ Imagine the Maltese Cross in front of you and imbue it with all the qualities listed above – strength and power to do what you have come to do in life, wisdom to do it in a way that benefits all, and love to do it lovingly.
❖ Imagine your heart chakra as a ball of radiating light, a ball that is connected to all the other chakras which are spinning now as one column.
❖ Imagine either the Maltese Cross (or the Three- Fold Flame of freedom and truth) now seated in the centre of your heart chakra.

❖ Program: *"I now ask that this symbol of Divine Freedom radiate through my heart chakra permanently, the energies of Divine Love, Divine Wisdom and Divine Power into this world in a way that nourishes us all."*

Q10: What is the Dimensional Biofield view on how pranic nourishment is possible?

Answer Q9: Recently when I looked at the deification of the Gods throughout our time, I saw how each God is a grid point in a cosmic chakra system which mirrors our own, and how each grid point is a doorway that pulses a certain beat, and how some grid points radiate more powerfully than others and hence can reach deeper through the fields. I saw that the reason that our sun can nourish all life is because it too is a God that attracts and radiates Divine power. And so the worship of the sun can also attract field nourishment and pranic light.

In terms of Divine Nourishment – as being like taping into a source of cosmic electricity – let's look at grids and cabling, and matrixes and drives. Metaphysicians know that our sun receives its power from the Central sun in beats of ten and then diffuses this to a seven beat to feed all life on Earth. We know that the Central Sun –which radiates a beam of sustaining love and wisdom into the heart of our physical sun – receives its own power via the cosmic computer via a pulse of 33 and then diffuses it to pass it down to our sun as a beat of 12. Each sun acts as a store house with a circuit breaker, a grid that receives and diffuses and disperses light to feed life in each dimensional system.

Is this still metaphysical theory? Yes.

Does it explain how we can be pranically fed? Yes, as the more light filled and powerful the grid, the more refined realities each grid point can beam through – more complex = more refined, more subtle = more depth and more doors = more choices. 33 is a more complex number than 7 which is the beat our Earth operates at to sustain a third dimensional reality field. Another major grid point is our human bio-system with its seven major energy centers or chakras. Our bio-system is the most complex computer we know.

Yes it's true that altering our lifestyle can alter our brain wave patterns which in turn will expose us to energy beams of light so that we can access our internal and external grids. There is nothing too complicated with this idea nor is it hard to fathom the idea that each sun, as a God and as a grid, is a doorway to another dimensional field.

Why is it easy for a Dimensional Biofield technician to accept this?

Because every bio-system runs on a matrix that also has grid points. These inner grid points are acupuncture points in our meridian system that mirror a universal pattern which is an inner plane system of cabling that looks like a gossamer web of light. This web has layers and planes of light and sound that we can access and see depending on what level our brain wave patterns are anchored into. Our 7 level system represents the Beta field, the 10 the Alpha, the 12 the Theta and the 33 the Delta so in order to access the Cosmic Computer or Creator God of our system we need to get refined enough to match its beat. Obviously a person who is anchored in the Beta field will have a limited awareness of the virtues and gifts that they possess that are only revealed when they move into the Alpha or Theta fields. Gifts like telepathy and other paranormal powers become real and blossom further when we commit to the practice of virtue and act as the masters that we are.

Chapter 11 – Part 3

Research Done and Research Recommended

Divine Nutrition Findings

As more and more individuals tune themselves to the Divine nutrition channel and allow it to provide Level 3 nourishment for them, our curiosity regarding the type of research that needs to be done in this field expands. It's one thing to have experiences and hypotheses and another to understand the science behind it all.

We have discussed previously our theories on how if a person tunes their brain wave patterns via their daily lifestyle to the Theta – Delta field then miracles happen and how a number of researchers now postulate that this is how Divine Nutrition – and Its gift of freedom from the need to take physical nourishment – happens.

Over the last decade of my own research in this field I have experienced many things that I would like answers to and I offer these for scientific postulation as these are things that many Divine Feeders have also experienced. Other experiences I offer just for elaboration on the subject.

Level 2 Nourishment Research required:
- ❖ Firstly I would like to see research dollars exploring all of the ideas put forth in this book particularly the effects on our health and happiness levels of the 8 point Luscious Lifestyles Program as the sooner the benefits of the total lifestyle package are confirmed and taught in schools via a holistic education package, the sooner our world will be in peace.

Level 3 Nourishment Research required:
- ❖ It has become obvious that since – on the purest level – Divine Love feeds us, that then when we spend time in a hostile energy field where there is heavy skepticism and even derision, we can lose weight and also feel quite tired.
- ❖ We know that the energy field of pranic nutrition is very powerful yet very subtle and that it can be overwhelmed by a denser field which can then interfere with its nutritional delivery. So field weaving and dynamics need to be addressed and studied.

- ❖ We know that even though we may no longer take physical food, that our weight can be maintained by the surrender of the body's cells to our DOW provided we also use the specific programming codes as discussed earlier.

- ❖ We also know that as in the research done with Hira Ratan Manek that even if programming re weight stabilization is not applied, the body will eventually stabilize itself if we keep holding the thought-form reality that we are being nourished.

- ❖ We know that body weight reprogramming does not work for everyone particularly if they do not live a suitable lifestyle to maintain themselves in the frequency field where Divine Nutrition flows easily enough to nourish them properly or if they have past life cellular memories that are powerful enough to over-ride the new programming codes.

- ❖ We know that once the pranic flow is established that if/when we begin to eat again, our weight balloons which is obviously due to the fact that a) our metabolic rate has slowed right down and also because b) we are now absorbing two sources of nourishment – food and prana.

- ❖ We know that to combat this we need to either stop 'nibbling' or increase our exercise program to burn off the extra calories.

- ❖ We also know that many individuals – who channel Divine Love as in Reiki and Pranic Healing – are now also putting on weight as the reality that the Universal energy can feed us has now been anchored in the morphogenetic field. The influence of the global morphogenetic field on an individual's personal Biofield needs more study.

- ❖ We also know that going back to the ingestion of physical nourishment makes us tired and not as strong, and we have found that if we eat we go back to needing more sleep and are less clear in our thinking and creative processes. In other words when we exist solely via Divine Nutrition we are stronger and healthier and more mentally alert and creative which we assume is a natural by-product of being anchored in the Theta field.

- ❖ We know that there is a corollary between extra ordinary abilities and brain wave patterns and that the Beta field dampens these natural abilities while the Theta field enhances them. These abilities may include clairvoyance, clairaudience, clairsentience as well as the ability to be pranically nourished.

- ❖ Research to date shares that going for long periods of time on one or two hours of sleep a night, is detrimental to the human bio-system yet the ability to exist healthily on minimum sleep seems to be a natural by-product of being nourished by the Divine Channels. It appears that the physical bio-system functions with such ease and minimum effort that it becomes more energized and has less need to rest via sleep. Whether this has any detrimental effects on the human need for dream-time and REM needs to be explored.

- ❖ We know that the pineal gland regulates our body thermostat and that prana feeders feel the cold more easily than many – is there a correlation here?

❖ We can begin with the above, and when our scientists and doctors attain Level 2 of the Divine Nutrition program and expand their consciousness through the Alpha – Theta and Delta waves, then we will discover even more….

Interview with Dr Shah

Dear Jasmuheen,

As desired by you, I am sending answers and notes on your questions. My credentials:
(1) Hon. Neuro-physician to His Excellency Governor of Gujarat
(2) President: Assoc. of Physicians of Ahmedabad '97-'98
(3) Hon. Associate Prof. of Neurology at K.M. School of PGMR and NHL. MMC
(4) Hon. Neurologist: V.S. General Hospital, Ahmedabad
(5) Panel Neurologist: ISRO, PRL, NID
(6) Fellowship at Houston and London on stroke and Parkinsonism
(7) Writer of Books (A) Epilepsy (B) The disease of brain and nervous system
(8) Lectures on stress, religion and other spiritual aspects at different parts of world.

1. Firstly, what led you into this field? (of studying chi or pranic nourishment)
ANSWER: Nature. I had an opportunity to monitor prolonged fasting as per the Jain religious method of Shri HRM for 411 days; on a scientific basis. That led me to postulate alternative ways to sustain the body when a person is not on routine food-calories. There was only one explanation, and that is – cosmic energy utilization.

2. What led you in to analyzing the thousands of brain scans, or ECGs, and MRIs that you have in the course of your normal medical practice?
ANSWER: To study the normal anatomy physiology and understand the functioning of brain. So far so I am unable to draw concrete conclusions from it. But, it is just fascinating and there are enormous possibilities. I have noted that the pineal gland and its connections with the pituitary gland and the hypothalamus – autonomic nervous system all have a very important role to be documented in the future.

3. What have you been looking for, and what have you found?
ANSWER: The pineal gland, pituitary, hypothalamus and frontal lobe associations are my areas of focus. Possibly the pineal gland and its connections have some answer to offer. The pineal gland is a psycho-spiritual body, and it has something to do with the functions of the mind and the occult powers and spiritual capacities are some way expressed by it. It has also possibly an important role in cosmic energy – pranic nourishment utilization capacity of a human body. It has some connection with the cosmic mind.

4. What have you concluded from these findings?

ANSWER: There is as yet no conclusion, but everything is at the hypothesis level. There are indirect indications, but no direct scientific proof so far, for me to conclude. The pineal gland was found to be enlarged in our studies on certain special subject of people…e.g. people living on no food or very low calories, or those who are highly spiritual or those who live very long. However, we need to study the pineal hormonal levels further and correlate. Only further research can lead us to a definite answer.

5. Can you tell us where your research project with solar nutrition is currently at? I believe Hira is also in the US and that you have connected now with some medical practitioners there. Can you tell us a little about this?

ANSWER: I am crystallizing my thoughts about a research project on solar nutrition. We are creating volunteers and want to follow them up. We have to reproduce the same findings in different human beings in different races and of different age groups. We are also going to study different methods of cosmic energy utilization apart from classic H-R-M method of sun gazing. We are also examining other potential sources of cosmic energy, e.g. air, water, plant, Earth. Apart from the eye-retina, there could be other recipient organ-structures in the human body, e.g. skin, lungs etc. so there are enormous possibilities and depending upon facilities, funds and resources research will go. At present we have ideas and some preliminary data. Shri Hira-Ratan-Manek is in the USA and has also been examined by highly qualified doctors and scientists of Jefferson University and University of Pennsylvania at Philadelphia. He was examined by an ophthalmologist to study his retina and eyes. His psychometry was done. Numerous blood tests and x-rays are done. Hormones and neurotransmitters levels are studied. Brain imaging and SPECT have been studied. Energy levels by EAV method are studied. His nutrition and metabolism is also being studied. Most studies are done at 3 levels. One before fasting, second during his on-going fasting and last level will be repeated at the end of his 130 days continuous fasting as per the Jain method. We will know the results of tests then.

6. In simple layman's terms, what sort of research do you feel still needs to be done in the area of prana as nourishment or what I call Divine Nutrition?

ANSWER: Pranic nourishment, cosmic energy, and Divine nutrition – all these things are new for science. Scientists and people in medical fields have started sensing the presence of such energy fields, but in view of difficulty in documenting them and quantifying them, things are so far occult. We can't measure them with present tools. That is our limitations. The problem is exemplified because of western mind set. A real barrier! Things can change and will have to change. A new understanding has to follow. This will be a quantum jump for science. The main concentration of research should be on documenting energy fields, then to calculate energy equations and conversion formulae. This will be followed by application of cosmic energy or pranic nourishment in day-to-day life and for specialized purposes. This will take few years, but will change the future of mankind.

Chapter 11 – Part 4

The Alchemical Action & Science of
Weaving the Fields

I include the following information here as I feel that for successful and continued living purely via Level 3, Divine Nutrition, it can be helpful for some readers to understand the alchemical art of weaving and influencing the fields which can drain us or be strengthened to support us.

Via our moment to moment reaction to events in our life, we are constantly redefining our inner energy field, our personal biofield – that auric space that surrounds us – and also our community biofield. We know that every thought, word and action that we have leaves an energy imprint in these fields, and that the sum total of it all also leaves an impact on the planetary fields. We know that just by our very existence alone, we are influencing fields.

Field creation or the fine tuning of an existing field requires us to address a few important issues such as how we wish to retune and imprint each field and the outcomes we would like the new imprinting to deliver. The first law of alchemical action requires us to be clear about what we wish to change in a field and why. Sometimes this means creating a new field or just adjusting an old one. Personally I feel that this is important as it allows a prana eater to tune any field into a supportive nourishing one and hence be less dependant on Bio-Shield Devices.

Field Construction:

After we've decided that we do wish to weave a new field and also what we intend as our outcome, we then enter into the next stage which is basic field construction. Field construction begins with an energetic matrix that can take from moments, to years and lifetimes to create. All fields have degrees of subtlety to which sensitivity is a key. Our field sensitivity, as we discussed, can be adjusted via our lifestyle for how we spend each moment of the day is what determines our strength at field imprinting and our ability to maintain our power and position within a field.

We know that a Bio-Shield device holds a space in a field and sets it into a specific frequency to achieve specific outcomes. Thus the manipulation of fields becomes both a gift to be used with integrity, and also an art, for the outcomes of field control can be quickly evident to all. The main reason for the alchemical action of field reweaving is to create a more personally and globally nourishing environment.

Weaving a successful field requires many virtues and attributes for the field weaver and to have the perfect influence on a field, we must have an alignment that is perfect with perfect programs, and perfect action plans to create perfect outcomes.

The next step to field weaving requires the conscious retuning of us for our bio-system is constantly reweaving the fields.

Part A: Tuning us.

Divine Nutrition Program Technique no. 32: Personal Tuning

Step 1 – First we need to **plug into a never-ending Source of power**, so that we can access everything that we require to radiate out the perfect nourishment into all fields. (As per Chapter 7 exercise.)

Step 2 – Next we need to **surrender the control** of field imprinting and weaving to our DOW as the true guru and boss of our being. This recommended program is to be said with sincerity. *"I now surrender every cell, every atom of my being to my Divine Self, and I ask that I be nourished on all levels of my life now and forever more. I also ask that this be done in complete alignment with the Divine self and the highest nature of all beings of this world, so that we can all co-exist as one people in harmony on one planet. So it is. So it is. So it is."*

Step 3 – Begin to **tune yourself** to the Divine Nutrition channel by developing your own levels of refinement and sensitivity by using the steps already discussed throughout this book and in particular the 8 point Luscious Lifestyle Program in Chapter 6 technique 5. The more tuned our bio-system is to the Divine channel of Love and Wisdom, the easier it is to correctly tune the fields around us and the more support we have to do so.

Step 4 – Use the inner realms of love, light and sound, and creative visualization, plus your will and intention to create, **activate or refine your internal field**. This means taking control over your life now, moving into another level of mastery now, applying particular tools that will achieve the health and happiness, peace and prosperity – Level 2 – agenda. All tools given in this book throughout this manual will achieve this outcome if applied as recommended.

Step 5 – Once a field is in place and running, as per the guidelines to be given soon, this step then requires for us to just **relax and chill out and enjoy the game**. Hold the focus of the outcome we are seeking with the intention of it happening with fun. Adopt also the attitude of maximum output, minimum effort – "I ride the wave of Grace" mantra. Understand that once fields have been created, laid down, activated, charged, plugged in to the most nourishing source of power and programmed, then outcomes are guaranteed. All it takes is power of concentration and the more you do this, the quicker this becomes a reality among the status quo as this attitude alone has the power to influence the fields. When it emanates from someone well tuned to the Divine Nutrition Love channel, it has even more effect as alchemy can magnify both our positive and negative field aspects.

Summary: The most effective way to weave or influence a field is by our Presence and the energy we radiate which allows us to constantly be tuning the external fields around us to a beat that mirrors and nurtures us all. The above steps allow us to radiate more love and hence stimulate the release of more love in others.

Part B: Tuning the World to the field of Harmony, Peace and Love:

The next question might be, is the co-creation of the One People living in Harmony on One Planet – OPHOP – agenda so difficult? The answer is no it's not difficult. It is extremely simple. We just need the correct nutrition for our people on all levels of their being which the food of Gods will provide as creative nourishment for our bio-systems. Because of the frequencies we are applying with the basic field foundations – which are Divine Love, Divine Wisdom and Divine Power rays of the Violet Light grid – this outcome is assured because of the resonance of the underlying field. It is also assured because of the purity of hearts and intentions of the creators and manipulators and supporters of the field. In field reweaving, it is helpful to have attained at least Level 2 status in the Divine Nutrition Program and yet the reweaving of a field can help us also to achieve and then maintain this status.

So once we are all plugged in to the Divine Love field via our 3 cosmic cables and lifestyle habits, what comes next in the field weaving game?

Divine Nutrition Program Technique no. 33: Global Tuning

Step 6 – The next step is recognizing the need for us to **reach out**. We are not islands, we are all cells in the human field of the Divine, we are atoms of God, kept alive by the will and pleasure of this God, who we can recognize and love as It breathes us. The more we recognize It, and that we are all interconnected then the stronger we become and the more we ignore It the weaker and more dis-eased we become.

Step 7 – To reach out we first need to be aware of what is around us, to acknowledge what has gravitated or been pulled into our field via the law of resonance. So step 7 means taking the time out to **assess life** honestly – for our life mirrors it all, just as how we see and relate to the world is a mirror of our own consciousness.
- ❖ Is our personal world as we wish it?
- ❖ If it's not as we wish it to be, then why not?
- ❖ How do we fit in the planetary game?
- ❖ How do we see the world?
- ❖ What do we want for humanity?
- ❖ For our children, our future?

This step requires us to get clear so that the universal intelligence that surrounds us can support us more easily.

Step 8 – Next, we **identify the target**. For example, in answering my call to be in a sanctuary at the beach, I assigned the angels to find me the perfect place, giving them a detailed list of my requirements – it took them 2 weeks. So, obviously the need to relocate was to be imminent. Then having located and secured a new living field, I began field extensions and preparations.

While my target was the tuning of my new apartment to a supportive and nourishing grid, a global target, may be creating a love field for the people of the world to feed from, and both apply the same principles. So write a list of what you want for this world, how you would like to see it – for example, with the objective of there being more love and light in the world to stimulate the radiance of the DOW in all, and imagine every one being happy and kind and giving etc. The target of field reweaving may also be your work place, or a government centre etc. Once you have identified the target then think of how you wish for the new field to operate and the outcomes of this change.

For example: a) If the field is a government building, you may wish to feed the new field enough Violet Light so that the institution is more supportive of the Level 2 health and happiness, peace and prosperity for all agenda.

Or b) If the field is a family home environment, you may wish the outcome of the new field imprint to be one where everyone is more loving and supportive of each other and their choices in life, particularly of anyone who is choosing the Level 3 nourishment aspect of the DNP.

Step 9 – **Field Extensions**: The strongest field to extend a new grid from is your current base, and although I have become a citizen of the planet, my home base is powerfully plugged and tuned, and it maintains itself as a valuable imprinting tool in the global field. In other words, my home base radiates particular frequencies into the global field to imprint it and achieve certain things. My home base also radiates a particular frequency for the people who live within it so that they can be supported, loved and given all the strength and nutrition that they need to do what they need to be doing.

Divine Nutrition Program Technique no. 34: Field Extensions
Extending into a new field is quite a simple procedure.
❖ First, you visualize the current field of your home base.
❖ Next, having secured a strong visual image of your home, create a Bio-Shield of love and light around it, a ball or cocoon that is plugged into the Cosmic from which it will be fed.
❖ Visualize a beam of light going from the home base directly to the new home. In my case it was my beach apartment. For others the 'new' home; may be a love filled world, so visualize a beam of love extending from your current home base and wrapping itself around your community, then extending out around your country and then out around the planet. (more details re how to do this is in BB2) If you have not

done your own home yet, do not worry because you can also apply the following techniques to it before you extend the field out to a) an office or b) a beach apartment, as in my case, which is another family residence, or c) to a government building, or d) a hospital for healing, or e) an orphanage, or f) any place that you feel would benefit by having the 'love' field placed around it.

❖ So visualize your home base, visualize that it is connected to Source and cocooned in a ball of love and light and that this cocoon is being constantly filled with Violet Light.

Note: Your home base is a wonderful field to send out field extensions from as you feed it daily by your presence, however by plugging your home base bio-shield into its own power Source you can maintain a constant radiation level with or without you.

❖ Visualize the field of your home radiating out a beautiful beam of pink light. See this light wrapping itself around the new premises or the object of your intended field of reweaving and encase it with love; visualize a perfect concentric circle being manifested around this new field now via the pink light. Imagine this is like weaving string around a ball, and imagine that this first level of light is pure Divine Love that comes straight from the heart of the Mother Father God.

❖ Next visualize projecting a golden light beam from your home base, and wrapping this around the extended field of the place to be encased. Just imagine as you are doing this that this light beams naturally wraps itself horizontally, vertically, diagonally, like string around a ball, and that this is adding the next crucial layering field of gold white light which is imprinting this field with the Divine Wisdom frequency. Imagine all the wisdom, all the knowledge, all the intelligence, all the resolution, all the ingenuity, all the compassion, everything that is needed now for your home to operate, or this new biofield to operate, well enough to deliver the desired outcome.

❖ Just see these in your mind's eye, this pink field and this golden field now intermingling and firing up. For the next layer, visualize now a blue beam being projected around the new field being created. Imagine that as this blue energy wraps itself around vertically, diagonally, horizontally, that it is weaving through this extended field all the power, all the strength, all the courage, all the conviction, everything that is required to achieve the desired outcome. For example, you may wish to weave a field around the White House with the intention that the President and his government members can access enough love and wisdom to make decisions that benefit the whole planet.

❖ Next visualize in your mind's eye that this extended field is now pulsating with the pink, the gold and the blue light, which is all merging together and is now cocooned in a bubble of Violet Light

❖ Imagine this bubble has its own three streams of Divine Love, Wisdom and Power to hook this new field into its own never ending stream of power as in Chapter 7 meditation.

Basic Field Creation after the energy grids are in place:

Step 10 – **New Field Imprints**. Next you have to think more on what it is that you need in this field once you have the foundation grid in place. What are the attributes you wish the new field will radiate out into the world? What are the intended outcomes of your field reweaving work? Begin to feel the results of these outcomes.

Step 11 – **Emotionally imprinting the field**: Each field extension can be represented just on the inner planes, it is more effective when it is physically webbed into this realm and to do this effectively we need to imprint the new field or grid with emotion. For me, personally, with my new living space, my new field was to be a spiritual sanctuary where I could be tuned to the 'health and happiness, peace and prosperity with joy, and ease, and Grace' – Level 2 and 3 – agenda, and so after setting up the field gridlines, I placed this program with intention, with feelings and thought into the field. Using a yoga type sacred dance, I sang and danced my hopes and prayers and wishes with love flowing from my heart and emotionally imprinted this new field with these ingredients.

Unless we wish to experience what I call a dry space, all fields need specific not random emotional imprinting. I personally like to exist in fields that are warm and inviting where people feel comfortable and where they feel nourished, cared for, appreciated and loved – including myself.

The yogis among the Dimensional Biofield Technicians know that the true sanctuary lies within us, and that when we simply sit in silence and turn ourselves inward, we can access an island of deep and nurturing peace and the Shaman know the importance of imprinting our surrounding fields.

Emotional imprinting can lovingly stimulate the appropriate movement and rhythm into the new field to make the desired outcome a success. Loving stimulation is food for the soul of the bio-mechanism, it enables the bio-system to experience emotional sensitivity and thus provide another depth in life. Hence the importance of all the steps we have already discussed.

Step 12 – **Honoring bio-diversity and field inter-dependence**. Next, once a field is established and operational it can then be accessed as a support system for a new field, which is what we were discussing with having a home base and then sending out a field extension to encase another dwelling for example. This is basic grid networking and requires field merging and sharing. I prefer, actually, that the field status in this exchange be one that is positive and nurturing and inter-dependent as all fields operate better this way. *It is important that we recognize the uniqueness of another field and the gifts of bio-diversity and not seek to dominate and control another's field.* Again we cannot stress enough that the type of field techniques we are discussing are far more powerful and will bring amazing outcomes if used by people who are working with love and are in their integrity and have made the commitment to live impeccably. Also for all the fields to operate inter-dependently and harmoniously we need to assure that all field extensions are also plugged into their own limitless Violet Light Divine Source supply. A base (or home) field can have as many extensions as it wishes as long as it is generating enough power to maintain its own strength while it helps to support and feed the other fields. One way to ensure this is to also work with nature spirit bridges as in step 14.

Step 13 – Next, we need to use the DOW power, the **"DOW Match", and paradise code tools** of Receipt 2000➔ as outlined and elaborated on in the book *Four Body Fitness: Biofields and Bliss – Book 1.* (We also provided appropriate community and social field turning techniques in *Co-creating Paradise: Biofields and Bliss Book 2.* While it is not imperative that you read these books, it will help in your understanding of Dimensional Biofield dynamics.) Briefly, the "DOW Match" code allows us to operate DOW to DOW with all that we meet in all the fields. Sending everyone we connect with a beam of pure heart love and sincerely chanting "DOW Match" 3 times is enough to hook in on this level.

So once each field is woven and activated then the field can be set to extend itself as via bio-feedback looping it can then make connecting bridges. The driving force of this is the magnetization of different fields, via the energy pull of like minds; like attitudes; like lifestyle and sometimes the magnetism from past lives. There are many reasons for why fields magnetize apparently magically with little effort on our behalf. But generally it's just the mathematical codes of like attracting like.

Step 14 – A feature of the new field may also be the **invisibility tool**. This would be such as was required when I decided that I wished for my new sanctuary to be a very low-key presence in the social field surrounding it. I was wishing that my new field would merge peacefully into the existing environment rather than make my presence felt. However, at the same time, I also wished to imprint the surrounding field in a way that was harmonious to all. So, to do this I successfully used the **nature spirit bridge**.

Step 15 – **The nature spirits** represent a specific molecular combination of the Gods of the elements and so does the bio-system of man, which is re-arranged into a different pattern in comparison to the energy fields of the Devic worlds. For example, if your base field has a giant tree like mine does, we can communicate and connect into the spirit of the tree and set up a mutual support system. We can merge the field of the tree's bio-system with our own bio-system in a way that the tree can dominate and even obscure the beat of our own, and hence we can become invisible by tuning into, then being hidden in the more dominant field. Being invisible is sometimes very appropriate and opportune and is a great tool to use for travelers. I have long drawn nourishment during my travels from my nature spirit bridges even though I have been based in city fields, for the nature spirit bridges work with us on the etheric realms and can cross constraints of both time and matter.

Bridging and merging with a tree spirit for example means that we open our fields to be flooded with the Devic* energy of the tree spirit whose essence is so huge in comparison to our own physical form bio-system that we can easily disappear into the tree field and become nothing more than a small leaf on one of its branches. That way it is easy for us to be overlooked when other technicians are scanning the fields.

Part of the program of the new field may be that in any moment or situation that it is good for you to be seen, then the Nature spirit field can let you go and the fields will begin to pulse with their different frequencies and separate again. Invisibility also requires the ability to be the watcher and also one who can move through a field and leave little trace, as even watching a field changes it.

I used to think that invisibility actually meant dematerializing the molecular structure so that we were no longer able to be seen in someone's physical presence by their physical eyes, but I have since learnt that field control allows us to merge into and be over-shadowed in ways that, even though we can be close to somebody, they simply do not see, or sense, or feel or recognize our presence, even though we may be physically not invisible.

Before we move on I wish to elaborate a little on this by an example of an experience I had some years ago. I was once in an environment where not only was there no food nor water, but the air I was breathing was filled with toxic carbon dioxide fumes that had begun to overwhelm and poison my system. After a few days of this I managed to connect with a large tree and hooking in to its core via a beam of love from my heart and telepathic intelligence to intelligence connection, I asked the tree Deva for its support to draw out the poison from my system and to release its nurturing energy as oxygen back to flood into my fields. This occurred in a mutual exchange of energy that was so rewarding that the spirit of the tree then showed me in my inner eye of the support bridges and of dominant fields and invisibility. The shaman among you know that this type of communication and field sensitivity is common in the Theta field where we know and experience that all is one. Talking to all of nature with gentleness and love as if it is part of us just as we are part of God, opens the doorways to this field of possibility.
* A Deva is a member of an order of Angelic Beings who serve the elemental forces of nature. They hold the matrix for the Christ consciousness on Earth among the nature and human kingdoms.

Step 16 – Personally I feel that also **connecting our Bio-Shield to the Cosmic Nirvana Network** – C.N.N. – is imperative, as like our DOW, it truly provides us with an incorruptible network and focus on the common goal which is paradise for all. This is as simple as imaging this inner plane network and asking our DOW to connect us in a mutually beneficial way.

Step 17 – Additional Field Programming: Next, I feel that a field needs to be set to the **success and harmonious abundance program,** if that is required, so that resources such as wisdom, love, clarity, discipline, faith, finance, Earth and cosmic team power, plus streams of Grace and chi can merge together as a formula for success of basic field imprinting. As we have always stressed, fields need to be created and then programmed to achieve certain outcomes and the success and harmony program adds a layer of ease to life.

The above steps are just some of my personal fields of exploration as I have sought to strengthen my own nutrition channels. Beta world existence for a Theta field feeder can be tough when we submit ourselves to the random signals of each field. Hence the reweaving of the fields we spend time in can give us the support we need until the morphogenetic field becomes more supportive. For example today there are a myriad of support systems for vegetarians who are no longer seen as 'off beat', and in time the same will occur with the pranic Theta field feeders. In the meantime – as masters of reality creation – we can just adjust our internal and external energy flow to be a little more supportive.

More Questions & Answers

Before we complete this chapter, let's look at a few more commonly asked questions.

Q1: How can we deal with people or situations that have either dominating or overwhelming fields? How much power does one individual have over the many? And what has this to do with those who choose the path of pranic nourishment?

Answer Q1: As I have already shared, my personal agenda over the years has always been on providing social and political nourishment for the manifestation of inner and outer peace and many have been annoyed at this telling me not to mix spirituality with politics. To me spirituality is political as everything is spiritual, everything is God and nothing is separate from God. Every thought, word and action that we do is done as Gods in form, and yet somewhere along the way we disconnected from the food of the Gods and began believing in the maya of illusion and in the reality of duality and separation. When the food of Gods flows freely through our system, these realities can no longer be maintained for we 'know' better. Nor can we remain oblivious to the suffering of others for the role of a true leader – as an individual or as a nation – is to act always with an awareness and compassion that considers and fulfills our needs, and respects the greater good of all.

Consequently, I believe that the true service of the light eaters is to support the co-creation and manifestation of paradise via a mass ascension and a mass demonstration that we are all masters in form. Obviously, an individual can be restricted by how much we can access, hold and radiate of the Theta – Delta fields. For the one to have power over the many and to be able to rebalance or over-ride negative field imprinting by the less aware (i.e. political leaders whose motives are questionable), our bio-system needs to be strong and each cell of our body needs to be tuned to the powerful Violet Light spectrum which brings Its gift of transformation.

When applying Dimensional Biofield Science various factors come in to play when we look at field influences. For example, even a very pure and well refined being can only have a certain field of influence and radiance if they are existing in a predominantly Beta field world, as the strongest frequencies always overwhelm the weaker.

However, the Delta and Theta waves in themselves have a far greater range of positive influence than the Beta – Alpha field. When we are dealing one on one, or when we have one Theta – Delta person swimming in a sea of thousands of Beta – Alpha people, then our signals can be too easily absorbed by the hunger of the greater field. Hence to have any sustainable long term influence and be effective, we need to be as pure and powerful as we can be and even then, our field of influence, although sustainable, is restricted in its range.

Even a being such as the Christ or the Buddha, if in the flesh today, would find their field of influence restricted by the 6 billion plus predominantly Beta – Alpha beings in this world. However, when working with Theta – Delta frequencies, one plus one equals so much more than just two, so the more who choose to tune to the Theta – Delta field and radiate the Violet Light spectrum, the sooner the Beta – Alpha field of mass consciousness can be flooded and imprinted and nourished on all levels – cellular and soul – and transformed. This is just a science of the fields and when I am fed by the food of Gods and you are fed by the food of Gods and another joins us and so on, then our field of influences increases and all are nourished in this world; for the power of one who is well connected is greater than the power of many who are weak in their connection.

Hence, the power of one is in the desire to personally maximize our intake and efficiently utilize our intake, of chi, by living an impeccable lifestyle that keeps our brain wave patterns tuned to the Theta – Delta field. When we do this we become not just fit on all levels but we also become a far more effective and empathetic human being.

The power of many comes when individuals who choose to be tuned like this gather together with a common vision that is beneficial for all. This also requires each individual to have the courage to alter any model of reality they hold that is not beneficial for all. A common vision, a benevolent model of reality, a desire to co-create communities that work for the good of all, plus access to and utilization of the Violet Light spectrum can only bring a result of global peace and harmony. However as is commonly understood by all – in order to refine a world – we first need to refine an individual. Inaction is still an action as we all imprint the fields.

Question 2: So you are suggesting that through using the various tools in this book, one individual can access enough power to redirect the course of history and transform the world?

Answer Q2:   As naïve as it may sound – yes. I keep hearing the words of the Christ saying that everything I have done you can do and more, that I and my Father are one and I believe them. I believe them because I have researched enough of quantum science and experienced enough of Dimensional Biofield Science and meditated enough to know this to be true. I choose to believe that we are Gods in form, here to flex our creative muscles and that we are now being given the opportunity to co-create a world that we can be proud of – this is the greatest gift of the food of Gods as, via DOW power, It gives us the fuel to do this.

The global and personal rewards of Theta – Delta field feeding are revolutionary and when fully understood and applied will bring a huge economic, social and environmental transformation – one that perhaps our current world is not yet ready for. Thankfully, there are many steps required before this can come into being and each step will implement a gradual transformation without creating too much chaos. The first of course will be the redistribution of our world's resources to address the issues discussed in *The Madonna Frequency Planetary Peace Program* Biofields and Bliss book 3. This will be followed by global vegetarianism.

Global enlightenment is a journey about the advancement of human consciousness as a mass, and as mentioned, this can now be measured by the Schumann resonance, which currently is measured at 7.4 hertz. This demonstrates that the Earth itself, Gaia, as a living energy field is already being held in the border of the Alpha – Theta zone. Now we just require human consciousness to match, and maintain, the consciousness of the Earth so that the transition can be complete. This explains the birth of spirituality on our plane with people now being driven by a deep desire to know more and to have a real spiritual experience and connection with their Divine Source. We are all so hungry because the spiritual 'come to dinner' gong has sounded and our Divine appetites are seeking satiation.

There are two more exercises that I would like to gift to you and our world.

Field Re-Setting – Divine Nutrition Program Technique no. 35

Exercise: Checking our personal radiance levels.

❖ Look in the mirror, where is your shine?
❖ How bright with the spark of life and passion does your DOW's light radiate from your eyes?
❖ How radiant, how fulfilled, how gracious, how loving do you feel? *Remember that by our lifestyle we can increase or decrease the level of love that we experience through life.*
❖ If your light is not shining,
❖ If your heart is not singing,
❖ Then have the courage to apply the tools in Chapter 6.

Personally I want to be a player in the fields of a 33 level Theta – Delta world as it is a field where I feel completely nourished. In the 7 level Beta field world, I can slide into being a victim as it is tough and our choices are much too limited as I don't have the perception that I need to recognize it all and see the world and live in the world in a way that feeds me and so I am always hungry for more.

This constant hunger inspires an initiate to begin the journey through the fields and to make adjustments along the way – the fields respond, you respond, I respond and things change. 6 billion plus 'field fiddlers' – we're all doing it anyway, yet a change of focus, a clear desire, a common goal, a few good tuning tools and a different outcome is assured.

I love the fact that my work is focused on working on the foundation grids, for in order for us to be a true union of nations on Earth, we need to have a level playing field. It is hard for intelligent discussion to gain respectful support when so many are still starving and when the basic rights that would provide a healthy existence for all of our people are still being ignored.

Some people complain if I discuss such things and say I'm being too political yet to me everything is spiritual and our true political agendas need to shift from war to eliminating all of our hungers, for only then will we find ourselves in peace. How we conduct ourselves en mass is symbolic of the state of our emotional, mental and spiritual evolution and our physical progress we can see for our selves – just as our local and current world affairs reveal how we are doing as a species. And yet it is easy to look back in retrospect and judge ourselves and chastise and criticize and sometimes we do this so that we can learn and then move on but to keep repeating patterns that don't manifest lasting and positive change is simply a waste of our time. We need to do much more.

When we remerge with our DOW we enlist a source of purity and power that will transform us all, deeply, from the inside out – morally, politically, compassionately and lastingly.

I recently realized that there was one more act that I could do that would guarantee an immediate change in my future. It is so simple that it's easy to overlook but let's do it anyway.

Field Re-Setting – Divine Nutrition Program Technique no. 36

Exercise: Change our future by changing how we see the past.

- ❖ Look back over your life and look at the gifts that you've been given. Look at every major imprinting, life changing situation and look at what you learned, what it taught you – the pain of suffering or the joy.
- ❖ What were the moments that delivered the greatest understanding, the clarity or insight that you needed?
- ❖ What were the events that triggered that feeling of "Everything is right with my world"?
- ❖ When did you first feel ecstasy? Or see a wave of Grace?
- ❖ What about those moments where everything just flowed, in a harmony and a rhythm and a graciousness of its own?
- ❖ Then give thanks to it all, bless the fields of life for coming together to allow you to play and to learn. Own it all, savior it all, pat yourself on the back with a "well done, I've learnt so much – this is who I am and its OK" kind of way.
- ❖ Make the commitment of: "From this point on I am the best I am."
- ❖ Then program with sincerity: "DOW, run my life, tune my bio-system through the Beta – Alpha – Theta and Delta fields so that I experience personal paradise and manifest and witness health and happiness and peace and prosperity for all, by all."
- ❖ Then support this by knowing and loving your DOW.
- ❖ Reclaim your DOW for Its 'God'ness, claim It for Its position on the Throne, for the knowing that it has a direct line to the very heart of the Divine Mother.
- ❖ Do the love breath meditation enough to prove that your heart is a mirror of Hers as you feel Her love pulse throughout all the fields.
- ❖ Then hold the intention that we may all ride through life on a wave of Grace, supported by joy and laughter. And lastly – if you look for God in all as you walk through this life then God will be revealed.

Chapter 12

The Greatest Gift

Over the past 33 years of my conscious exploration of the Alpha – Theta – Delta fields, I have been gifted with many things. Born with an immense hunger I could never settle for life in a Beta field world as I always knew that there was so much more to experience and explore. Each of us is born with a seed of Divine growth in our field, a seed of potential that when nurtured into blossoming will open the doors to our paradise-based soul. These seeds germinate by time spent in all the fields – the Beta field provides the soil, the Alpha field the water, the Theta field the sun and the Delta field provides the love to flower and then reveal the sense and beauty of it all. In it we see with inner eyes and hear with inner ears and feel with senses that have taken lifetimes to refine; and with our refinement comes a knowing that words can not define.

Yes it's true that we can flood our bio-system with so much food from the God within that all of our questions disappear. To walk this Earth and no longer be seeking is a miracle in itself for it allows us to appreciate the moment that is now.

Yes it's true that the God within can flood our bio-system with so much joy and so much love and so much light that we are fed on the deepest levels of our being and freed from any need.

Yes it's true that when we bathe in the Theta – Delta fields we are given such insights to the mechanics and wonders of creation that we are left permanently in awe, touched in a way that is unexplainable, that makes us lose our words as we recognize the perfection of it all.

Yes it's true that we can be with Holy beings of great light and wisdom and love who walk with us through the planes of paradise in the state of samadhi and bliss. And yes it's true that there dwells within us a Holy being that we can call the Divine One Within, a being of freedom who knows no bounds and whose greatest joy is to breathe us and love us and nurture us as we seek to wake and remember who we are.

Yes it's true that as we remember who we are, one of the gifts our DOW gives us is the illumined experience of ascension, an experience of being filled with light and an indelible knowing of the 'Is-ness' of it all, and the joy of having been in the Presence of the Supreme Splendor and always feeling It in the now. In this state of being, we see everything from a divinely inspired perspective and hence everything makes sense – everything has a rhythm and a reason for being and all is perfect as it is. In this state of awareness we can understand the bigger picture and see all life as cycles in time, unfolding naturally, driven by the Divine DNA that dictates the evolutionary nature of life.

Yet the experience of ascension is not the greatest gift of being fed by the light of the food of the Gods, for ascension is a never ending experience, it is a journey not a destination for our experiences within the ascended Delta field are only limited by our capacity to receive and handle the frequencies of our own DOW's radiation. Even the Christ and Buddha and Mohammed continue to become more illumined as they journey through the fields, loving and being fed in turn by the love we give in gratitude to their presence.

Other gifts of being fed by the food of the Gods are the revelations and insights that we gain from the Theta – Delta field of consciousness where many have received explicit information on how to bring our planet back into a more enlightened way of being.

Yes it's true that there is an opportunity for Earth to enter into a millennium of great peace and to bring this into being many metaphysicians are being instructed to not just bridge Heaven and Earth, but to also flood the Beta – Alpha fields with the virtues of the Theta – Delta fields. Other individuals who have discovered and explored the benefits of Theta – Delta zones are Shaman many of whom are guided to act as bridges between the worlds. This means allowing our bio-systems to operate as Divine transmission stations, to hold and radiate the Violet Light and in doing so, be transformed as well.

Yes it is true that people nourished purely by the Violet Light gain access to amazing levels of both creativity and stamina making us push, and stretch, and grow, and expand, and move forward in ways that defy imagination. It's as we become free of illusions of grandeur and are filled with a knowing that things are simultaneously perfect yet can also be tuned in a slightly different way to deliver outcomes that are actually good for us all. These are insights that have fed many for so long.

Perhaps the only point of creation of life on Earth at this time is the experience that comes when we develop our more compassionate levels of emotional sensitivity, for the Divine Mother Love spectrum provides an amazing range of experiences for us to be nurtured by. And yet we know that it is no longer enough to nurture just ourselves for we have entered into a cycle of time where our presence must now nurture others. To do less is to deny the sacred nature of our soul and to do less will keep us always hungry.

It is good to end this book as we have begun, which is with the acceptance and knowing that *the greatest gift of the food of Gods lies in the nurturing field of Its love.*

Omraam Mikhaël Aïvanhov once said: "Wisdom consists in understanding that love is more important than anything else…. Intelligence that fails to grasp the fact that love must be given priority, that everything must be for love, with love and because of love, is not really intelligence at all … love is the heart of everything and if they (*mankind*) make it the one motive power behind every aspect of their lives, the intense heat of their love will be transformed into dazzling light and their intelligence will be illuminated. Illumination can only come from love."

In Dimensional Biofield Science everything is temporary, transient, supported by fields of energy that constantly merge and dance and pulse with their own rhythm to form worlds. And the foundation of the grid that supports it all, that binds it all together, is Love. So to many the greatest gift of our journey through the fields is to discover and feel and truly know the depth and range of this Love for we are born to feed from the Divine Nutrition channel. To know of, yet ignore, Its Presence is like living with a pre-programmed time bomb as DOW power is a love seeking missile looking for recognition. The key to Its magical kingdom is our purity of heart and to the pure of heart all the kingdoms are given.

Love can never be an intellectual affair yet nor is it enough to feed our world the nutrition that it needs. To do this we will need love's partners – wisdom and compassion which are gifts that lay as dormant seeds within the heart of every being, ready to sprout with our return to the field of Love. And the science of love is in the BEing it.

The Deification of our DOW:

For weeks I have sat on my favorite beach reflecting on the "Food of the Gods" waiting for the final point of this book to be revealed. The symbolic meaning has not been lost on me with the fact that I had to return to my base in the city to receive the final download and that the point of it all would come as I sat on the couch with my well loved husband. My time in my beach ashram has strengthened me, given me reflection time and some retuning pain. Yet a mega dose of Surya yoga has recharged my fields and allowed more light into the deeper, darker spaces of my whole, for I had begun to feel the weight of the constant challenging of the status quo which had often seemed like being in the 'Mohammed Ali' boxing ring of life.

For weeks I had tried to write this final chapter as personally I feel that we need to go beyond such statements as "all we need is love" and "let us act with wisdom and compassion when we deal with one another in life". I don't think that mouthing platitudes is a grounded enough reality. We need more. We need instructions, recipes, quick easier fixes (yes they do exist) and a lot of faith and trust. We also need inspiration and a deeper level of nourishment for our DOW to expand and grow. All the tools, thoughts, programs, discussions and questions in this book are sources of food that are designed to deliver one particular outcome – the deification of our own DOW.

And to the world the DOW, as it unites us, will bring a lasting peace.

I think the world has stated clearly that we are ready for a different beat, for war and violence have fed our desire for change. Many ask now: What does it take to tune a field to lasting harmony and peace? What does it take to entice a human heart back to the fields of kindness and compassion? What are we really hungry for and where does true food come from?

The teachings of Buddha and Mohammed and the Christ and all the Holy Beings are all woven together with common threads of truth for we are in fact all One. The more refined we become the easier it is to understand the essence of them all yet we too are equipped to be Masters and the choice to demonstrate this is ours.

So much of what the Holy Ones have shared with our world has great appeal to my inner being.

Is it naïve to trust in human nature so much, or to expect and know, that we will and can choose to support the greatest good? Is it too arrogant to say we are born in the image of the Divine and that while we have spent lifetimes deifying all of the messengers and the Gods, that we have somehow not seen the greatest revelation in our world and that is to witness and be fed by the blossoming of our own DOW?

If we are to deify anybody – Gods, Gurus, Presidents or Saints – let it be because we recognize within them all a light, a love and a wisdom, plus a kind and compassionate heart. Let us love them by their deeds and we will unmistakably see when we look into their eyes, how lit up they are – and yet we can only recognize in another that which is in ourselves for the pure of heart can always be recognized by their inner light.

Yes it's true that a little Bhakti yoga would go a long way in our world and that devotion to our DOW is easy when we experience Its gifts. Deification is the act of making something Godly. Deification of our DOW means our alignment with the Solar Logos, which is the light behind all life and DOW devotion increases the radiation levels of Divine Mother Love through the grids allowing the fields to nourish us all and fulfill our hunger for love and unification. And when we have deified the DOW in us then we will naturally deify the DOW in others which will bring health and happiness and peace and prosperity to everyone in our world.

Only we can fulfill our hungers and yet the nourishment is there – wanting it is a personal choice, finding it is easy and experiencing it is a joy.

My personal journey through the fields continues like a dance where I continually learn new steps, for the fields of life are constantly changing as we expand into more refined levels of the game that we call life. All of it goes on in cycles and through it all we are constantly reborn.

As I sit with my father and hold his cold thin hand I see the light in his deep blue eyes and how his skin is becoming more luminous as he surrenders his hold on his life. Each day has become so precious for us as we know there will be so few, yet I also know that when he passes we can call each other through the gridlines of love that will always connect our hearts.

Namaste to you all – Jasmuheen

I dedicate this book to the light that I see shining in my Heavenly Father's eyes.

And to my father Arnie who passed from this Earth in June 2003
and to my first grandchild who will enter it in April 2004.

Personal Calibration and Testing methods for safely fulfilling the freedom agenda:

Post-script with Jasmuheen – January 2005

In 2002 a book called *Power vs. Force* was released and read with great interest. In it the author David Hawkins, a psychiatrist and spiritual teacher, shared his research findings on a simple method to calibrate levels of human consciousness and the various spiritual paths that many of us undertake plus much more. An in-depth twenty-year study using the applied science of behavioral kinesiology, I highly recommend this book.

Excited by the possibilities that his calibration system offered as far as a way of checking our freedom models, I began to apply it during my October/November 2004 tour. Quickly recognizing that we can use this system as a base to move into levels perhaps unexplored by David Hawkins, during this tour I took advantage of testing and confirming my findings with hundreds of special test subjects from four different countries – France, Italy, Germany and Switzerland.

In order to understand what I'm about to share in this post-script, it is important for you to read and understand what David Hawkins is talking about in his *Power vs. Force* book, nonetheless I will provide a brief synopsis here so that its relevance to our own findings is a little easier to understand.

Hawkins sees the potential of kinesiology as "the 'wormhole' between two universes – the physical, and the mind and spirit – an interface between dimensions ... a tool to recover that lost connection with the higher reality and demonstrate it for all to see".

Founded by Dr George Goodheart and given wider application by Dr John Diamond, Behavioral Kinesiology is the well established science of muscle testing the body where a positive stimulus provokes a strong muscle response while a negative stimulus provokes a weak response.

Using Diamond's system, Hawkins developed "a calibrated scale of consciousness, in which the log of whole numbers from 1 to 1,000 determines the degree of power of all possible levels of human awareness." In this model 200 represents emotions of positive stimulus where muscle response remains strong and below 200 is where muscle response weakens as emotions anger, fear, guilt or shame, begin to influence the body.

200 is the energy of truth and integrity, 310 is the calibration for hope and optimism, 400 is the energy of reason and wisdom, 500 is the energy of love, 540 of joy, 600 is perfect peace and bliss and 700 to 1000 represents even higher levels of enlightenment.

Hawkins shares: "The individual human mind is like a computer terminal connected to a giant database. The database is human consciousness itself, of which our own cognizance is merely an individual expression, but with its roots in the common consciousness of all mankind. This database is the realm of genius; because to be human is to participate in the database, everyone, by virtue of his birth, has access to genius. The unlimited information contained in the database has now been shown to be readily available to anyone in a few seconds, at any time in any place. This is indeed an astonishing discovery, bearing the power to change lives, both individually and collectively, to a degree never yet anticipated.

"The database transcends time, space, and all limitations of individual consciousness. This distinguishes it as a unique tool for future research, and opens as yet undreamed-of areas for possible investigation." He is of course talking about accessing the universal field of intelligence which is within and around us all.

Applying the Kinesiology principle and test results re the freedom agenda:

When I start to download a book from universal mind, information that is needed to be incorporated is always given to me, particularly when the research is beneficial to my findings. Consequently I experienced great joy when I read David Hawkins's work as I realized that I was finally able to provide a safety check for the freedom model, particularly for someone who tests yes as per the questions asked meditation 4 in Chapter 16.

For example, among the hundreds of people that we tested in the countries mentioned:

- ♥ 80% tested yes that it is part of their blueprint to create a disease free life.
- ♥ 70% tested yes that it was part of their blueprint to learn how to be free from taking nutrition through food and access it through feeding from the divine nourishment flow within.
- ♥ 18% tested yes for setting up the reality of being free from the need for fluid, this lifetime, by again allowing that divinely nutritional source of prana within them to hydrate their body quite perfectly without the need for external fluids.
- ♥ 40% tested yes that it was part of their pre-agreed service blueprint to demonstrate physical immortality;
- ♥ 15% tested yes for pre-agreeing to learn, and demonstrate, the art of dematerialization and rematerialization and
- ♥ 70% tested yes for developing the ability to stop the ageing process.

As you can see from these figures the type of people that are attracted to the freedom agenda and the workshops that I do are a very particular group of a very specific calibration. Hence having a model that can ascertain our calibration level before we enter into the release of these types of limitation adds a very beneficial layer.

What I would like to offer therefore is the use of David Hawkins work as one layer, in a three layer testing system, some of which we have already touched on previously in the sacred support systems chapter.

A THREE LEVEL CONFIRMATION SYSTEM

This three layer testing system is outlined as followed:

1) DOW – Divine One Within – our inner voice. This must always be our first method of testing in that it is the only reliable source of confirmation that is completely incorruptible. This requires us to establish a clear line of communication between ourselves and our divine nature – whether we call this our DOW, Monad or Atman or whatever. This level of communication comes via our sixth and seventh senses of intuition and knowing and needs to be, in my opinion,

our first barometer of guidance in everything that we do in life; particularly in accessing and manifesting our pre-agreements. Our DOW is the only thing that all humanity has in common, It is pure, It gives us life, It breathes us, loves us and guides us to evolve into our perfection. Learning to listen to It and trust Its guidance is a basic part of self mastery and self knowledge.

2)   The second level of testing is to use the art of kinesiology to gain information confirmation using muscle responses in the body. Kinesiology, as many trained in this field know, has its limitations because it depends on how it is used and how strongly people's muscles test. It also depends on the calibration purity of the one being tested, the one doing the testing and the questions being asked. Reading David's book on this subject will provide a deeper understanding. I also recommend that when we use kinesiology that we ask the Divine One Within to confirm data, using the muscle testing system through the body, rather than asking the body's consciousness itself.

3)   The third level of testing that is a wonderful support system for us as we journey through the freedom agenda, is to ask to receive clear confirmation from the universal field of intelligence which is all around us. This goes back to the story of people who, looking for answers, walk into a book shop, find that a book falls off the top shelf and hits them on the head, then spirals around and falls at their feet, open, the right way up and when they pick this book up, there is the answer to the very question that they had been thinking about. This is one way that the universal field of intelligence responds to our telepathic thought patterns when we have a strong desire for further knowledge, particularly when the knowledge that we are seeking is supporting our own evolutionary path in a positive way and is also beneficial for the world.

So these three levels of testing 1) accessing and listening to the divine voice within then 2) confirming its guidance or your query through muscle testing with kinesiology and c) asking for further confirmation from the universal field; these are three wonderful ways to provide a very clear system of guidance and a safety mechanism for human beings who are ready, willing, able and who are preprogrammed to display 'freedom from human limitation' to the degrees that we have discussed in this book.

When people go through the testing program in Chapter 16 to ascertain their pre-agreements, and if they receive a clear yes, then they will find that the universe will provide them with all the support that they need to fulfill this. There are many different ways to move into this agenda and setting the intention that we fill our preagreed agendas with joy and ease and Grace, allows the universal field to deliver whatever information and tools that we need to do this. Also as time goes by and the calibration of the mass morphonogenic field changes, then the way to attain and demonstrate these freedoms will become easier.

We have often had people receive an answer of 'no' during the meditation even though their own inner feeling was that these freedoms were something that they would like to embrace. Receiving a 'no' from the testing mechanism simply means that it is not part of your 'preprogrammed' blueprint, however as a being of free-will you may choose to exhibit these freedoms anyway as a side issue along with your main service agenda.

We also had people test the following using the David Hawkins *Power vs. Force* system, and I recommend that you may like to look at these yourself in more detail. These are:

a) The testing of your birth calibration.
b) The testing of your current calibration.
c) The testing of your home field calibration – which will allow you to see how supportive your home field environment is for you to move into these agendas.
d) The testing of your work field calibration.
e) The testing of your current biological age plus
f) the testing of the biological age your body is happy to support you into demonstrating.

From these tests we also found some interesting things. Firstly it is imperative that if someone tests 'yes' for a fluid free agenda then we can only recommend that they let go of fluid when the bio-systems calibration can support this in health and safety.

By first checking if it is in your blueprint and then checking, after intensive preparation using the methods discussed in *The Food of Gods* and *The Law of Love* books, when/if the bio-system is ready and able to sustain this, we then have a safe system to advise us. To attempt to do this without the support of the right calibration is only asking for potential physical trouble.

Other points to note regarding testing calibration levels:
Calibration limits: While David Hawkins shared in his book that most people in general society rarely move more than 5 calibration points per lifetime, this is not true for the spiritual student who lives a lifestyle that allows them to download and radiate more of their Divine essence or their DOW power; for this essence is able to create instant change provided that our bio-system can handle it.

Another anomaly with David Hawkins system is a process that I call weaving.

Field Weaving: This relates to a discovery I made when I wanted to test my youngest daughter's calibration. The first thing I did was to check with her own divine force if it was okay for me to be given this data to which I quickly received a 'yes'. However when testing her calibration using muscle testing on my body I kept getting some very strange readings which intuitively I felt could not be right. Switching to Erik's body, who was testing with me, we realized that because I had an emotional attachment to her, sometimes the readings can be incorrect, but more than that we also realized that because I have been consciously weaving my energy through her energy fields to support her these last few years, by the conscious weaving of my field with hers, then her calibration was changing, because of how I calibrate, and so we had to look at the question differently. Using Erik's body to check, we procured a truer reading which we then confirmed using additional methodology.

Interestingly enough the calibration was still quite high even though at this time she does no meditation or yoga or the practices that I recommend in *The Food of Gods* book, however what this particular being does have is an incredibly open, loving, caring and compassionate heart. She is someone who has a huge network of friends and is always there for others. This in itself will bring a human being into wonderful calibration levels and can sometimes compensate for a lifestyle that maybe not as supportive of the physical bio-system as it could be.

The process of weaving is also very interesting because it can allow conscious access to other beings of great light and great love. For example, when we connect strongly through the doorways of love and devotion, to Mother Mary or to any of the other Holy Ones, that opens up an energetic path through our will and intention, for us to connect to their energy field, which then can weave back through into ours as we are all one and connected.

The recognition of this type of connection and possibility allows the weaving to begin and also is a way of fine tuning our calibration and strengthening it quite quickly. For people who do play with these realities, who are not living the sort of metaphysical lifestyle that we recommend in our previous manuals, then David Hawkins sharing that most people will only move 5 points in their calibration per lifetime is truth.

Personal Calibration Requirements for the Law of Love Freedom Agenda:

When originally tested, via two test subjects using kinesiology and David Hawkins system, and confirming this via an additional two sources using the pendulum and inner plane Divine One Within confirmation, thus using a triple blind test with metaphysical tools – we originally found the following regarding the freedom models. These calibrations were then confirmed by approximately 500 test subjects and this is what we have noted:

- ♥ In order to establish a disease free existence where there is no physical, emotional, mental and spiritual disease a human bio-system needs a personal calibration of 635.
- ♥ The creation of an ageing free system where the ageing process is literally stopped a human bio-system needs a minimum calibration of 637, which is interesting as this is very close to the calibration of a disease free existence.
- ♥ In order to safely exist on purely a pranic flow for nourishment and no longer need to take physical food a human bio-system needs to calibrate at 668.
- ♥ In order to safely exist with the fluid free existence a human bio-system needs to calibrate at 777.
- ♥ The calibration for physical immortality for a human bio-system is 909
- ♥ and the calibration for successful dematerialization and rematerialization is 1367.
- ♥ I then asked for the calibration of classic miracles; to really witness the flow of Grace in such a powerful way, that the majority of people would deem it a miracle, the field around it needs to calibrate at around 1450.

For the last two calibrations, which are over Hawkins's 0-1000 scale, these are possible due to field weaving and coming into the consciousness of pure Oneness.

I do recognize in these results that we have been given, that as the general morphonogenic field of the mass of humanity changes, then the hundredth monkey system kicks in to change these calibration levels. According to Hawkins, while 78% of people calibrate at less than 200, mass consciousness as a whole registers at 207 due the process of entrainment where 22% of people of higher calibration are dominating the field enough to shift it into the level of truth and integrity en mass.

Another thing that we asked the bio-systems of the groups was to ask the body consciousness at what weight, in kilograms, that their body would stabilize at, once they entered in the food free and then later the fluid free existence. I felt that by asking the body consciousness this question this is another wonderful way to affirm our readiness. For example, a few years ago when I checked where my body weight would stabilize at with a fluid free existence I was told 45kgs. For me intellectually and emotionally I rejected this simply because I felt that it was not good for me to look so skeletal, and perhaps the health that I was seeking would not be maintainable, and so I held off on my decision to go onto a fluid free existence. When testing this same question this year, I was told that my body can now sustain a fluid free existence at 51kgs because my calibration has changed over the last few years. This is a lot more acceptable for me and therefore makes the movement into this level of freedom far more attractive.

Hence if you get a confirmation from your body of a weight that you feel is unacceptable to you then the advice is to wait and increase your personal calibration levels before going into this additional level of freedom.

The quickest way, as we all know, to increase calibration levels is simply to love a lot in life, for love is one of the most powerful feeding mechanisms that we have to match our calibration levels with our DOW because the divine essence is a being of pure and limitless love.

As we mentioned in earlier chapters, setting the home field calibration and refining it, is something that is easily done through the art of Feng Shui, and also through how life is conducted within the home field. It is important to have a field calibration in your home of a minimum of 200 which is, as David Hawkins has shared, the beginning levels of operating in truth and integrity. The higher the home field calibration then obviously the more supportive the environment is for you to move into and maintain these levels of the freedom agenda.

When Hawkins book was first published in 1995, his research shared that only 4% of the world's population calibrated at over 500, while in 2004 it is now 6%; and in 1995 only 1 in 10 million calibrated at over 600. Nonetheless a person calibrating at 300 has the enough DOW power radiation to energetically influence 90,000 people; at a calibration of 700 we can counterbalance the energy of 700 million. These figures confirm that if all we do is refine our personal calibration levels to radiate maximum DOW power, this in itself is a valuable service, for not only does it deliver us naturally into the freedom agenda but it will also allow our presence here to positively influence the world.   ♥ Namaste – Jasmuheen

THE BLISS OF BIGU & much more …
September 2014 Update:

It is interesting to see how things can sink in and stick to us if they are meant to … every day I keep hearing the words "It's better with Bigu" or BIGU is best - words spoken by Qigong Master Tian Ying who I first met at the end of 2013 and then again this year when I worked with her at the Rainbow Spirit Festival then again in Berlin and during our German Retreat allowed us to share with each other and others, the unique blend of our personal research and also watch the way that we both present this. Feeling her BIGU transmission, the programming songs she uses during this, then talking to those who experienced this afterwards was also very enlightening.

While I know that meditation and the lifestyle we encourage people to live to stay in the zones of health, happiness and harmony, can deliver so many insights and rewards, Tian Ying loves to state that being in the state of Bigu is better, at least for her. After receiving a BIGU transmission in the early 1990's from a qigong master in China, she was healed from a long term disease and has gone from strength to strength. As some know the first recorded case of someone entering into the Bi Gu Fu Chi state was around 6,000 years ago so it was nice to tap into this ancient lineage.

According to the Tiangong website, "Bi Gu is a millennia-old Chinese method which allows a change of diet, so that one will be able to live wholly or partly on cosmic energy and to correspondingly renounce earthly food. Bi Gu can be practiced phase wise as well as continuously. Bi Gu Fu Qi, which is the full term, literally translated means: "Renunciation of grain, except for Qi."

"In Chinese culture, Bi Gu Qi Gong has been practiced for thousands of years. Several schools have developed special Qi Gong practices to achieve this capability. Nevertheless, in today's China there are only a very few people living in the state of Bi Gu. The main reason is that the ability to cosmic diet was traditionally very difficult to achieve. Often it took several decades of intensive practice. The phenomenon Bi Gu is also known under different terms outside China. The Indian yogi are practicing prana nourishment, in the Western spiritual world it is often spoken of as light-nourishment and within the Western Christian traditions, there have been people who have lived for years without any food and drink.

"Bi Gu in Tian Gong - In the 1980s Tian Gong's founder Letian Shi Fu has begun to pass the Bi Gu information down to his students on using a special energy transmission - with surprising results. The practitioners have not only experienced a very high degree of Bi Gu, but simultaneously Bi Gu has also accelerated the physical healing processes as well as the development of mental abilities such as telepathy, clairvoyance, and energy breathing. This was also the case with Tian Gong Master Tianying, one of Letian's first students and founder of the Tian Gong Institute in Berlin. She has been cured from her severe liver disease by Bi Gu and within the subsequent period, she developed a series of remarkable Qi Gong skills. Since December 1993, she lives in the state of Bi Gu."

So, is life better with or in the Bi Gu state of awareness and experience?

Firstly, how would people know unless they have experienced the difference? As I answer emails and look at Google alerts that inform me when people have added their remarks to some of our research data on YouTube, this makes an interesting question for we are all so quick to dismiss or judge as impossible things we do not understand or have had no exposure to.

Education into other fields of possibility can require endless patience at times yet thankfully we know that new information cannot be absorbed unless people are ready and open! For example a friend of mine has been recently diagnosed with bone cancer, but only loves and listens to allopathic medicine and so she dismisses all non-allopathic practices as not for her. Other friends of mine are the opposite and so they only adhere to non-allopathic treatments for disease, dismissing all allopathic treatments as incomplete. This is something I have witnessed time and time again, how being so limiting in our understanding can create such discomfort for so many in life and how their lives could have been so different if they had been a little more open to other methodologies. What about a combination of both where this is applicable? What about investigating and then utilizing whatever methodology works to allow us to enjoy freedom of disease on all levels?

The ancient qigong masters know that when we increase our chi or life force we get healthier and also happier and need to take less from planetary resources, all of which is beneficial for us and our world. After years of research we also know that our day to day lifestyle is the key to health and happiness but we must be open to change if and when required. And sometimes all we can change is our attitude for things are always unfolding for so many reasons, many of which we cannot see or fathom until much later.

So ... Is being in the state of Bi Gu Fu Chi better? I think that this is a fact that is becoming impossible to deny by those who have experienced the difference between being nourished directly from Source and having to go through the physical food systems for sustenance but then when our Essence is strong in Presence within us there are undeniably many benefits for us all!

In 2006, I began to film the documentary *In the Beginning There Was Light* with Austrian film critic P.A. Straubinger. Six years in the making, Peter filmed over 200 hours of footage as he interviewed countless of people about their experiences of being able to be physically nourished by prana. For me it was wonderful to be able to share about these ones with him during this interview, as in 1993, when I underwent this initiation there were no books of reference and virtually no one that was in the public eye who did this and who was also involved in positive global education about this phenomena. To arrive in 2006 and be able to talk of all the others I had discovered who were now also active was wonderful!

Released at the Cannes film festival in 2010, the movie invites a skeptical viewer to understand a little more regarding the power of our mind, using the examples of people living on prana as a physical body nourishment source and it has been instrumental in educating many about this field of possibility.

So, we hope you enjoy this new 2014 version of this book and all that it contains; as what we share here has many benefits on health, hunger and environmental levels in our world. It is also part of human evolution but let's look at this from another perspective as we provide a quick summary and update and a look at the various categories that people are now moving through and into quite naturally all around our world as consciousness continues to blossom upon her.

OUR ESSENCE AS A SOURCE OF COSMIC MICRO-FOOD
Excerpt from *BEing Essence*

As we move into a higher dimension of expression, which is a result of BEing more imbued with our Essence, we find that It can also provide us with a type of physical body nourishment that I have come to call *Cosmic Micro-food*.

Due to the beneficial effects that our research has found, that this can have on both our health and our environment, we will include some of the basics of this here on a bigger picture level.

To me, one of the most fulfilling journeys a soul can make while anchored in the plane of duality, is awareness of and full reconnection and perfect union with their I AM Essence.

Yet unity consciousness allows us to feel-sense that Essence as being everywhere, the very fabric of creation, the baseline frequency of life.

Apart from being able to nourish us physically via its cosmic micro-food flow, it also aligns us to a rhythm of such peace and contentment, that we find ourselves forever transformed.

Its gifts are endless.

Its ability to love, guide, heal and nourish us completely, is natural yet profound. It reveals itself in Its own way, in Its own time, when the energy streams can match It within us and around us, and yet we are never separate from It, It is always there, just Its volume alters, the strength or subtlety with which It flows.

All of this we can control by understanding the science of pranic living, which is the science of being Essence.

While we have already written five books on the being-physically-nourished-by-prana reality which share much more detail about this; the key to being able to be free from the need to take physical food and fluid, is to be anchored in the versions of ourselves that are most imbued with Essence.

This makes the Breatharian reality a spiritual journey and not a diet, for this intake of cosmic micro food comes from direct access to our Essence and its multi-dimensional nature.

Everyone has a version of themselves that has this freedom. We all have multi-dimensional, inter-dimensional versions that are already the true Breatharian, versions that exist without form as a flow of intelligent loving consciousness.

We all have versions of ourselves that are also so light-filled yet still in form, that prana as Essence, is the natural source of nourishment.

It is impossible to live without physical food or fluid intake if all we focus on is our personality self with its beta brain function living in a dual-natured world.

Yet a breatharian is said to be a breather of God and God as Essence breathes us all. As we shift identification to our Essence nature, feel It, experience all Its gifts including the choice of where we wish to take our physical body nourishment from, then we find that not only is our Essence as a God-like force, breathing us, but that we are in Essence the pure I AM that some call God.

Our Baseline Essence
Resource of Nourishment (Living on Light) - a quick summary

Our Essence is our life force which is pure prana.

To understand how we can utilize our Baseline Essence (B.E.) as an internal resource, we need to understand its composition, i.e. what our B.E. contains.

As an energy source, our B.E. holds all the building blocks of life and all creation has the same baseline Essence woven through it.

For example, a cotton shirt cannot be made until the cotton has been sown as seeds, then grown, harvested and woven, and from this fabric many types of garments can be made. Our baseline is like the cloth, a weave that runs through all.

Similarly the fabric of creation can be woven in many different ways. Some is woven into universes, galaxies, solar system, planets, human and other life forms.

How the B.E. expresses Itself, and Its very existence in everything, then becomes the common denominator of all as It is in all.

As the supporting fabric of creation, our Baseline Essence has every vitamin, mineral, element, chemical, electro-magnetic pulse potential and much more than a human body could need to utilize.

Therefore feeding our body and living purely on prana – or our Baseline Essence - is not about *creating* an alternate source of nourishment.

Instead we just need to tap into what is *already* in our Baseline Essence, and allow it to do what it has always known how to do even though we have forgotten this.

Merging our awareness and aligning our bio-system back with our B.E. brings many additional gifts apart from our Its ability to physically nourish us.

We tap into our B.E. in many different ways, yet the process begins by our acknowledgement of our B.E. as an internal resource that we all can access.

Acknowledgement of our B.E. is easier also when it is not just an idea but a tangible experience.

Experiencing our B.E. comes from matching frequencies with it, which we do via the Luscious Lifestyle Program that also emphasizes Baseline Essence identification and conscious alignment.

Due to the Universal Law of Resonance, our B.E. also grows via our focus upon it.

Our B.E. contains a field of infinite intelligence. In this field is the innate knowing of how to keep a life-form alive and healthy on all levels.

In fact, our B.E. holds pre-programmed data flows on how to access anything we need to be self-sustaining and feel whole and complete.

Thus it is the perfect teacher.

Our steps then so far are:- attitudes of acknowledgement, allowance, and lifestyle alignment on a day to day basis.

Allowance requires a mindset shift, holding the awareness that we only eat for pleasure not for need as we know our Baseline Essence can feed us.

While food is wonderful to consume, it is nice to know we do not need it and to have a greater choice in how we wish to be nourished.

Next we need to lovingly invite our physical body system to open to receive a perfect blend of nourishment from all healthy sources including Cosmic Micro-food (or Chi, as prana) which is also our Baseline Essence.

We can also lovingly instruct our complete bio-system to open to our Essence as a source of perfect nutrition.

We can intend this to occur within our physical, emotional, mental and spiritual systems.

We can further ask our intelligent B.E. for us to be so well nourished on all levels, that we exist with Grace and ease in the rhythm of health, happiness, harmony and mutual enhancement with all.

This program of intention allows us to be a self-sustaining mechanism on all levels not just physically.

Next we need to learn to talk to and listen to the physical body. Stop eating out of habit. Eat only when and if you are hungry while you hold firm in the knowledge of what your B.E. can do for you.

Begin to eat less and eat more live and light foods. Go from 3 meals per day to 2 then 2 meals a day to 1. Put less on your plate – eat only until you are no longer hungry and not until you are full, as research has shown that this is better for you.

Via meditation, tune to your body consciousness and ask it what it wants you to eat, rather than what you think it needs.

Learn the B.E. Guidance breath test technique that we have already shared and use it to check your prana percentage on a regular basis and improve this percentage via your lifestyle. (This breath Test system is available in our Being Essence booklet.)

Using this method make the statement …

"Prana now provides more than 50% of my physical body nourishment!"

If the breath confirms this, then check using the same statement for more than 60% and so on until you ascertain your exact prana percentage.

Anytime you get a no response with the breath test, then drop the percentage amount you are checking, down as maybe your prana % is 40%, or even 49% for example.

If you get a yes to 50% then you can safely reduce your physical food intake by that % amount.

However if you do this, you must also hold the intention that:

"All my vitamins, all my minerals and everything I need to be a healthy, self regenerating, self sustaining system comes directly to me from prana as my Essence."

Full conversion to living purely on prana and our B.E. cannot be attempted until this level reads 100% and your complete bio-system is hooked in.

Note: while your mental and physical systems can often handle a quick conversion, the emotional body system can take much longer.

Conversion rates vary within our own bio-system, as well as person to person, as each is unique.

The embodiment of certain virtues is also important as a mode of accessing a stronger flow of Essence energy to the degree that a pure, pranic flow can feed us.

Use the B.E. Guidance System to assess your required virtue components for an easy transition. Which ones need more attention and development?

With sincere hearted intention, ask your Baseline Essence to guide you into this experience of nourishment organically, in the rhythm of joy, ease and Grace, in the right way and time for you.

Know and trust that your B.E. is your perfect energy resource of love, wisdom and true nourishment, by using meditation to experience what your Essence really is!

Be more conscious of the Divine Resource within and use It to free you from, or lessen, your dependence on the world's food resources.

TREAT YOUR BODY WITH LOVE AND CARE.

THE BREATH TEST - Here is an additional tool for you that we were unaware of when I first wrote this book. Keeping Your Body Safe by Testing and Knowing Your Prana Percentage:-

As I travel I continually hear of all the different ways people have elected to do this and some of them just aren't physically safe. **Physical safety and health with this needs to be our number one priority as no initiation is worth losing our life for!**

Also it is now well known that I do not recommend that people do this initiation any more as the energies on our planet are now very different to what they were when this initiation was downloaded in late 1992. Still while it cannot guarantee the gift of being nourished purely by prana as only our personal resonance can do this, many people are being called to do this process. For those of you who are, then we stress again, please follow the guidelines as offered.

Also use the following breath test to check to see:

a) if it is in your divine blueprint to live purely on prana physically this life and

b) to determine exactly what your current prana percentage is. If your current prana percentage is say 60%, then if you stop taking physical food then your body will go into fasting mode for the additional 40%. You will also not be able to stabilize your body weight post process unless you are at the 100% nourishment level.

The following Breath Test is an excerpt from my book *Being Essence.*

Apart from trusting our initial intuitive reactions, there is a simple method we can use to do this, for this Baseline Essence breathes us and when we make a statement that is not in alignment with Its' will, then It will change the way that It breathes through us.

We call this method of testing the Breath Test.

Remember we live in a time now of great chaos and change, it is a time of self-reliance, self-responsibility and learning to trust and listen to that divine voice of infinite wisdom and love within.

So let's practice this breath test now …

Baseline Essence Guidance System - Breath Test

Just think for a moment about something simple that you know is a complete lie for you, something simple like, "My body really loves meat" for example, which for a vegetarian is not true.

As you chant this over and over as if it is a truth, just watch what your breath does …

breathe normally as you watch what is happening in your body as you keep chanting this lie over and over as if it is a truth.

Now take a moment to think of something that you know to be absolutely 100% true for you, something simple, like perhaps the statement, *"I really love my family"* or find something else to chant that is absolutely true for you

then begin to chant this simple truth over and over as a statement of fact while again you watch what your normal breath does

be very aware that there is an energy force breathing you and how it is reacting to this chant …

Take a moment to practise this before you read on.

Results or signs:- Many people find that when they make a statement that is true for them, that is 100% in alignment with the will of the Essence that is breathing them, that physically it feels as if the breath drops right down to the stomach, or to the intestinal area, and that the organs, especially the lungs, seem to expand or open up.

They also find that when they make a statement that is not a truth for their Essence, then the Essence that is breathing them lets them know by allowing the breath to rise up towards the nose or else it seems to get stuck in the throat, often with the feeling as if everything, including the lungs, is closing down or contracting inside. Others can also notice a change in the beat of their heart or sense other signs in the physical body that are a clear physical response as directed by their Essence, to a statement they are making.

Just play with this rhythm for a while, thinking of something that you may not be sure about in your life that you would like confirmation for, always make it as a statement as if it's true for you, whether you know that it is or not, and then watch what your breath does.

I like to always start this breath test with ...
"It is beneficial for me to ... (insert the statement)."
Or
"It is for my highest good to ... (insert the statement.)"
Or
"It is for my highest good, and the highest good of my work in this world, to ... (insert the statement.)"

While many long term meditators are great at receiving clear inner guidance, sometimes tuning ourselves into true stillness, to be able to hear our inner voice, can take time.

This breath test technique is a quick and simple way for us to receive inner guidance from our Essence wherever we are and whenever we need quick confirmation without having to go into deep meditation. It also means we never have to give our power away to anyone again, as through this simple technique we can always know what is true for us.

If there is no response when you are well practiced at receiving results from this technique, it may simply be that regarding this information you are seeking confirmation on, that it is not your time to know the answer yet, or that what you are seeking to know is none of your business.

However this technique tends to work very well when we check information for others and when we seek data that is for their highest good as well, for our Essence is their Essence and it is all knowing, all loving, all wise, existing everywhere and breathing through us all in every moment.

So practice this technique until it becomes a quick response mechanism for you, where you find that you can simply make a statement once or twice in your head telepathically to Essence within and see how the breath responds ... breathing always naturally ... always making a statement as if it is true.

This technique can be used before making any important, potentially life changing decision.

So make the following statement and watch how your breath responds.

"It is in my divine blueprint to demonstrate being physically nourished purely by prana this life."

Keep chanting this over and over until your breath responds. If you get a yes then trust that as is this a pre-agreement prior to your taking embodiment then you will be given all the support you need to bring this into truth.

If you get a '*no*' then why do an initiation like the 21 day process, which for some is very challenging?

Also then check the following:

"It is beneficial for me and for my highest good to undergo this 21-day initiation."

Again if you get a no then do not do it.

Also now using this same method, make the statement …

"Prana now provides more than 50% of my physical body nourishment!"

If the breath confirms this, then check using the same statement for more than 60% and so on until you ascertain your exact prana percentage.

Anytime you get a *no* response with the breath test, then drop the percentage amount you are checking, down as maybe your prana % is 40%, or even 49% for example.

If you get a yes to 50% then you can safely reduce your physical food intake by that % amount.

However if you do this, you must also hold the intention that:

"All my vitamins, all my minerals and everything I need to be a healthy, self regenerating, self sustaining system comes directly to me from prana as my Essence."

Full conversion to living purely on prana and our Baseline Essence cannot be attempted until this level reads 100% and your complete bio-system is hooked in. Now let's take this reality to another level.

RESEARCH AND UPDATE ON NUTRITION FOR OUR WORLD
From carnivore to breatharian and the evolutionary stages in-between – the effects and benefits on our personal health and on our global environment.

FEEDING FROM THE OUTSIDE IN OR THE INSIDE OUT - OR BOTH

Figures now abound on the internet regarding the rising cost of obesity, resource misuse and over consumption, especially on global health and our environment, plus the global obesity epidemic itself that now touches every country in some way. Independent of the fact that a child still dies every 2 seconds from malnourishment, according to the World Health Organization worldwide obesity has nearly doubled since 1980. In 2008, more than 1.4 billion adults were overweight as well as 40 million children under the age of five and 65% of the world's population live in countries where overweight and obesity kill more people than being underweight.

The question now stands … is there another way to feed the growing population of our world? Is there another nutritional resource that we can all access that improves our health and lessens our carbon footprint by using global resources more conservatively? Have the yogi's of India, the Jain's, the Bigu Qigong Masters and other traditions that are more metaphysically inclined discovered an alternate way of being physically nourished? According to research at the Embassy of Peace and those interviewed in the controversial documentary *In the Beginning There was Light*, the answer is yes.

This ancient, free and easily accessible alternate resource is called prana, chi or the universal life force and understanding more about this nutritional energy source plus how to access and increase this internal source of nourishment is well documented in our research manuals *The Prana Program* and also this book *The Food of Gods*.

Now, after 20 years of personal experiential research and travelling constantly to share our research into this field of alternate nourishment, and connecting with the various people whose journey this is, we have now been able to classify nourishment as being delivered to us in various ways and from a variety of sources. After decades of hearing people talk about living on light, or people who do not need to physically eat, we wish to first state that everyone must have physical body nourishment or else the body will die. The only issue to be discussed now is from what source and also what is the cost to our health and on our environment from these various sources of nourishment?

FEEDING FROM THE OUTSIDE IN – absorption and atrophy.

Category 1 – TRADITIONS & HABITS. Category 1 is based on traditions and habits which are about being fed from the outside in. This category covers the usual method of taking physical body nourishment such being a meat eater, vegetarian, vegan, on raw food, fruitarian etc. In this category people live in the reality that the physical system needs to ingest physical food to survive and most are unaware of the "inside out" method of nourishment and feeding. Due to the substantial health issues that are often associated with the traditional carnivore and/or heavily processed food diet, many are now turning to a more plant based vegetarian lifestyle and reducing their consumption of animal products.
Category 1 fallout: The main problem with 'feeding from the outside in' – especially when excessively 'meat, animal product and processed food' based - is that it often leads to more rapid aging, dis-ease and physically system breakdown plus it adds significantly to global warming and to over consumption of both medical and planetary resources. For example, a meat eating diet consumes 30 times more of the world's resources than a vegetarian diet.

Category 2 – SUBTLE SHIFTS. Category 2 is a substantial movement occurring for many who also live a holistic lifestyle that is also naturally increasing their chi or prana levels. This is when people begin to lighten up their diet intuitively without being aware why but knowing that it just feels right to them. This 'subtly shifting' in what and how often they feed from the outside in, is usually a result of their day to day lifestyle changes as these ones are beginning to naturally be fed from the inside out yet are unaware of this. Holistic education into prana as cosmic micro fuel allows these ones to relax and know that this is a natural progression and option due to their lifestyle. Category 2 also takes into account the new children being born who are intuitively aware of this alternate form of nourishment and hence display very little interest in the 'feeding from the outside in' methods of nourishment.

Category 2 fallout: The main problem with this is that lack of education into why this is happening causes many to worry about what is occurring and hence not trust this natural transition or get aligned more healthily to it.

Category 3 – TRANSITIONING WITH AWARENESS. This category is when people are conscious of prana as an alternate source of nourishment and so they consciously begin to adjust their lifestyle to be fed more from the inside out – the successful transition into this is completely depending on their own frequency field and their ability to be more at one with their own pure Essence nature that is breathing them. In this category people begin a conscious detoxification process of the physical, emotional and mental systems via a specific lifestyle shift; and/or they may begin solar gazing practice and/or qigong practice to increase their chi flows.

Category 3 fallout: The main problem with this is people's impatience and lack or physical system readiness. Health problems can occur if people try to transition into categories 4, 5 & 6 before they are fully ready.

Now let's address 3 more categories that support the reality of being nourished from the inside out rather than being nourished from the outside in; categories that require safe, careful preparation, that are also completely dependent on mindsets and more importantly a person's day-to-day lifestyle which can either increase or decrease the flow of chi through their physical system.

FEEDING FROM THE INSIDE OUT – radiation and regeneration

Category 4 – TRANSITIONED & FREE TO CHOOSE. This is the category for those people who have converted their system successfully to being fed in a healthy way from the inside out. They have achieved this via their lifestyle and good holistic education into this field of possibility. Having had this experience and given themselves this freedom by the living of it, they may then decide to enjoy the pleasure of taking physical food from time to time. Some do this once a week, others once a month or once a year while others in this category may eventually move onto category five or even decide to drop back to category 1 and enjoy a light vegan, raw or vegetarian diet. Imagine the impact on our global environment if people could safely even halve their current physical food intake as they are healthily fed from the inside out for all their nutritional requirements?

Category 5 – FREEDOM & PLEASURE. This is when people are being nourished completely from the inside out yet they still like to take liquids for social or pleasure reasons, or just for the pure enjoyment of this. Many in this category express no interest in category 6. I have called these ones 'liquidarians'. The redirection of the energy we normally use for digestion when feeding from the outside in, and instead being fed from the inside out, leads to many improvements in the human physical, emotional, mental system functioning. Our research has found that for these ones less sleep is required, more mental clarity and intuitive visionary ability is gained and people's general health rhythms improve significantly with some people experiencing the eradication of all dis-eases.

Category 6 – the TRUE BREATHARIAN – although these people are still relatively rare in our world, this is the category for the people who take nothing from the outside in as they no longer require either physical food or fluid since they obtain all that they need to be healthy on all levels of their being, from the inside out. This includes being hydrated as we have found that the body is capable of hydrating itself also from the inside out when it requires. Noted breatharians are Zinaida Baranova and Prahlad Jani.

Category 4, 5 & 6 fallout: None if people stay well tuned to what their body is telling them and adjust accordingly. If unprepared people can die if they attempt to enter into categories 4, 5 & 6 unless they are ready. To do this successfully their prana percentage must be at 100%. Our book "Being Essence" shares how to achieve and measure this.

On a final note, what category people will eventually end up settling into will depend on their Divine Blueprint and what they have agreed to obtain and demonstrate in this life time. If someone is pre-programmed to be a Category 4 or 5 they may never feel the natural pull to go into category 6; similar it may not be in people's blueprint to move beyond category 1.

Pre-programming is also connected to our service agenda and as of mid 2013 there are now more than 50,000 people enjoying and exploring the freedom of categories 4, 5, and 6; as I myself have done over these past twenty years. More in-depth research into this alternate source of nourishment will not only improve global health but also substantially reduce our global carbon footprint as will a return to a lighter, vegetarian diet and a change in basic lifestyle via good holistic education programs.

Additional Obesity Facts

According to the Sydney Morning *Herald*-Lateral Economics Index of Australia's Wellbeing … "The cost of obesity to Australia's collective wellbeing has reached $120 billion a year - the equivalent of about 8 per cent of the economy's annual output" and with 28.3 per cent of the population considered obese, and 2 in 3 people overweight, their research now shares that "The negative effects of obesity are growing faster than … net national income, environmental degradation, inequality, life expectancy and job satisfaction." In the USA the Harvard School of Public Health claimed that some sources calculate that the current trend of obesity, and its economic cost, will rise by between $48 to

66 billion per year, up from the $190 billion spent in 2005. The Harvard report also states that one estimate says that "the health care costs of obesity are responsible for nearly 21 percent of total health care spending in the U.S." Researchers from Johns Hopkins Bloomberg School of Public Health have also addressed the current obesity epidemic and … "expect that by 2030, 86% of U.S. adults will be overweight or obese, with related health care spending projected to be as much as $956.9 billion." According to the WHO "Based on the latest estimates in European Union countries, overweight affects 30-70% and obesity affects 10-30% of adults." and this figure is rapidly rising.

New stem cell research funded by Google's co-founder, Sergey Brin, has now delivered the world's first hamburger made of meat grown from scratch in a laboratory, at a cost of more than €250,000. Production of meat in this way is considered by many to be more ethical and may also one day hopefully cease the slaughter of billions of animals and reduce our carbon footprint.

While some predicate that by 2050 our global consumption of meat will have risen by 70% and we will need three planet earths to continue to be able to provide for this; still the process in stem cell meat production is time consuming and also fails to address the health issues arising from a heavier meat based diet compared to the long term health and environmental benefits of being vegetarian.

If people can also increase their chi or prana flow via their lifestyle, then they can consume less of our external world food resources and be fed instead by a blend perhaps of being nourished from the inside out as well as from the outside in! As many can imagine, the global environmental and health impacts of this will be astounding!

Yet the ability to physically feed us from the inside out is just one gift of many that our Essence has for us and personally I feel that too much emphasis is placed on this one aspect. Other gifts our Essence provides as it nourishes us on all levels are permanent peace, deep contentment on mental and emotional body levels plus a life filled with Grace and a heart filled with gratitude! When we increase our chi we get healthy and happy!

JASMUHEEN - Biography & Background
www.jasmuheen.com

Jasmuheen's main service agenda is the raising of consciousness to create a healthy, harmonious world. To support this she is the author of 38 metaphysical books that are published in 18 languages; the Founder of the Embassy of Peace and implementer of its Personal, Global & Universal Harmonization Projects; she is also an Ambassador of Peace for the Madonna Frequency Planetary Peace Program; Pranic Living & eliminating global hunger; international lecturer on metaphysics, ascension & interdimensional energy field science. Jasmuheen is also a leading researcher on the controversial pranic nourishment reality & Darkroom Training facilitator; founder of the Self Empowerment Academy; facilitator of the C.I.A. – the Cosmic Internet Academy; publisher & film-maker; artist presenting Sacred Art Retreats, musician & President of the Global Congress – Pyramid Valley, Bangalore, India.

A meditator for over 42 years, the lifetime President of the GCSS in India, Jasmuheen, specialises in deep inner plane journeys using the alchemical meditative process to allow people to merge even deeper with their own enlightened nature. As an Ambassador of Peace for the Embassy of Peace, she has travelled for over 20 years and achieved many positive things in the world with her work with tribal cultures in Colombia, the Amazons and also the slums in Brazil plus working with various levels of government including presenting her work again at the UN in Vienna in 2013. Through this time she has been instrumental in helping to educate millions into better global resource usage via developing a stronger connection to the Divine resource within and since 1993 has been personally nourished by prana and for over 20 years has lived without the need to take physical food. In her tour time this year she will share an update into her research on this, provide deeper connections and insights into the powers of the Pure Love channel, that feeds us all, discuss spontaneous healing, plus our current evolutionary status on earth according to the Divine Feminine and the Light Beings she works with and much more. A deeply peaceful person, Jasmuheen is light, entertaining and always filled with love and her gatherings are always inspirational!

JASMUHEEN'S BACKGROUND Timeline

- ❖ 1957 – Born in Australia to Norwegian immigrants
- ❖ 1959 – Began focus on vegetarianism
- ❖ 1964 – Began to study Chi
- ❖ 1971 – Discovered the Languages of Light
- ❖ 1974 – Initiated into Ancient Vedic Meditation and eastern philosophy
- ❖ 1974 – Began periodic fasting
- ❖ 1974 – Discovered telepathic abilities
- ❖ 1975 - 1992 – Raised children, studied and applied metaphysics, enjoyed a 10 year career in finance and computer programming
- ❖ 1992 – Retired from the corporate world to pursue metaphysical life
- ❖ 1992 – Met many Masters of Alchemy including those from the Great White Brotherhood the Higher Light Scientists from Arcturius and the Intergalactic Federation of World's Council
- ❖ 1993 – Underwent the Prana Initiation to increase her chi flow and began to live on light
- ❖ 1994 – Began an intensive 14 year research project on Divine Nutrition and pranic nourishment
- ❖ 1994 – Began her global service agenda with the Ascended Masters
- ❖ 1994 – Received the first of 5 volumes of channeled messages from the Ascended Masters
- ❖ 1994 – Wrote the metaphysical manual *In Resonance*
- ❖ 1994 – Founded the Self Empowerment Academy in Australia
- ❖ 1994 – Began to hold classes in metaphysics and Self Mastery
- ❖ 1994 – Began *The Art of Resonance* newsletter renamed later as *The ELRAANIS Voice*
- ❖ 1995 – Traveled extensively around Australia, Asia and New Zealand sharing Self-Mastery research
- ❖ 1995 – Wrote *Pranic Nourishment (Living on Light) – Nutrition for the New Millennium*
- ❖ 1996 – Invited to present the Pranic Nourishment research to the Global stage
- ❖ 1996 – Began an intensive re-education program with the Global Media
- ❖ 1996 – Set up the International M.A.P.S. Ambassadry – Established in 33 countries – held global elections for additional spiritual governance where people in each country elected the spiritual overseer of their choice such as the Christ, Buddha etc.
- ❖ 1996 – Created the *C.I.A. – the Cosmic Internet Academy* – a free website to download data for positive personal and planetary progression. Web address: www.selfempowermentacademy.com.au
- ❖ 1996 - 2001 – Traveled extensively to Europe, the U.K., the U.S.A. and Brazil with the '*Back to Paradise*' agenda
- ❖ 1996 - 2014 – Talked about Divine Power and Divine Nutrition to > 1 billion via the global media

- ❖ 1997 – Began to set up scientific research project for Living on Light
- ❖ 1997 – Began the *Our Camelot Trilogy*, wrote *The Game of Divine Alchemy*
- ❖ 1997 – Formed the M.A.P.S. Ambassadry Alliance – people committed to global harmony and peace
- ❖ 1998 – International tour to share the Impeccable Mastery Agenda
- ❖ 1998 – Wrote *Our Progeny – the X-Re-Generation*
- ❖ 1999 – Wrote the *Wizard's Tool Box* which later became the *Biofields and Bliss* Series.
- ❖ 1999 – Wrote *Dancing with my DOW : Media Mania, Mastery and Mirth*
- ❖ 1998 - 1999 – Wrote and published *Ambassadors of Light – World Health World Hunger Project*
- ❖ 1999 – Began contacting World Governments regarding Hunger and Health Solutions
- ❖ 1999 – International tour to share the Blueprint for Paradise
- ❖ 1999 - 2001 – Began M.A.P.S. Ambassadors International Training Retreats
- ❖ 2000 – International tour 'Dancing with the Divine' to facilitate the election of an Etheric Government in 28 key cities and also shared the Luscious Lifestyles Program – L.L.P.
- ❖ 2000 - 2001 – Wrote *Cruising Into Paradise* an esoteric coffee table book
- ❖ 1999 - 2001 – Wrote *Divine Radiance – On the Road with the Masters of Magic* and
- ❖ 2001 – Wrote *Four Body Fitness : Biofields and Bliss* Book 1
- ❖ 2000 - 2001 – Launched the OPHOP agenda One People in Harmony on One Planet
- ❖ 2001 – Wrote the book *Co-Creating Paradise : Biofields and Bliss* Book 2
- ❖ 2001 – Launched *Recipe 2000>* as a tool to co-create global health and happiness; peace and prosperity for all on Earth
- ❖ 2002 – Launched www.jasmuheen.com with its Perfect Alignment Perfect Action Holistic Education Programs; and its I.R.S. focus to Instigate, Record and Summarize humanity's co-creation of paradise.
- ❖ 2002 – Did the 'Divine Radiance FOUR BODY FITNESS – Unity 2002' World Tour
- ❖ 2002 – Received, wrote and launched *The Madonna Frequency Planetary Peace Program* as the free e-Book, Biofields and Bliss Book 3.
- ❖ 2002 - 2003 – Wrote *The Food of Gods*.
- ❖ 2003 – World Tour "Divine Nutrition and The Madonna Frequency Planetary Peace Project".
- ❖ 2004 – Wrote *The Law of Love* then toured with "The Law of Love and Its Fabulous Frequency of Freedom" agenda.
- ❖ 2005 – Wrote *Harmonious Healing and The Immortals Way*, then toured with the "Harmonious Healing" agenda.
- ❖ 2005 – Began work on The Freedom of the Immortals Way plus continued with writing *The Enchanted Kingdom* Trilogy & *The Prana Program* for Third World Countries.

- ❖ 2005 – Presented THE PRANA PROGRAM to the Society for Conscious Living at the United Nations in Vienna – Nov. 2005
- ❖ 2006 – International tour with THE PRANA PROGRAM
- ❖ 2007 – International tour focus on THE SECOND COMING and SECOND CHANCE DANCES.
- ❖ 2007 – Launched THE EMBASSY OF PEACE on 07-07-07 & began training programs for Ambassadors of Peace & Diplomats of Love.
- ❖ 2007 – Released the book *The Bliss of Brazil & The Second Coming*
- ❖ 2008 – Released *The Enchanted Kingdom* Series after 6 years of writing *The Queen of the Matrix, The King of Hearts* and *Elysium.*
- ❖ 2008 - Toured with the Future Worlds Future Humans agenda and begins more intense work in India.
- ❖ 2008 – Appointed President of the Global Congress of Spiritual Scientists Pyramid valley, Bangalore India.
- ❖ 2008 – Released the coffee table books *Sacred Scenes & Visionary Verse* plus *Cruising Into Paradise.*
- ❖ 2009 – Released and toured with the *Universal Harmonization Program* for the Embassy of Peace, focusing on research into extraterrestrial intelligence.
- ❖ 2009 – Released her book *Meditation Magic*
- ❖ 2009 – Began writing *Cosmic Wanderers* – book 4 in the Enchanted Kingdom series
- ❖ 2010 – Jasmuheen continued her work in South America and India and tours with the *Harmonics of the Heavenly Heart & Pranic Living Agenda*
- ❖ 2010 – From 2009 to 2011 Jasmuheen focused on providing free VIDEOs for education & entertainment on her YouTube Channel, plus creating education DVD's, art & music. Jasmuheen's YouTube channel now has over 500 free educational videos - http://youtube.com/jasmuheen
- ❖ 2011 – Released her *Pathways of Peace Pragmatics* book then toured and offered her YouTube videos on this.
- ❖ 2011 – Wrote then released her new children's series *Siriana's Adventures – Earth Bound* book
- ❖ 2012 – Jasmuheen released her *Being Essence* booklet and this was the focus of her world tour. She also completed her *Cosmic Wanderers* book the 4th in the Enchanted Kingdom series and her travel journal *The Rhythms of Love*. Both released towards the end of 2012.
- ❖ 2012 – 1st November - shared the work of the Embassy of Peace at World Peace Day Congress in Istanbul Turkey.
- ❖ In 2013 her focus was on her *YES Agenda* with theme of *Upgrading* all global systems of operation via her *Peace Paradigms and Programs.*
- ❖ 2013 - Delivered her *Feeding from the Outside in or the Inside Out or both – Cosmic Micro Fuel* system of nourishment.
- ❖ 2013 – 24th October – came back to the United Nations in Vienna to provide an update on her Cosmic Micro-Fuel Program.

❖ In 2014 she launched the first Embassy of Peace Retreat for those Affiliate to share the Luscious Lifestyles Program and the 12 Pathways of Peace.

❖ 2014 – Jasmuheen began her book *The Pure Love Channel with its Templates of Perfection* and toured with this theme.

Our Channels …
http://www.jasmuheen.com/embassy-of-peace-2/
http://www.jasmuheen.com/embassy-of-peace/#manuals
http://www.jasmuheen.com/embassy-of-peace/embassy-of-peace-other-languages/
Stay tuned to what we are lodging that is NEW at
http://www.jasmuheen.com/whats-new/
Also enjoy our …
http://www.youtube.com/jasmuheen
http://www.facebook.com/pages/Jasmuheen/187152512352
http://jasmuheen.blogspot.com/ plus http://twitter.com/jasmuheen

On Pranic Living Jasmuheen writes: "Pranic Living is not a diet - it is ascension into more refined evolutionary paths on both individual then global levels! As vast multi-dimensional beings, we have limitless access to a source of internal nourishment (prana-chi) that constantly bubbles champagne-like throughout the matrix of life. This pranic stream acts as a type of glue to bind our creations and help with our manifestations to bring more Grace into our lives. Meditation allows us to go deep within the inner silence to discover and experience this pranic flow in all its forms and as we focus upon it we become immersed within it and so find ourselves ascended and transformed. Increasing our personal internal & external chi flow like we do in our gatherings and retreats can rid our world of all of all its hungers and bring about a state of global harmony and permanent peace and so our international tours seminars and retreats continue with this focus."

As many are now aware, metaphysical author Jasmuheen has spent the last four decades studying the rhythms of the field of Divine Love to the degree that in 1993 she discovered its ability to provide nourishment on not just emotional, mental and spiritual levels but also on a physical level. She then toured extensively sharing this with all those open to experience this different way of being nourished, continually also offering deep meditations within the field of love that will align us more powerfully to this nourishing force so that our presence enhances human evolution in ways that benefit us all. Pranic living then gave birth to the Embassy of Peace with its pragmatic Programs & Projects of Personal, Global & Universal Harmonization.

Jasmuheen's books are now published in 18 languages.

BOOKS BY JASMUHEEN - A selection of JASMUHEEN'S research manuals can be purchased from her website.

1)   THE ENCHANTED KINGDOM Trilogy - 3 books in one.
2)   QUEEN OF THE MATRIX - Fiddlers of the Fields with Jasmuheen (book 1 in the Enchanted Kingdom Trilogy)
3)   KING OF HEARTS - The Field of Love - with Jasmuheen (book 2 in the Enchanted Kingdom Trilogy)
4)   ELYSIUM - Shamballa's Sacred Symphony with Jasmuheen (book 3 in the Enchanted Kingdom Trilogy)
5)   The Food of Gods
6)   The Law of Love & Its Fabulous Frequency of Freedom
7)   THE PRANA PROGRAM - Effective & Enjoyable Evolution
8)   PRANIC NOURISHMENT - Nutrition for the New Millennium
9)   Ambassadors of Light : World Health World Hunger Project
10)   The Bliss of Brazil & The Second Coming
11)   In Resonance
12)   Divine Radiance - On the Road with the Masters of Magic
13)   HARMONIOUS HEALING & The Immortal's Way with Jasmuheen.
14)   Darkroom Diary Downloads & The Freedom of The Immortal's Way
15)   Cosmic Colleagues – Messages from the Masters
16)   Biofields & Bliss Trilogy
17)   Four Body Fitness : Biofields & Bliss
18)   Co-creating Paradise
19)   'The Madonna Frequency' Planetary Peace Program'
20)   Meditation Magic
21)   Sacred Scenes & Visionary Verse
22)   Cruising Into Paradise
23)   Embassy of Peace Programs
24)   Siriana's Adventures – Earth Bound
25)   Pathways of Peace
26)   Being Essence
27)   Cosmic Wanderers – book 4 in the Enchanted Kingdom series

THE FOOD OF GODS
DIVINE NUTRITION – LIVING ON LIGHT SERIES
with Jasmuheen

The Food of Gods is Jasmuheen's 18th book on metaphysical matters and hopefully her last book in her Divine Nutrition research series. It is not necessary to have read the previous books on this subject which cover her personal journey and the solution for world health and world hunger issues as "The Foods of Gods" takes the pranic nourishment, Divine Nutrition discussion to another level and offers simple yet powerful tools to satiate all of our hungers.

Jasmuheen shares that the difference between the living on light and Divine Nutrition realities can best be summed up by the following points. She writes:

"The most important difference with our focus with Divine Nutrition is that It has the ability to feed us **on all levels** and that we can still benefit from increasing Its flow through our bio-system **even if we continue to choose to enjoy eating**. Allowing this Divinely Nutritional stream to be increased in our system means that we can be fed emotionally, mentally and spiritually and as such the techniques and guidelines shared in this book, will benefit us all by freeing us from our current personal and global emotional, mental and spiritual states of anorexia.

"Providing the tools and research to do this is my real focus in the world and just part of my life's work for I know that when we learn to nourish our selves enough - and from free and purer sources - then our planet will blossom into a state of paradise for all. Committing my life just to the issue of 'to eat or not to eat' is too limiting an agenda for me particularly since I have seen what really can be achieved when we access the food of Gods Divine Nutrition channel. I call this Level 1 of the Divine Nutrition Program.

"Once we have increased the intensity of this flow and directed it in a manner that will give us a pure and never-ending source of emotional, mental and spiritual nutrition, **we can then choose to refine ourselves further into Level 3 of this program and accept one of the additional gifts of this flow, which is It's ability to physically nourish our cells**. To me this ability is a very small gift of the food of the Gods and I feel that our focus needs to be on all of the gifts. However, while this may be an acceptable option for the bulk of humanity in our future, at the moment we are still in the pioneering stages of this in the Western world and much more research needs to be done. All pioneering work requires, 'guinea pigs' or test subjects, of which perhaps you – the reader – may be one. How do you find out if you are? Read this book and apply the technique for you to find out.

"Prana, or chi, or the Universal Life Force as in Reiki, all have as their underlying vibration, or base frequency, pure love and light and when these flood our bio-system, they stimulate the release of more love and light within us. These are the frequencies that can be directed to sustain and nourish us."

This flow of love and light is the true food of the Gods.

ISBN: 978-1-84799-847-7

Spirit
13 Holy Grail

DOW
14